IMAGES
of America

KELLER

I0806474

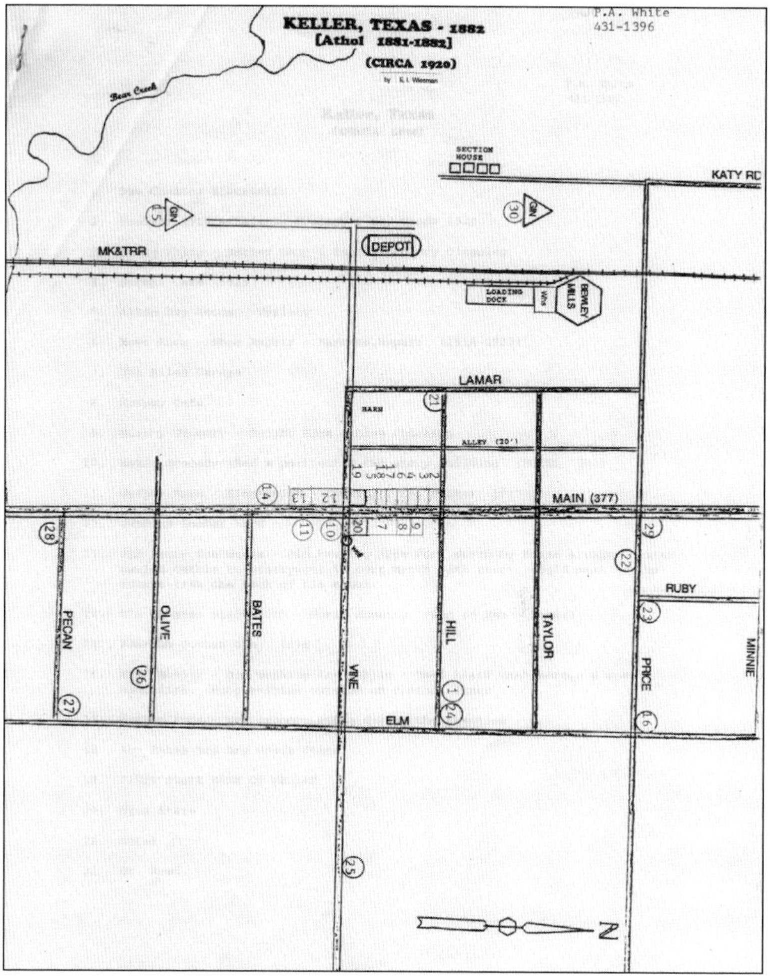

This map by E. I. Wiesman depicts Keller in the 1920s: (1) Sam Choates Blacksmith; (2) Pearson (1917)/Lavoise Grocery and Dry Goods (1920); (3) Emory White's Barber Shop and Bath, which did dry-cleaning; (4) Gorman Café (1925); (5) Allen Dry Goods; (6) Newt Knox, shoe and harness repair (1916–1923); (7) Don Biles Garage (1917); (8) Murphy Café; (9) Murphy Grocery, which bought eggs and live chickens; (10) Maxie Grocery; (11) Jasper Knox, a blacksmith and Chevrolet dealer (1917); (12) Jenkins Lumberyard; (13) Jim Perry Ice Cream House, did hauling from Fort Worth by horse and wagon and later hauled cattle to the stockyards in Fort Worth with a truck and sold meat to residents from the back of his truck; (14) Tim Choates Blacksmith; (15) Pearson Cotton Gin (1918); (16) Mrs. Hooper, a washerwoman; (17) Hatton Knox, a grocery store; (18) Abe Bates, who had a dry goods store; (19) First State Bank of Keller; (20) drugstore; (21) hotel; (22) Dr. Reed; (23) Dr. Jones; (24) Church of Christ; (25) Presbyterian church; (26) Methodist church; (27) Old Keller School; (28) Whitley Brothers cattle-dipping vat; (29) Baptist church (30) Charlie Johnson's gin. (Courtesy Joyce Gibson Roach.)

On the Cover: Mrs. Betty Lamkin presents Aaron Raper, of Vineyard, Texas, with an award for winning the Aged Mare Class, who is with his horse My Pal at the 1953 Keller Fair. The Keller Arena was part of the Keller Fairgrounds located on Keller Parkway (FM [Farm to Market Road] 1709) and Cindy Street, which held rodeos, races, and livestock shows. The Keller Arena no longer exists on the Lions grounds, but a new multiuse arena has been built on the grounds of the Keller Sports Complex just off Golden Triangle. (Courtesy Keller Lions Club.)

IMAGES
of America

KELLER

Rebecca Gallegos

ARCADIA
PUBLISHING

ISBN 978-0-7385-7946-7

Published by Arcadia Publishing
Charleston, South Carolina

Printed in the United States of America

Library of Congress Control Number: 2010917078

For all general information, please contact Arcadia Publishing:
Telephone 843-853-2070
Fax 843-853-0044
E-mail sales@arcadiapublishing.com
For customer service and orders:
Toll-Free 1-888-313-2665

Visit us on the Internet at www.arcadiapublishing.com

To Mom and Dad for suggesting I move to such a wonderful town

Contents

Acknowledgments

The Keller Lions Club has been instrumental in collecting Keller history, and without its archives this book would not have been possible. Unless otherwise noted, the Keller Lions Club graciously provided all images appearing in this book. I wish to thank Lions Club member Kurt Koster, who graciously trusted me with the Lions Club's images while I put this book together, and Donald Blevins for helping to place names with faces. A special thank you goes to Jay Cy Martin, for reliving his tales of Chisholm Trail and his stories as a railroad engineer, and to former mayor Ron Lee, for allowing me to literally take the pictures off his wall to be a part of this book.

Homestead Farms is a unique dairy farm and has been a part of Keller history for over 100 years. It was my distinct pleasure hearing the Browning family tales from brother, Michael Farris, and sister, Mindalyn Looper. Their excitement to keep the family history alive is being honored with their farm receiving the Century Farm Award from the Texas Department of Agriculture. Pollenzo's Pizza House in Keller deserves a particular thank you, as I spent many hours there writing this book and believe that the smell of great food prompted great literary moments of insight. A tip of the hat goes to Jon Paul Jordan at Copy and Ship Headquarters in Watauga for his assistance in the scanning process. Thanks, kindly, to the University of Texas at Arlington Library Special Collections and the use of the Lyda Smith White Collection, as well as to historical manuscript archivist Brenda S. McClurkin, whose help was greatly appreciated during my research. I thank Joyce Gibson Roach for donating this extensive collection of history.

I also wish to thank my editor at Arcadia Publishing, Hannah Carney, for her expert assistance and professional guidance in keeping me on task and to publisher Kristie Kelly for taking a chance on a new writer. Also, thank you to the *Fort Worth Star Telegram* and the *Keller Citizen* for access to their newspaper archives.

INTRODUCTION

In August 1881, a site was surveyed for a new town called Athol, which was to be located on 40 acres near Double Springs, an already flourishing community, in the lower eastern region of Cross Timbers. In a letter dated 1916, Dr. T. R. Allen, an original pioneer of Athol, wrote:

> Here we found the country which has been most wonderfully blessed by the Architect of Nature, a soil as rich as craving of man could wish for, and timber, water and grass in an abundance, and sufficient of the sunshine and the showers, besides the woodlands were lined with wild deer and turkey, and fine herds of antelope on the prairies the year round, the buffalo was there during the winter season. We found upon arrival in this section two small bands of natives, the Caddos and Seminole Indians, they were friendly disposed with us and so remained for many years.

Each farmer planned his crop to meet his own needs and provide seeds for next year's plantings. There was little reason to raise a surplus since there were no nearby markets to sell it. Since most of the area was unfenced, cattle and other livestock grazed on open ranges. When beef was butchered, the meat was divided among the neighbors.

On July 13, 1850, a meeting was held in the home of Daniel Barcroft with seven other charter members of the community to form Mt. Gilead Church, including John A. Freeman; Iraneaus Neace and his wife, Lucinda; Parmelia Allen; Abby Dunham; and two slaves, Ambrose and Carolin. A log cabin was built in 1851 and served as a schoolhouse on weekdays during the school term, which did not begin until the cotton crop was picked and had to end before the next planting season. American Indians roamed the area, and though few raids were made on settlements, a band of Indians burned the log church in 1859. Worship services had to be held elsewhere, and eventually the church was rebuilt. The Mt. Gilead Cemetery lies north and across the road from the church. Many of the gravestones bear the names of fourth- and fifth-generational descendents who still live in Keller.

Land grants varied in size: a single man could homestead 160 acres, a man with a family could get 320 acres, and a veteran who had served in the Texas War for Independence (1836) could claim as much as 640 acres. After the free land was claimed, later settlers could buy land ranging from 25¢ to $1 per acre.

In 1875, Isaac Roberts, a farmer who owned over 600 acres, left a parcel of his land to A. G. Roberts, who then sold the right-of-way to the Texas and Pacific Railway for $25. As rumors of the railroad spread, it was learned that the railway would extend north of Fort Worth. Keller received its name with the influence of a Texas and Pacific Railroad foremen, John C. Keller, who was able to influence the railway to put a stop in Athol. By 1882, the settlement, formerly known as Athol, became present-day Keller in honor of the railroad engineer. With railroad service now available, Keller began to flourish as a trade center for the nearby farming communities. The surrounding region of Keller attracted many settlers and their families with the supply of abundant game and water and plenty of land for raising cattle and farming. The post office was established in 1886 when the post office at Double Springs, located about 5 miles northeast of Keller, was discontinued and moved permanently. Mr. Charles Neace moved to Keller and served as postmaster for those years. He earned a salary of $6 per month and ran a general store in the back. His ability to extended credit to the nearby farmers helped Keller grow quickly.

As Keller developed, its water supply was harder to come by, and each family had to rely on collecting its own rainwater. In 1906, a new well was drilled on Main and Vine Streets and remained in service until 1960. Electricity came to Keller in the early 1880s, followed by a telephone system, which was privately owned until 1966.

In the first years, the closest school to Keller stood on Bear Creek Road and Elaine Street. By 1898, property was purchased on the corner of Keller Parkway (FM 1709) and College Street. The school was moved to this new location, where the Keller Education Center now stands. The Keller Independent School District was established in 1911. The first graduating class from Keller High School was in 1914–1915, which held 10 grades. It took the Great Depression and the government-sponsored Works Progress Administration (WPA) jobs for the Rock Gymnasium to be built. It was constructed as a community project on school property so the school could receive the benefit of the building, which was needed for the many athletic programs. Local residents supplied much of the native stone used in the construction of the gymnasium. Today the "Rock Gym," as it is affectionately called, serves as a meeting facility. A new school was completed in 1939 but burned in a fire in 1948, leaving only the gymnasium and lunchroom. While two new buildings were being constructed, students attended classes in wooden army barracks buildings that were moved onto the site. Some classes were also held at the Baptist Church, where the Veterans Memorial currently stands.

Keller benefited not only from being situated on the Texas and Pacific Railway, it also had the advantage of U.S. Highway 377 (Main Street), which runs north and south from Fort Worth to Denton. Keller was incorporated on November 16, 1955. True American "grit" has always run through the city and continues today with its vast array of local retail shops and restaurants. Old Town Keller is presently going through a new phase of revitalization while maintaining roots to the pioneers that once called Keller home. In 2009, CNN's *Money Magazine* ranked Keller as seventh-best place to live in its article "Top 100 Best Places to Live." As Keller continues to prosper, there are now over 39,000 residents, and many have been transplanted here from other states yearning to learn the history of their new homestead of Keller, Texas.

One

Keller Begins

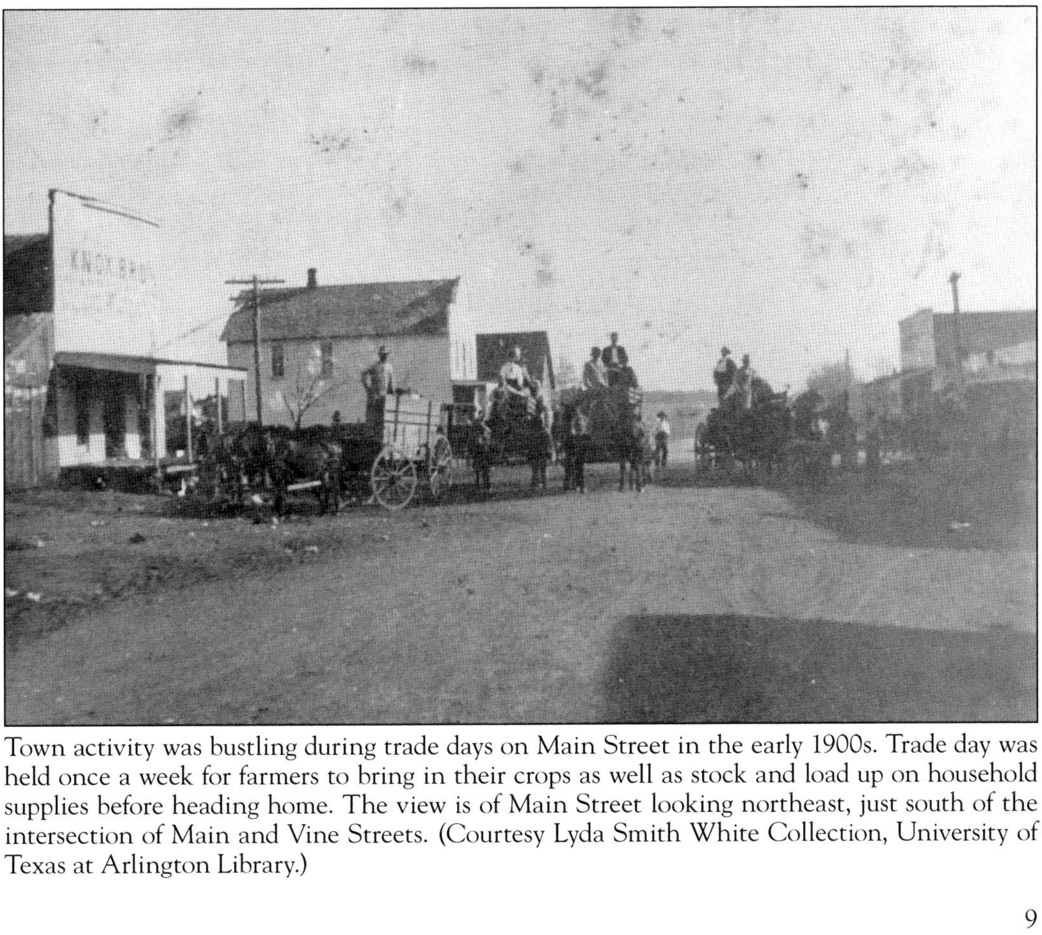

Town activity was bustling during trade days on Main Street in the early 1900s. Trade day was held once a week for farmers to bring in their crops as well as stock and load up on household supplies before heading home. The view is of Main Street looking northeast, just south of the intersection of Main and Vine Streets. (Courtesy Lyda Smith White Collection, University of Texas at Arlington Library.)

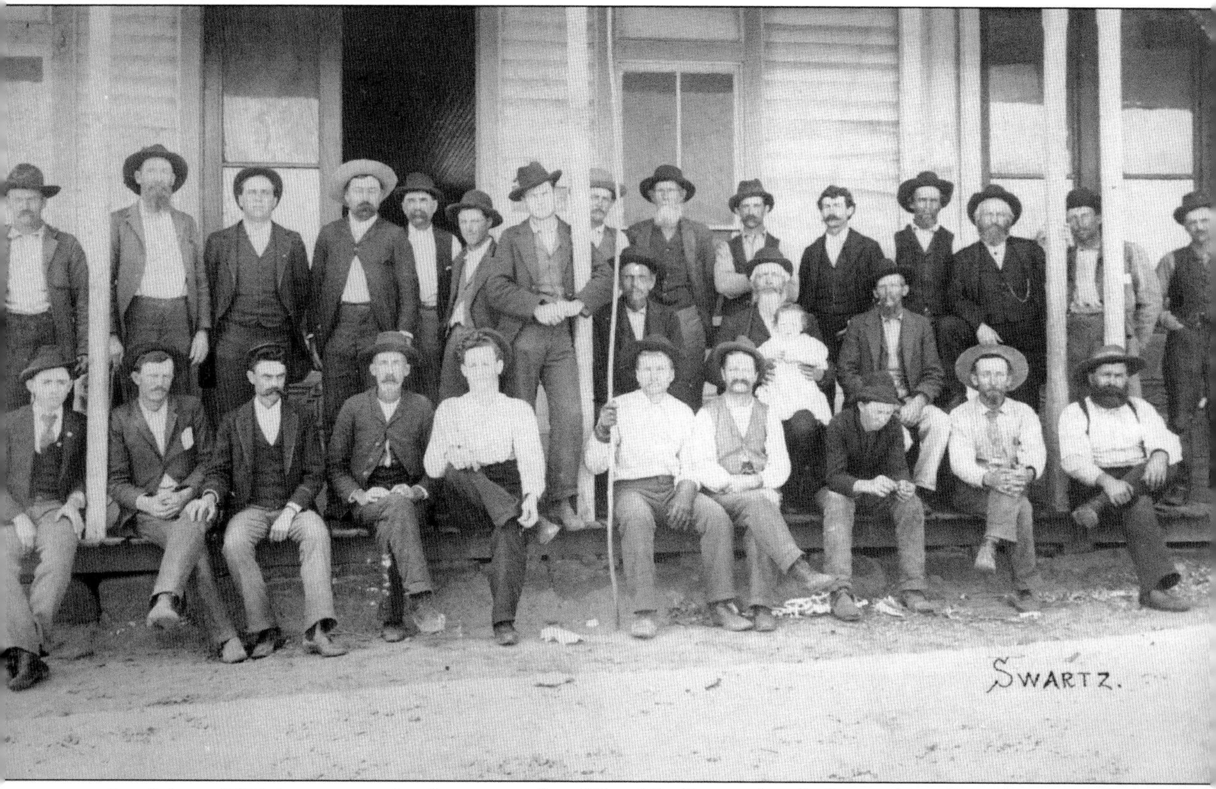

In this c. 1898 image on the front porch of Double Store that belonged to the Rippy Lumber Company and J. H. Prewett are, from left to right, (first row) possibly Asa Weaver, Perry Davis, barber Mr. Rudolph, possibly Charlie White or Mr. Ponder, Tom Meacham, Oscar McCain, Jule D. Myer, Fred Pippin, Jack Lavy, and blacksmith Mr. Brigance; (second row) Tom Neace, Rev. John Calvin Smith, Rev. Smith's grandson Billy Rippy, and Mr. Elson; (third row) unidentified, Harmon Cook, Dr. J. M. Reynolds, Tom McCain, Bruno Lavoise, John Mays, O. P. "Ollie" Rippy, possibly Lawson Stateham, Mr. Prosser, possibly Bob Wash or Mr. McCain Sr., J. H. Prewett, unidentified, Dr. J. W. McCulloch, unidentified, and Mr. Joy. (Courtesy Joyce Gibson Roach.)

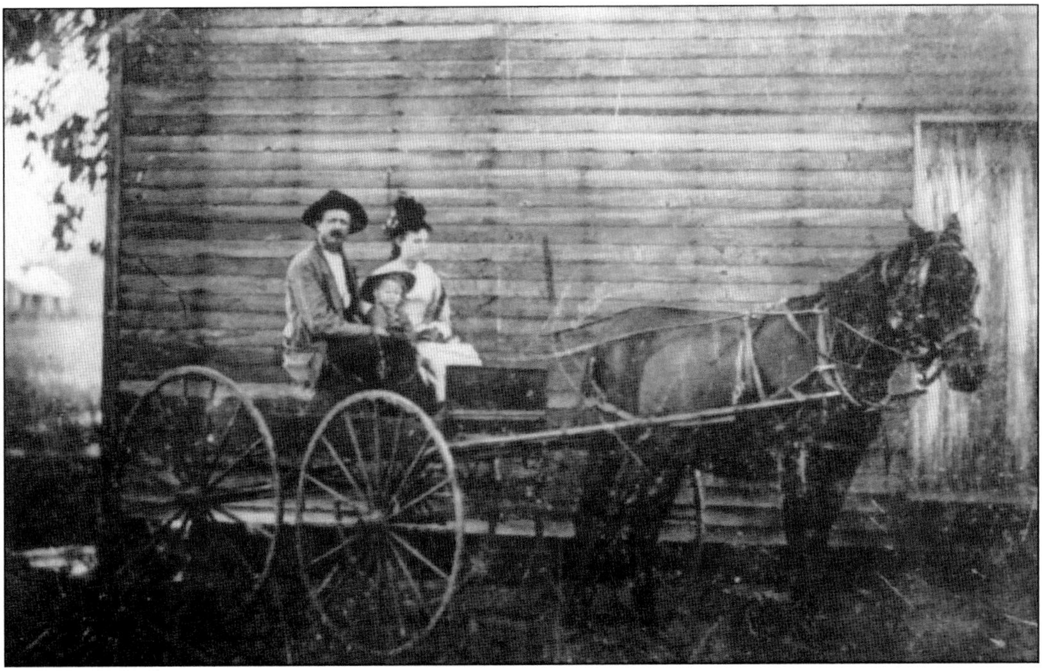

Pictured are Thomas Jefferson Jarvies, Annie Frances, and daughter Minnie Frances. Minnie, born in 1881, married Johnny Blevins and eventually moved to the community of Grapevine. (Courtesy Joyce Gibson Roach.)

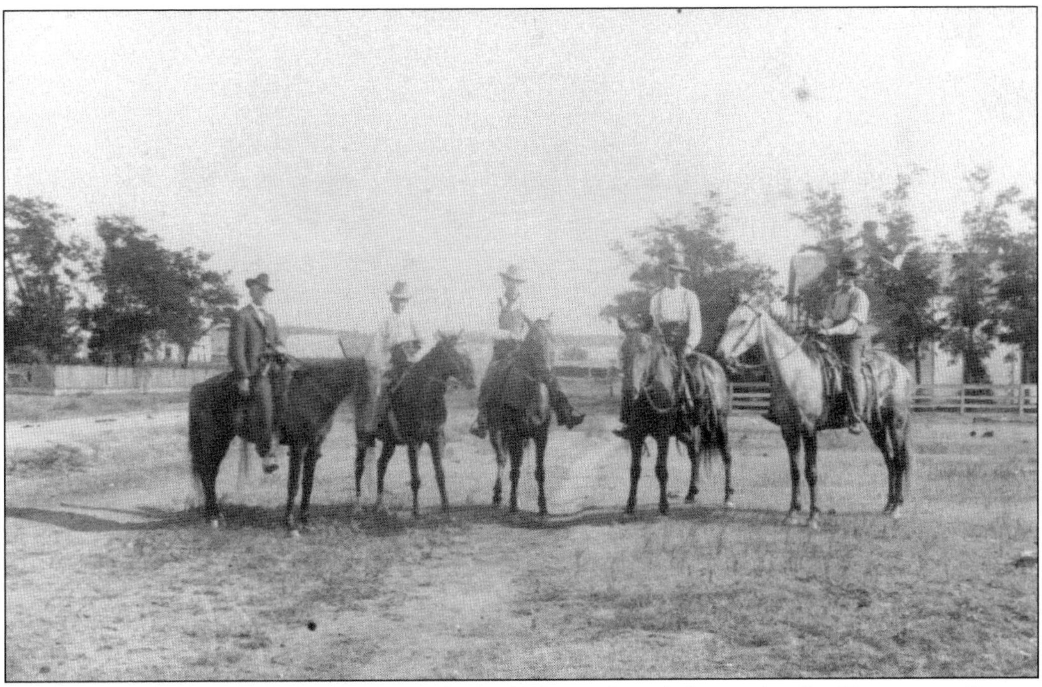

Looking south on Main Street (U.S. Highway 377) are, from left to right, Ike Flannigan, George Pipkin, Johnny Blevins, John Bourland, and Willie Weaver. The Prosser house is on the left and the Prewett house is on the right.

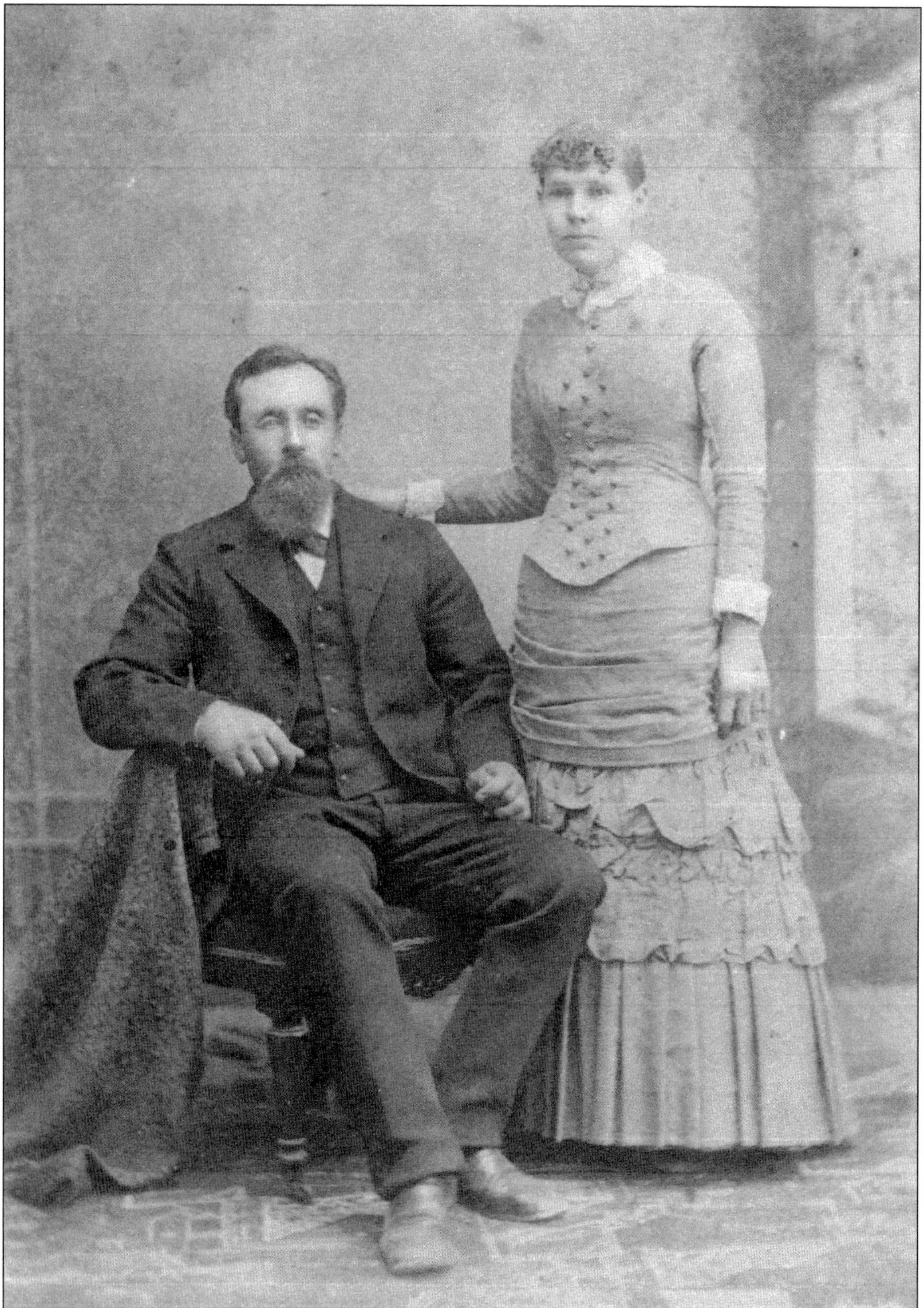

Posing in this studio portrait are Oscar and Ella Prosser Peterson. Oscar married a Virginia girl, Ella, and came to Texas in the early 1870s. (Courtesy Joyce Gibson Roach.)

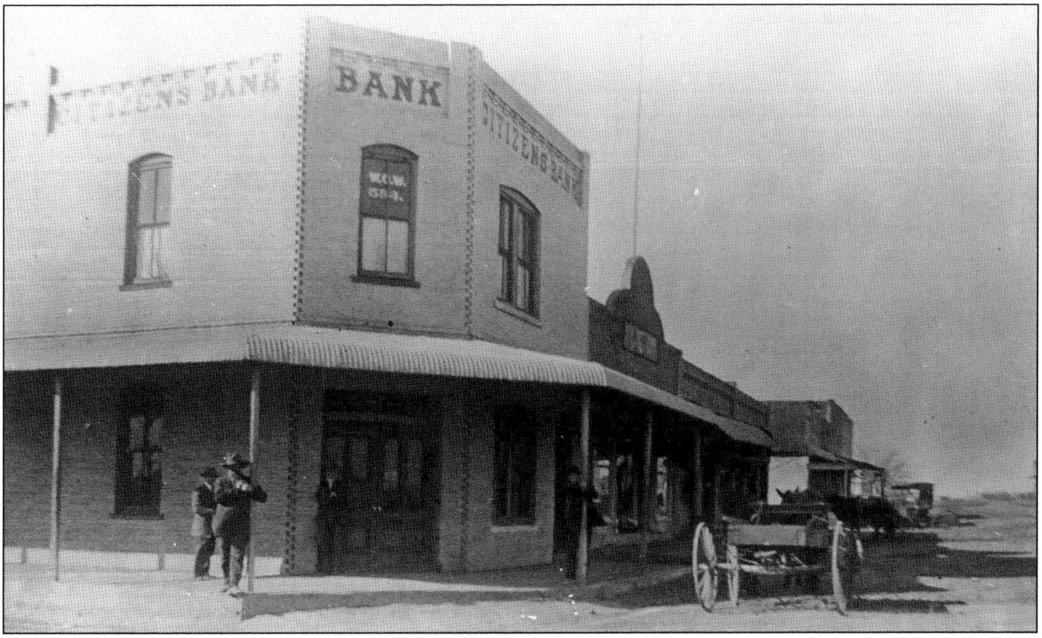

This is Citizens Bank, located on South Main Street, in the 1880s. The bank was originally a three-story building before high winds tore down the top floor. Today this building still stands and houses the Ann Gibson Insurance Agency. (Courtesy Ron Lee.)

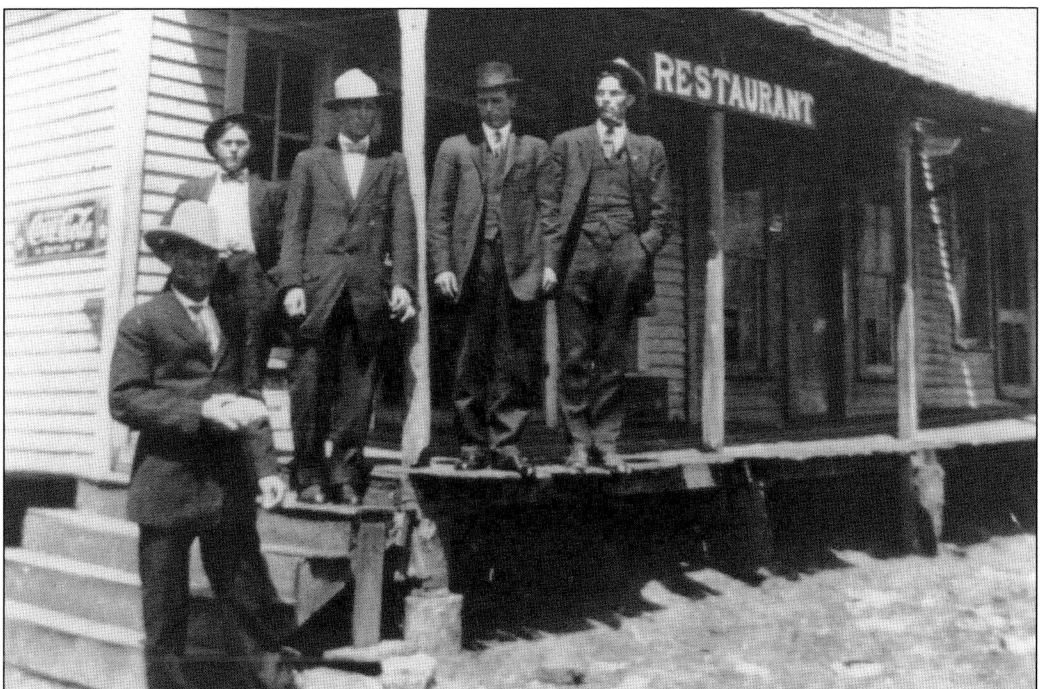

Men pose on the steps of a Keller restaurant. (Courtesy Joyce Gibson Roach.)

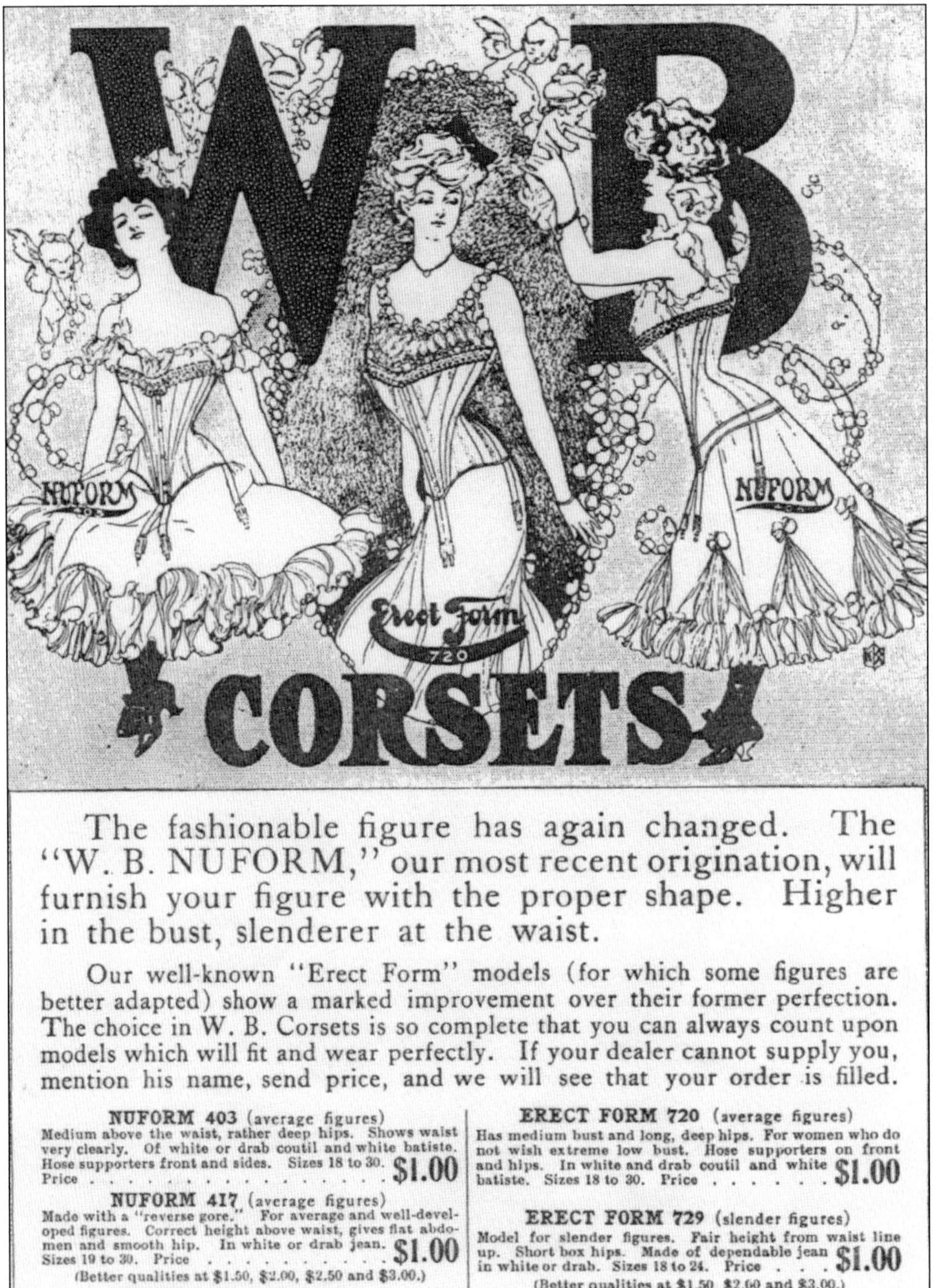

This is a corset ad from a 1906 *Woman's Home Companion* magazine that reflects the dress styles of the time. (Courtesy Joyce Gibson Roach.)

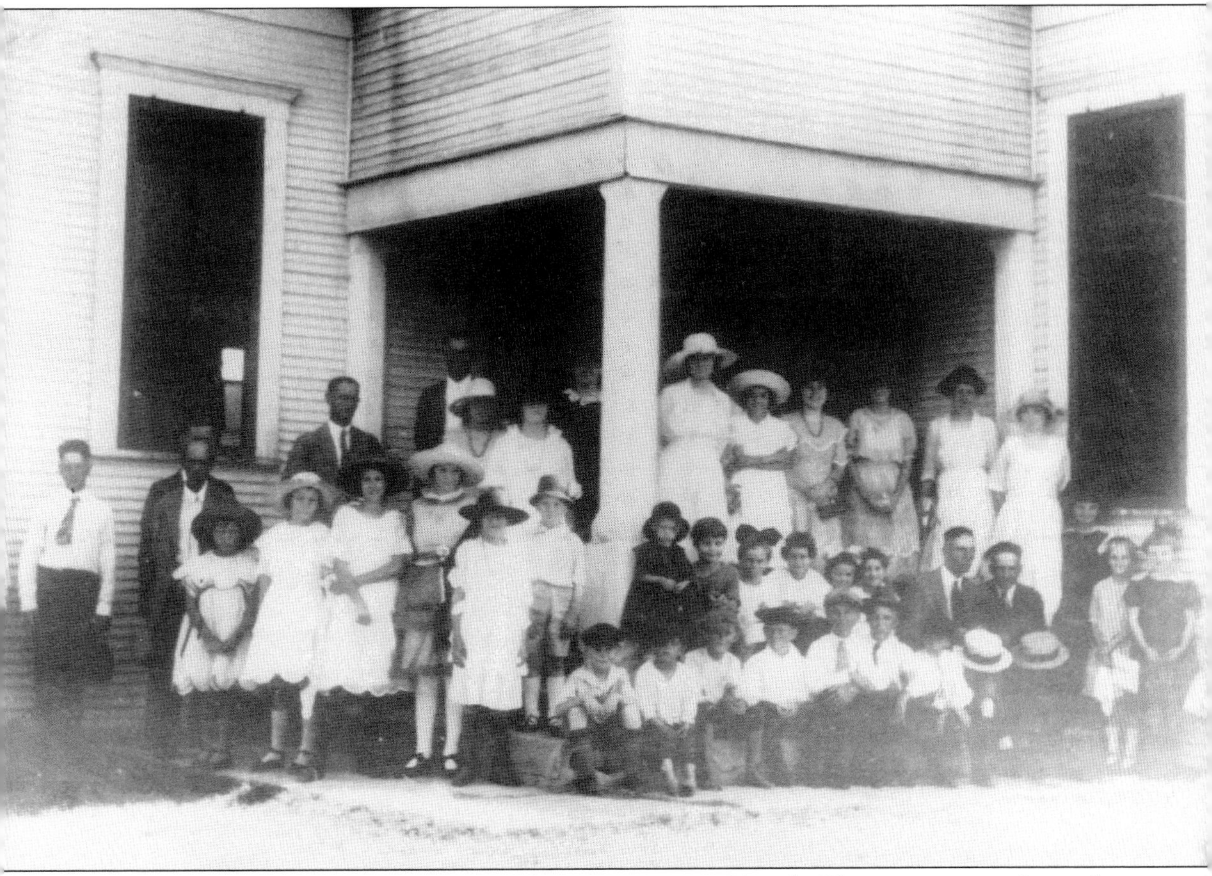

Pictured is a 1920s vacation Bible school of the First Baptist Church. The structure was located on the corner of Main and Price Streets. (Courtesy Joyce Gibson Roach.)

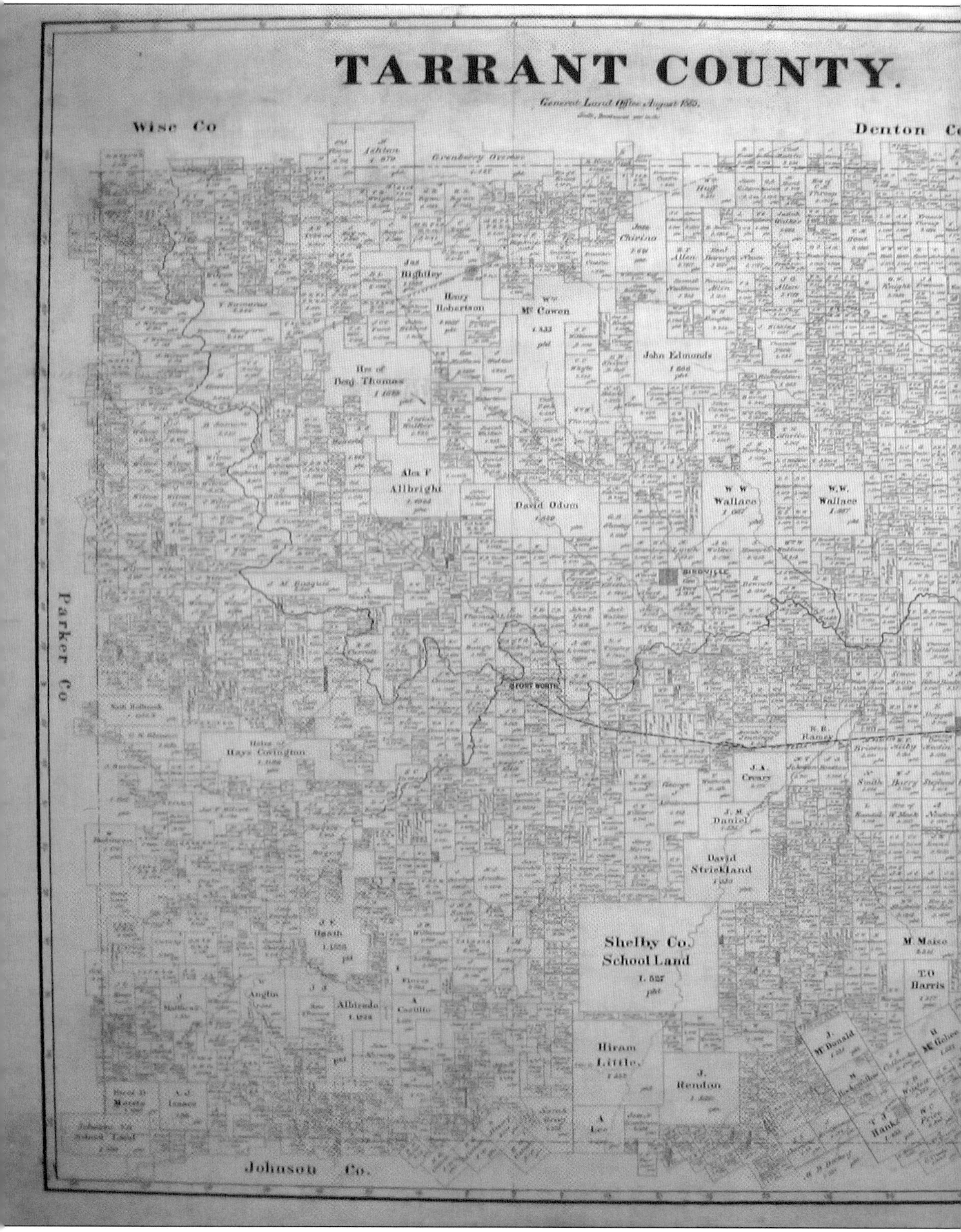
TARRANT COUNTY.
Wise Co
Denton
Parker Co
Johnson Co.
Jas Chirino
Henry Robertson
John Edmonds
Hrs of Benj. Thomas
Alex F Allbright
David Odum
W. W. Wallace
W.W. Wallace
BIRDVILLE
FORT WORTH
Heirs of Hays Covington
J.A. Creary
J. M. Daniel
David Strickland
Shelby Co. School Land
Hiram Little
J. Rendon
M. Maiso
T.O Harris
Johnson Co School Land

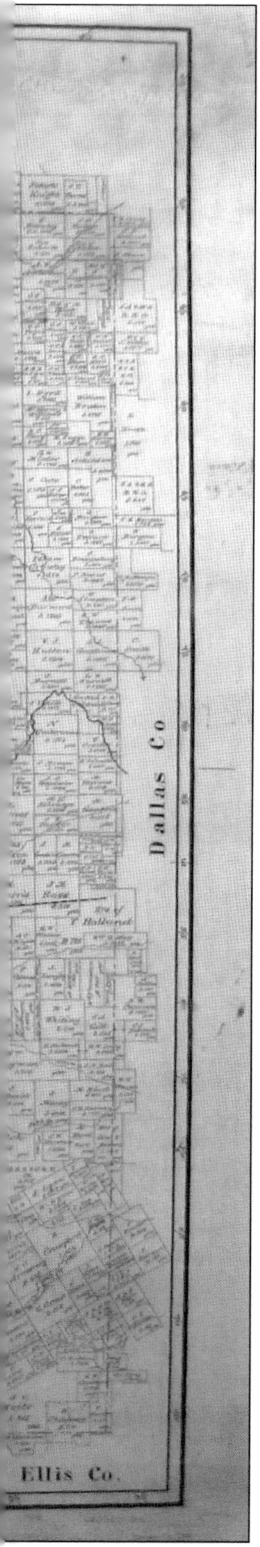

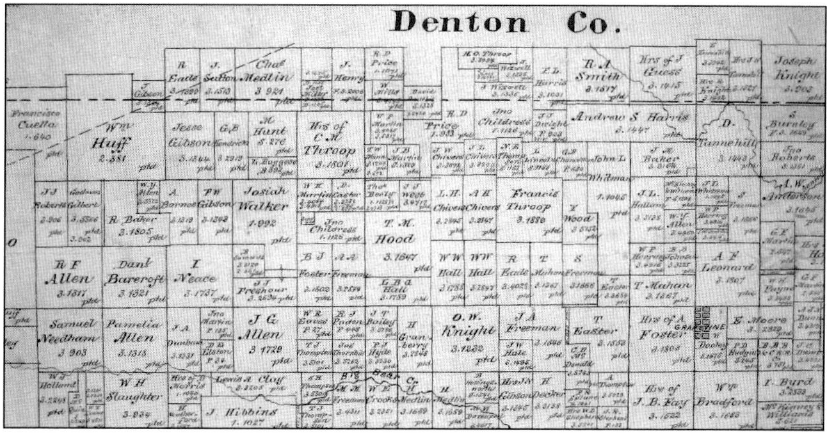

Site surveys were drawn to define family homesteads. Land grants varied in size, and a single man could homestead 160 acres, a man with a family could homestead 320 acres, and a veteran who had served in the Texas War for Independence could claim as mush as 640 acres. Once the free land no longer existed, settlers could buy land ranging from 25¢ to $1 per acre. Texas was ceded to the United States by Mexico in 1845, but land was still measured according to the Spanish varas; 1 varas equals roughly 3 feet. (Courtesy Texas General Land Office, Austin, Texas.)

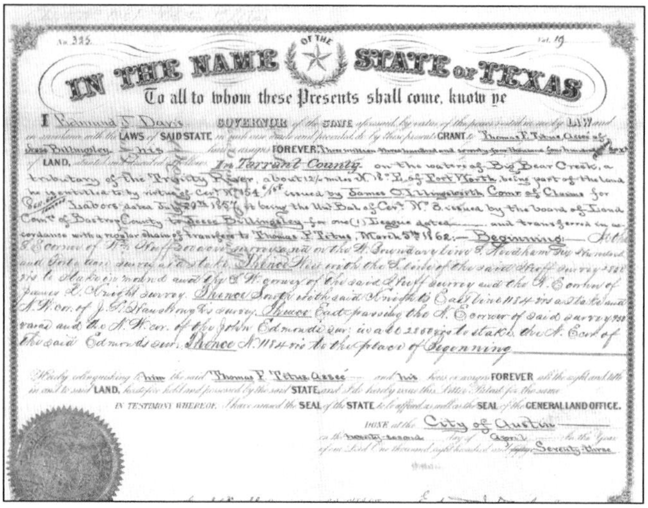
IN THE NAME OF THE STATE OF TEXAS

To all to whom these Presents shall come, know ye

Land grants were issued to families that explained how much land they had and where the boundaries were drawn. This land grant is for Jesse Billingsley, who was born October 10, 1810. Billingsley joined Sam Houston's regiment at the beginning of the Texas Revolution, and on March 1, 1836, he was elected captain. His left hand was permanently damaged during a battle, and the company disbanded in October 1836. Billingsley never settled in Keller and sold his land before he died in October 1880. (Courtesy Homestead Farms.)

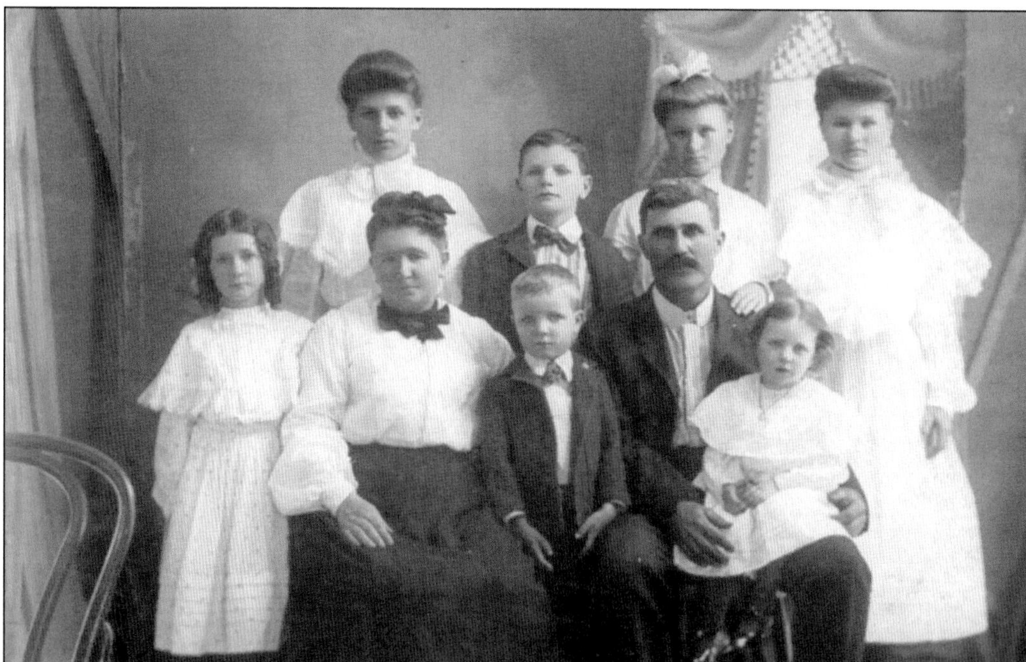

The Stateham family has owned land in Keller for over 100 years, and Homestead Farms is currently a working farm, owned by the descendents of the Stateham clan. Lawson Stateham purchased land in 1889 and ran a garage and grocery located on Main and Hill Streets. This 1903 Stateham family photograph shows, from left to right, (first row) Eula Alice, mother Rebecca Jane, Burl B., father Lawson Stateham, and Thelma; (second row) Ella May, William Harvey, Mattie Alama, and Maude Estelle. (Courtesy Homestead Farms.)

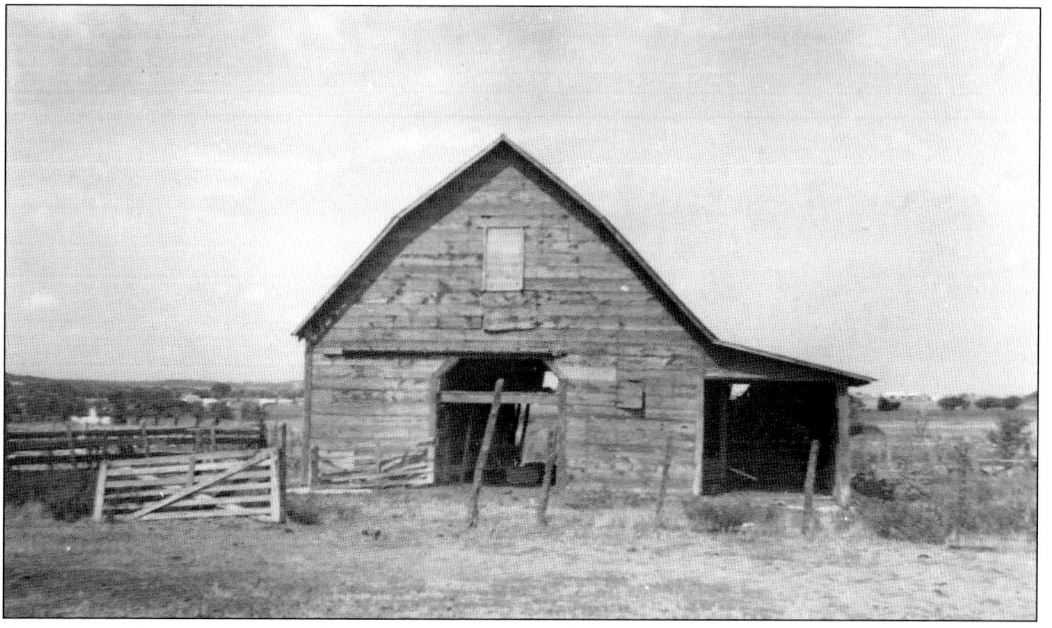

On August 9, 1873, Brother A. D. Bourland (1840–1904), a "hard-shell Baptist preacher" as he was known, purchased 86 acres of land out of the R. E. Allen survey, which was paid for with gold coins. He built the house and barn across from Bourland Cemetery. (Courtesy Ron Lee.)

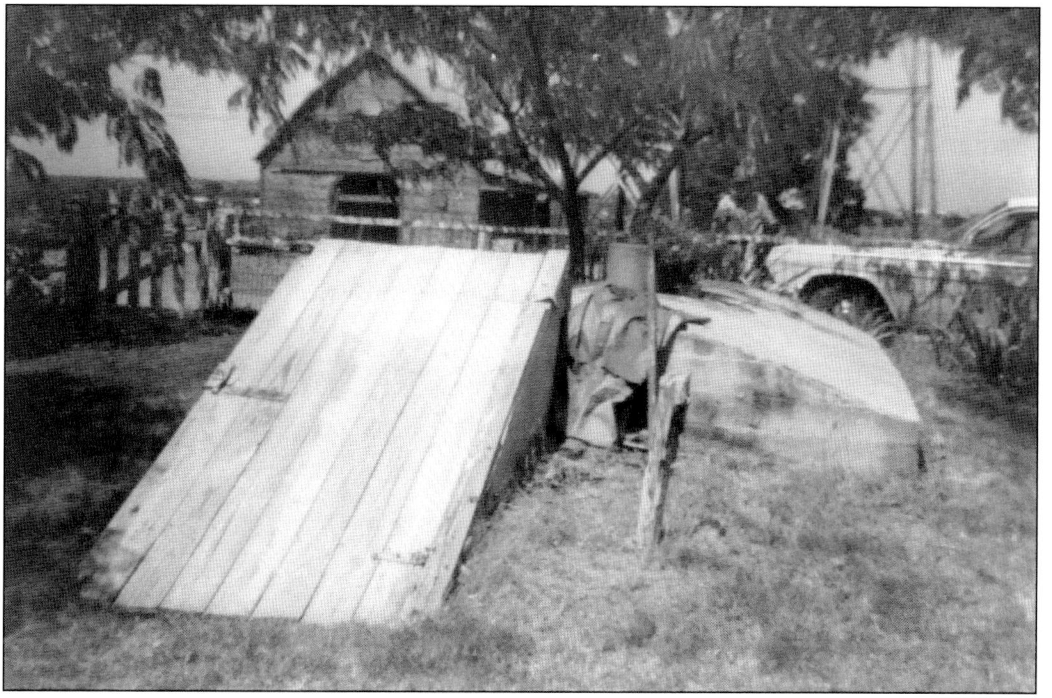

This Bourland farm photograph shows the storm cellar. (Courtesy Joyce Gibson Roach.)

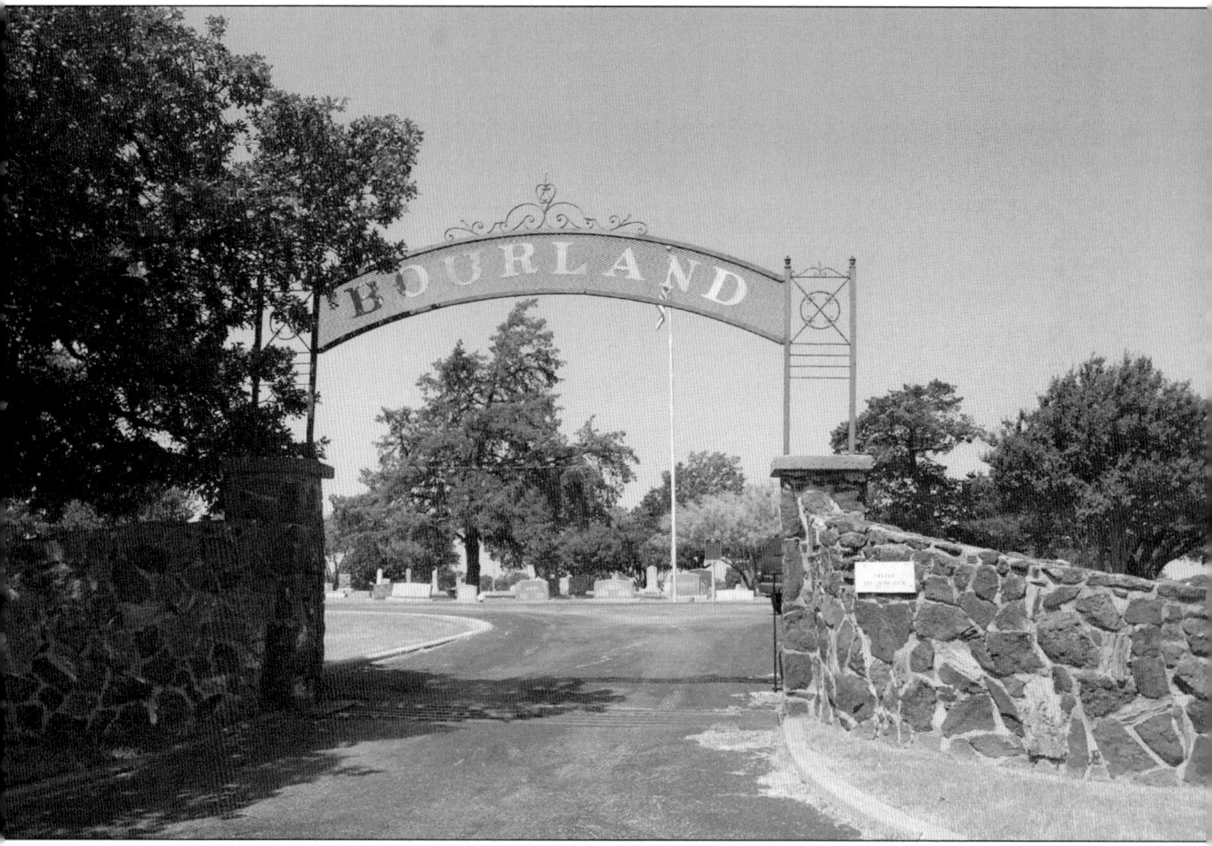

The WPA built the Gateway at Bourland Cemetery in 1935. In 1899, A. D. Bourland sold 2.5 acres, including the grave sites, to residents of Keller for use as a public burial ground. Bourland families donated additional land in 1947, and the A. B. Harmonson (1891–1967) estate donated land in 1977. (Courtesy Jennifer Featherston.)

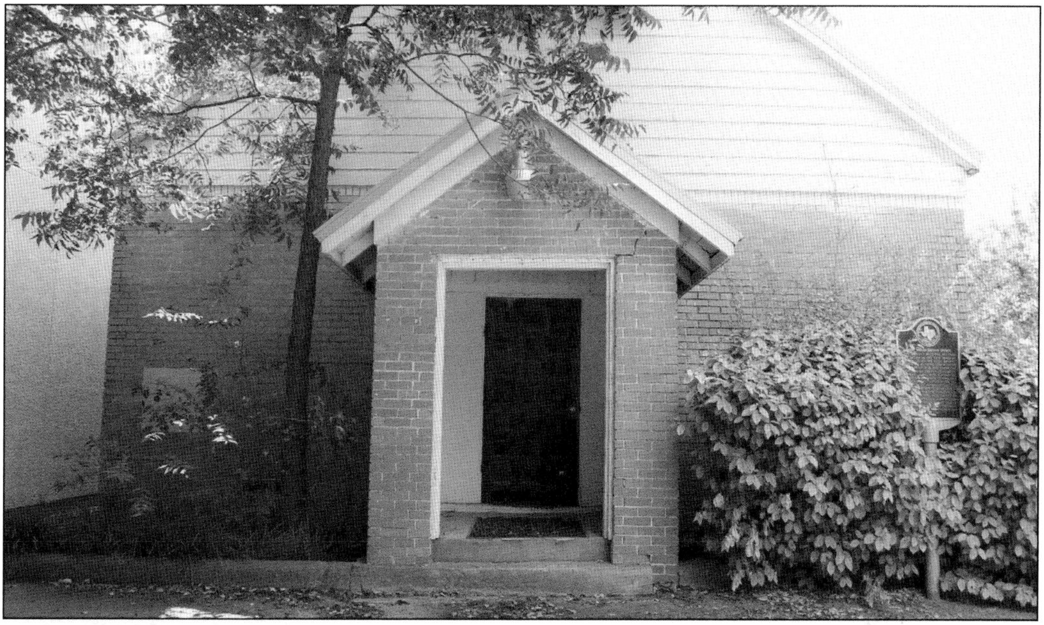

Mt. Gilead Church was founded on July 13, 1850, in the home of Daniel Barcroft. Besides Barcroft, the other charter members were John A. Freeman; Iraneus Neace and his wife, Lucinda; Parmelia Allen; Abby Dunham; and two slaves, Ambrose and Carolin. A log church was built in 1851 and served as a schoolhouse on weekdays. In 1859, American Indians burned the log cabin down, and church services had to be held elsewhere. The church was remodeled and modernized to its present state. (Courtesy Jennifer Featherston.)

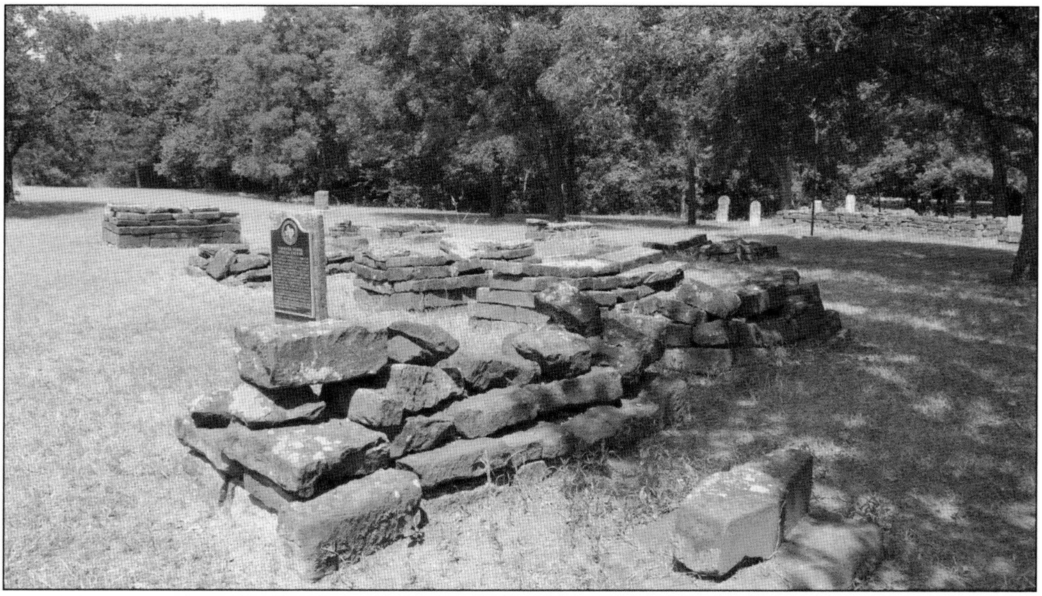

Mt. Gilead Cemetery lies north across the road from the church, and those who are buried here span over four generations of Keller residents. The burial ground originally served as a pioneer settlement of related families who migrated to the area from Missouri in 1847. The earliest marked grave is that of William Joyce (1836–1854). Homemade grave markers reflect the pioneer lifestyle of the early settlers. (Courtesy Jennifer Featherston.)

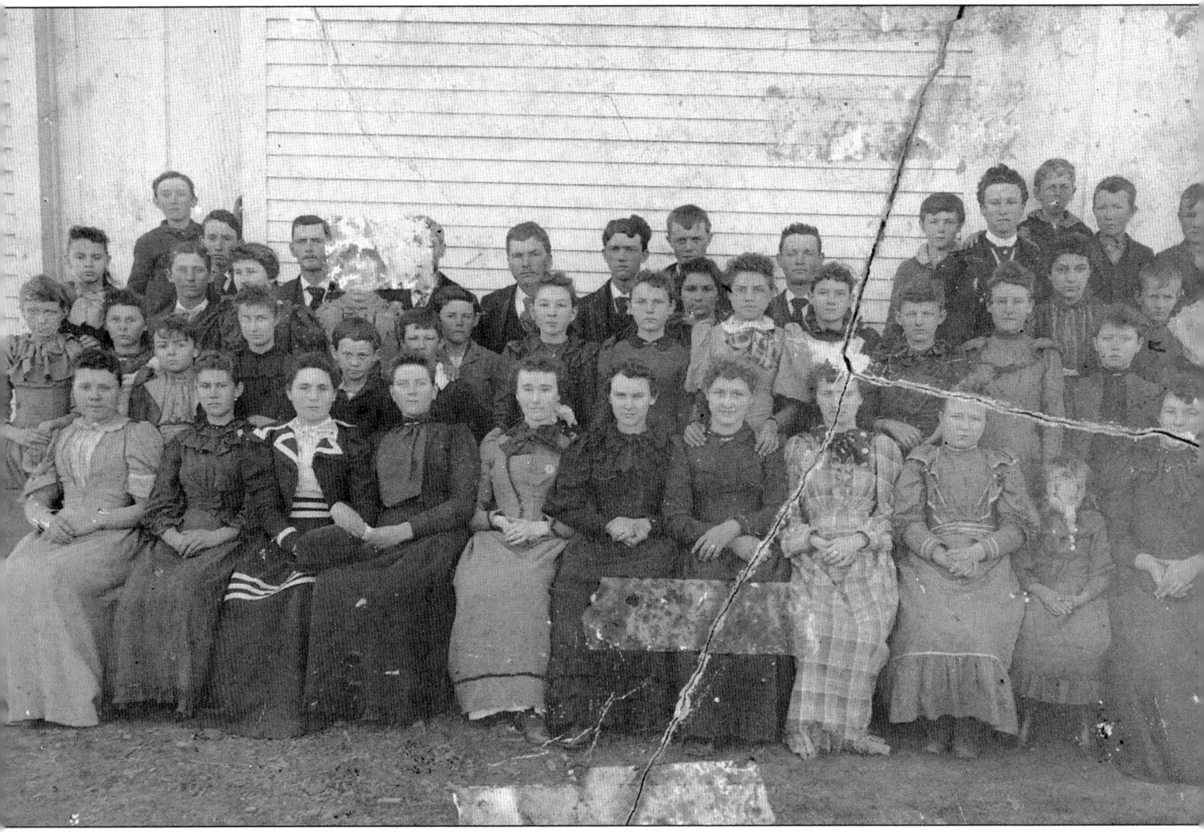

In 19th-century Keller, the school term did not begin until the cotton crop was picked, and it had to end before the next planting season. Once students were able to read the most challenging books available in the classroom, they graduated from school. These *c.* 1895 Keller School students are, from left to right, (first row) Nora McCain, ? Dewitt, Hattie Witten, Lenora Speer, Daisy Wallace, Johnnie White, Virginia Meacham, Virginia Wallace, Lela Ponder, Mary Pipkin, and Lenora Pipkin; (second row) Laura Price, Fannie Cantrell, Hattie Pruvett, Myrtle Merrell, Walter Douglas, Faris Burnett, Walter Hovenkamp, Laura McCain, unidentified, Clara Maxwell, Luten Perry, Lula Davis, Annie Price, Willie Maxwell, Octa Speer, and George Pipkin; (third row) Essie White, Alvin McCain, Ida Flemister, and Eliza Price; (fourth row) Sumpter Boone, Luke Ponder, Jim Speer, Dick Price, Oscar McCain, Ed Bourland, Perry Davis, Tom Meacham, Forest Pruvett, Hol Link, Earl Mays, Fred Pipkin, and Bert Pipkin. (Courtesy Lyda Smith White Collection, the University of Texas at Arlington Library.)

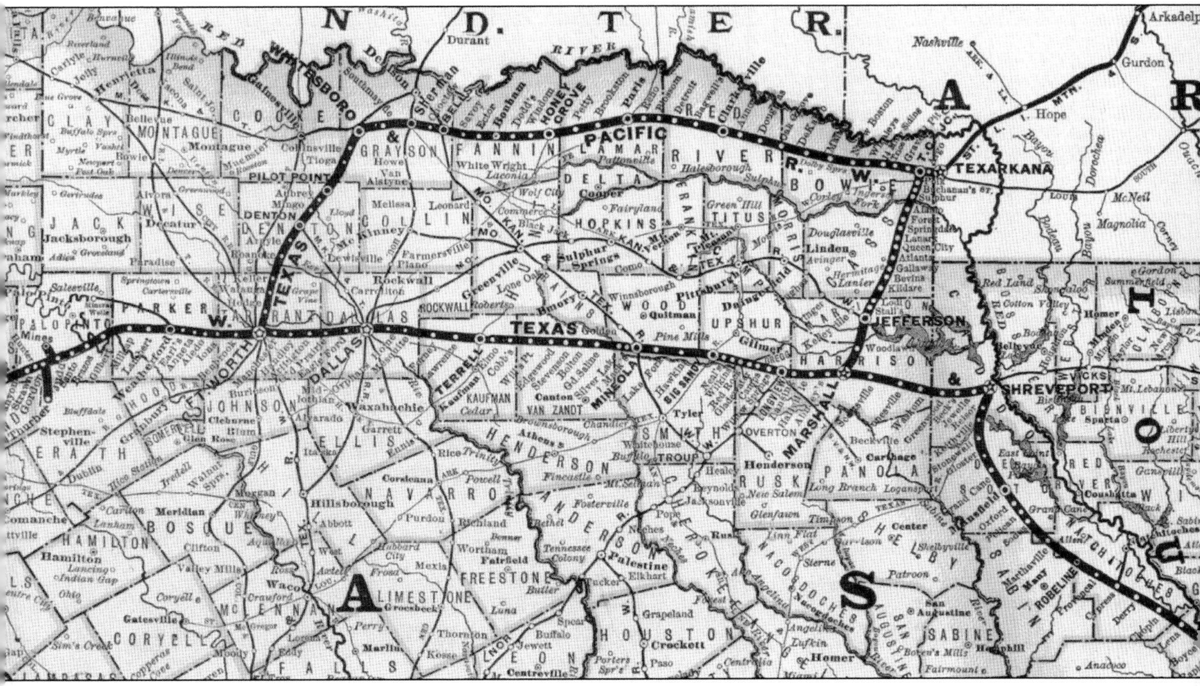

Chester Cy Martin was an aviator in the 1920s. He would fly into Fort Worth from Fort Smith, Arkansas, navigating by using the "Iron Compass," aviators' slang for the railroad. Prior to the Federal Aviation Administration and airways, radio, radar, and aircraft controllers, pilots didn't fly at night or in bad weather. According to Jay Cy Martin's Book, *Chisholm Trail, Déjà vu*, "Every town had at least one railroad, so you bought a map of the railroads and flew in the daytime and low enough to see the ground. You followed a railroad that led to where you wanted to go." This map is from 1897 and shows the railroad stops from El Paso to Shreveport. (Courtesy Texas General Land Office, Austin, Texas.)

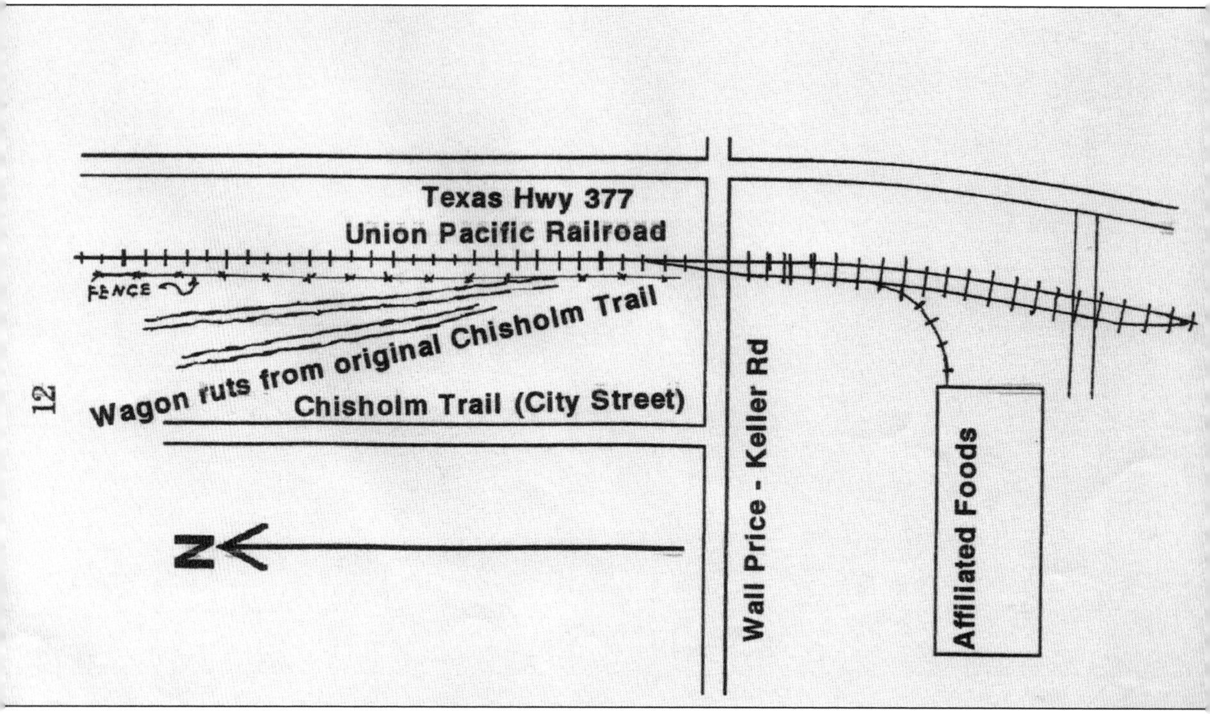

Chisholm Trail was used to move cattle in the late 19th century. The trail ran from South Texas, across the Red River, and up to railheads in Kansas. Many early settlers used this trail as well. Jay Cy Martin added, "The trails followed the shortest practical distance between two points, or at least the easiest grades. It didn't make any sense for a man to wear out his ox team or saddle horse going over a hill when he could go around it!" This map, drawn by Jay Cy Martin in 1992, shows how the railroad would directly stop at Affiliated Foods, what is known today as the Kroger Distribution Center. (Courtesy Jay Cy Martin.)

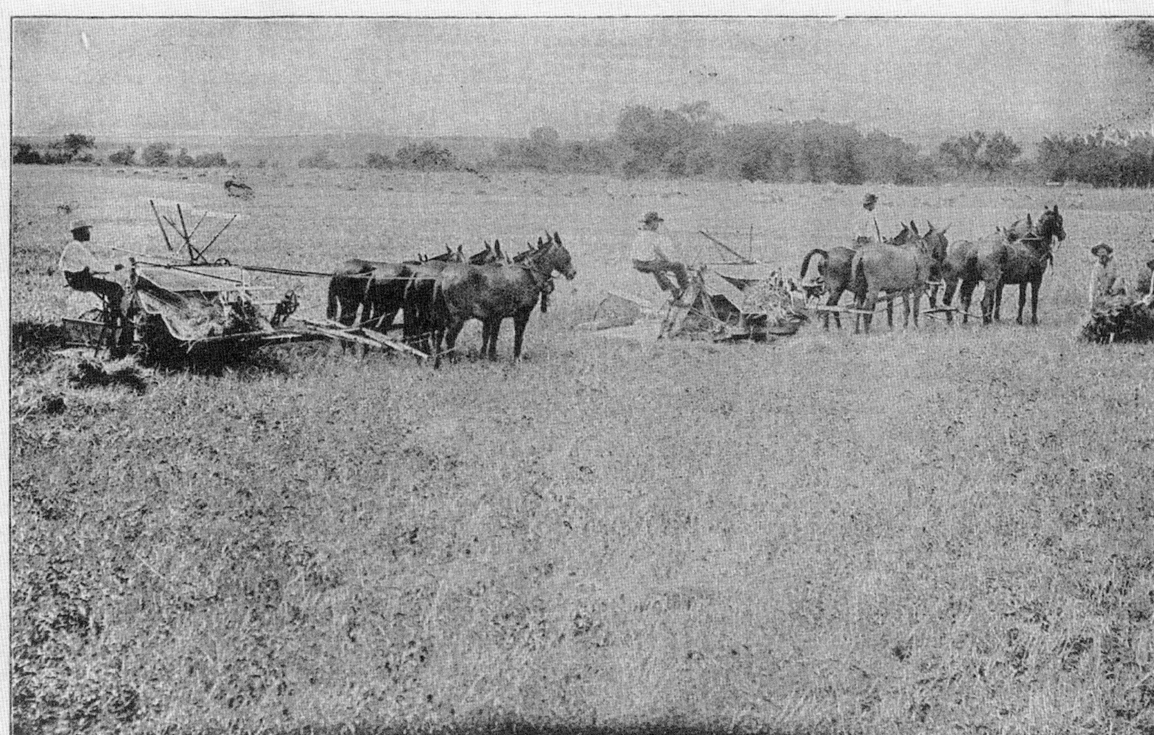

HARVEST SCENE ON LINE OF

THE TEXAS & PACIFIC RAILWAY IN TEXAS.

COME TO TEXAS.

The "Lone Star" is waving—the flag of the free-
Then strike for Texas, if men you would be.
No idlers are wanted, the thrifty and wise
To wealth and high station can equally rise.
Where corn, oats and cotton; the richest of loam,
Which yields to the settlers provisions and home.
Trees of every description arise on each hand,
From alluvial soil to the rich tableland.
Here springs are exhaustless and streams never dry,
In the season from winter to autumn's bright sky,
A wide panorama of prairie is seen;
Of grasses of all kinds perennially green.
Here millions of cattle, sheep, horses and goats
Grow fat as if stall-fed or fattened on oats.
No poverty is found in the mighty domain,
To the man who exerts either finger or brain.

Here are homes for the millions, the rich and the poor,
While Texas opens wide her hospitable door.
She has thousands of acres—yes, millions—to sell,
Yet can point without cost to where pre-emptors can dwell.
Her terms will be easy with those whom she deals,
While security all in their title can feel.
Buy land while 'tis cheap, and the finest select,
'Twill, young men, prove a fortune when least you expect.
Old man, for your children, buy, file it away;
A Godsend 'twill prove on some rainy day

For a handsome book fully describing this wonderful country, address E. P. TURNER, General Passenger and Ticket Agent, Texas & Pacific Railway, Dallas, Tex.

This 1897 advertisement describes a harvest scene on the line of the Texas and Pacific Railway. It reads, "The 'Lone Star' is waving—the flag of the free—Then strike for Texas, if men you would be. No idlers are wanted, the thrifty and wise to wealth and high station can equally rise. Where corn, oats and cotton; the richest of loam, which yields to the settlers provisions and home. Trees of every description arise on each hand, from alluvial soil to the rich tableland. Here springs are exhaustless and streams never dry, in the season from winter to autumn's bright sky, a wide panorama of prairie is seen; of grasses of all kinds perennially green. Here millions of cattle, sheep, horses and goats grow fat as if stall-fed or fattened on oats. No poverty is found in the mighty domain, to the man who exerts either finger or brain. Here are homes for the millions, the rich and the poor, while Texas opens wide her hospitable door. She has thousands of acres—yes, millions—to sell, yet can point without cost to where pre-emptors can dwell. Her terms will be easy with those whom she deals, while security all in their title can feel. Buy land while 'tis cheap, and the finest select, 'twill, young men, prove a fortune when least you expect. Old man, for your children, buy, file it away; a Godsend 'twill prove on some rainy day. For a handsome book fully describing this wonderful country, address E. P. Turner, General Passenger and Ticket Agent, Texas & Pacific Railway, Dallas, Tex."

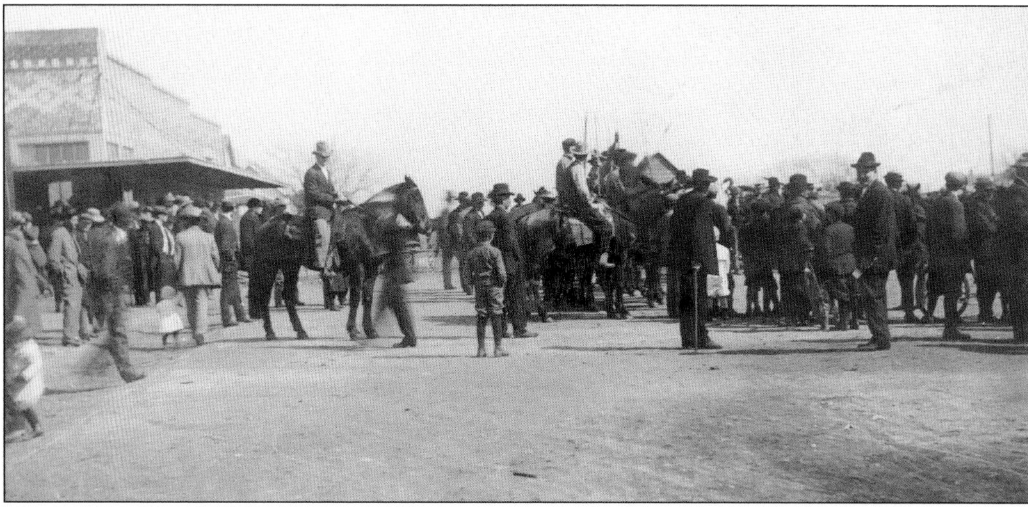

Keller was originally a community called Athol, and in 1879 there were rumors that a railroad was coming through northern Texas. The only way to travel up to that point was by horseback or wagons, and it was a two-day trip to the town of Fort Worth. Excitement began to build as the neighbors learned that the train would go as far north as Denton and to further parts unknown. Excitement built, and it was all anyone could talk about. Everyone who had influence was doing their best to bring the railroad stop to town. The construction boss and railroad engineer named John C. Keller suggested that if the community named the town after him, he would see to it that Athol received its train stop. (Courtesy Lyda Smith White Collection, the University of Texas at Arlington Library.)

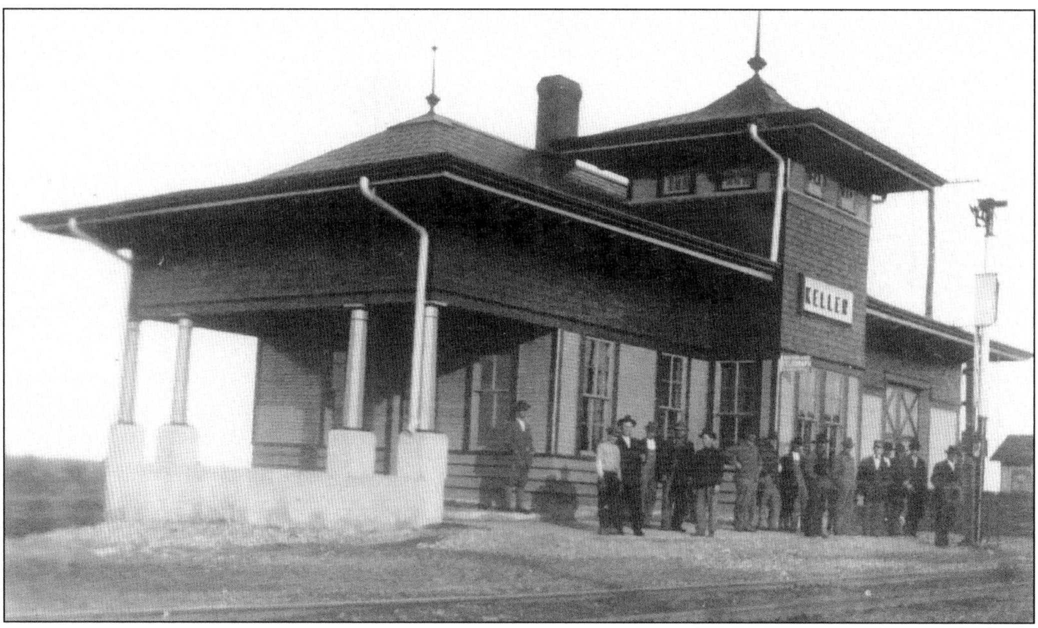

The Keller Train Depot was completed, and the first train came through Keller on May 9, 1881. It was a festive occasion, as people came from miles around to celebrate. Talk of the train drew settlers to Keller; proximity of nearby rivers and creeks, and vast amount of land to build on, were also huge draws. The town of Double Spring relocated to Keller—even the post office, which records show moved in 1882. (Courtesy Ron Lee.)

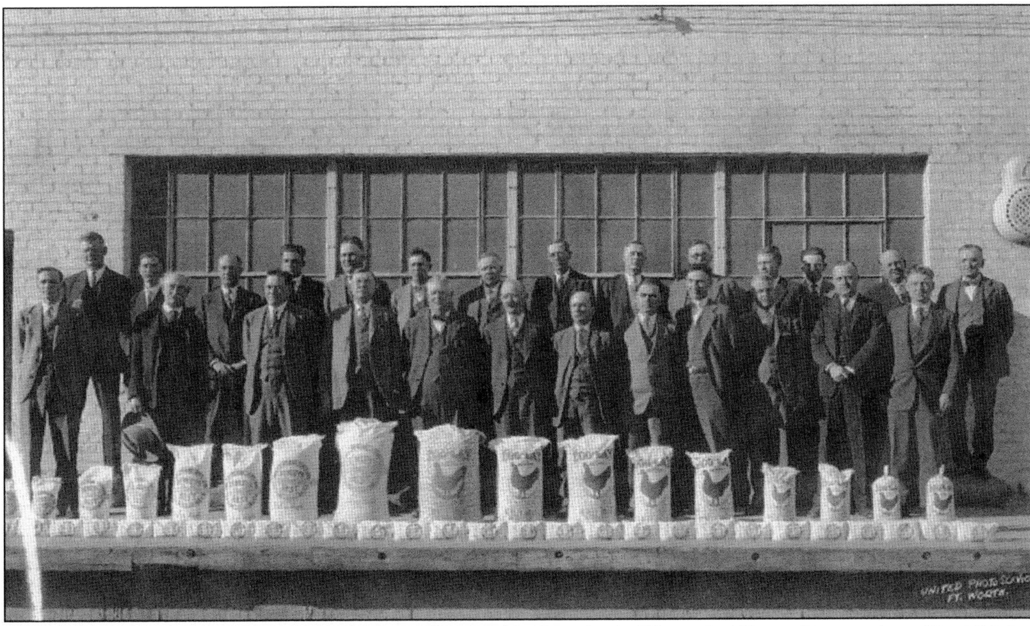

This is a sales meeting at Anchor Roller Mills Bewley's Flour Mill on December 31, 1926, a few years before "The Crash" that would be the worst economic disaster in American history. (Courtesy Keller Lions Club.)

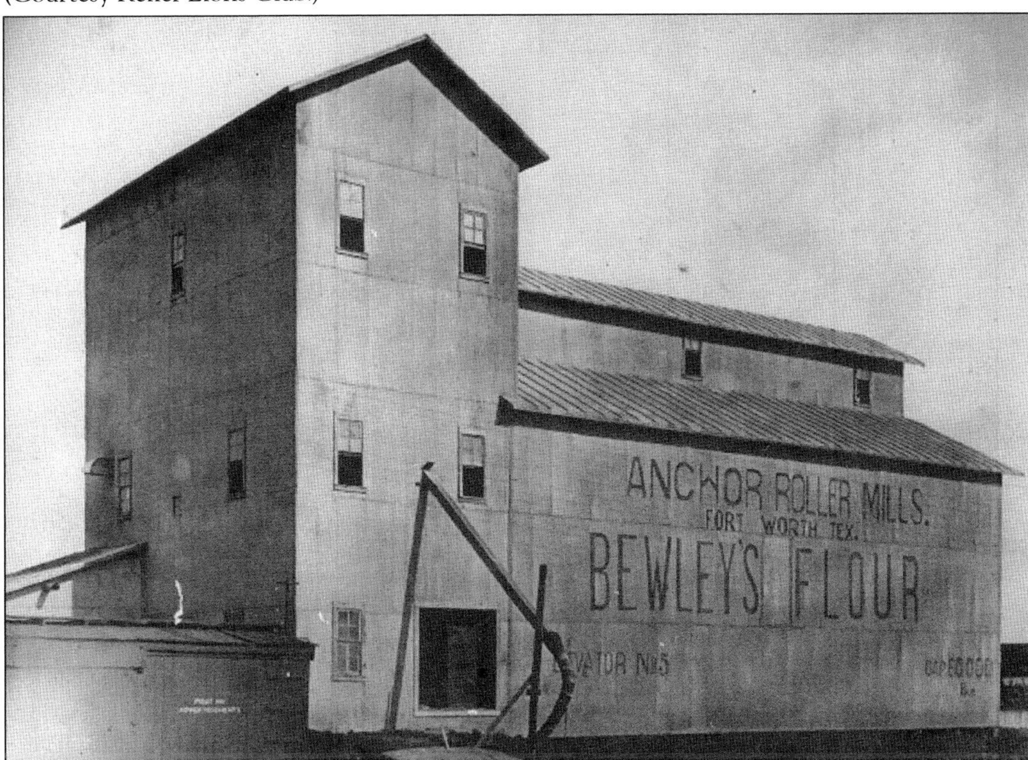

Anchor Roller Mills Bewley's Flour Mill was located adjacent to the railroad tracks just off of Main Street (U.S. Highway 377). (Courtesy Keller Lions Club.)

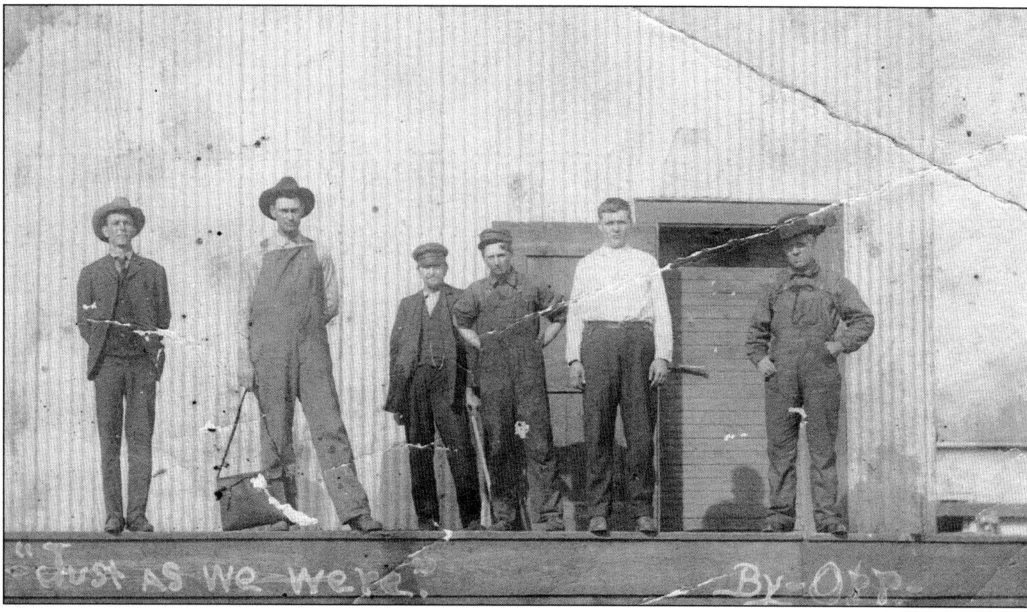

Men standing on dock of the Bewley's Flour Mill are waiting for the train. (Courtesy Joyce Gibson Roach.)

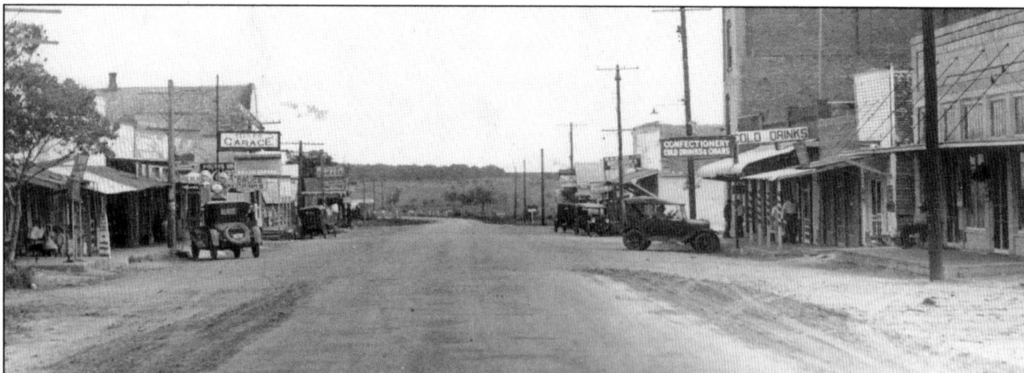

This is a Keller street scene in 1928 looking south on Main and Olive Streets. Model T Fords were the popular car and can be seen parked in front of stores. (Courtesy, *Fort Worth Star Telegram* Collection, Special Collections, the University of Texas at Arlington Library, Arlington, Texas.)

Two

GREAT DEPRESSION, GREATER HOPE

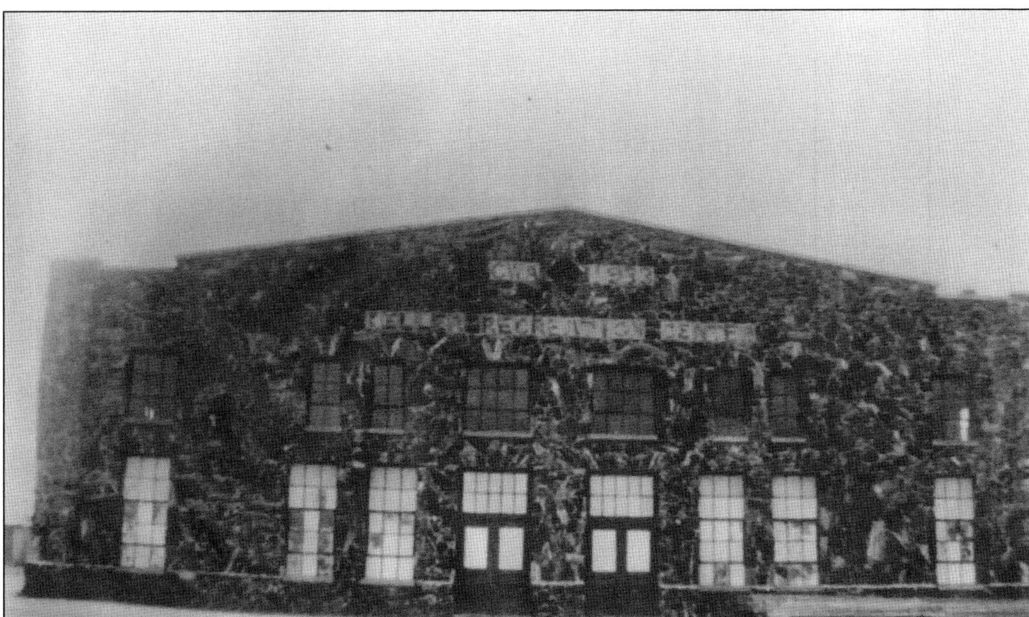

It took the Great Depression and the government sponsored Works Progress Administration to create jobs needed to build the gymnasium, or "Rock Gym" as it is affectionately called. The gymnasium was built as a community project on school property. Local residents supplied much of the native stone used in the construction. However, neighboring folklore states that most of the stone came from the White Farm off of Mt. Gilead and Roanoke Road, which was a turkey farm. The new school was completed in 1939 under the administration of R. L. Bray.

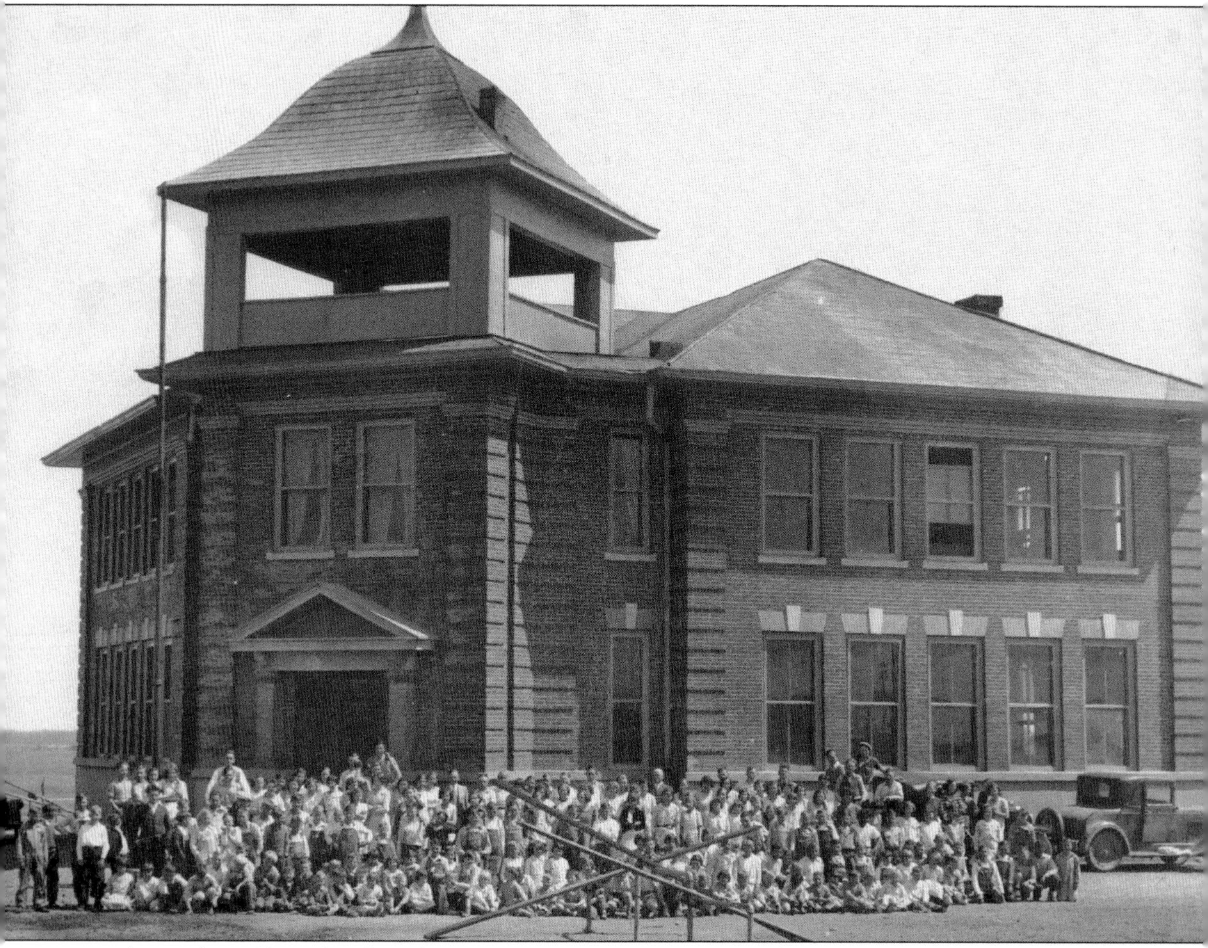

This is the Keller School graduating class of 1932. This larger redbrick school replaced the "Little Red Schoolhouse" on the Keller Waterworks site. It was two stories with three or four classrooms on the lower level and three large rooms on the upper level. The rooms were built with folding doors so the entire area could be opened up to accommodate public meetings. There was a small stage in the largest room, which also featured a small library. John White was the superintendent of the redbrick school, and one of the teachers was Mrs. W. A. Bates, who later became principal. The first graduating class was in 1914–1915 and only featured 10 grades. This school burned to the ground in 1938. (Courtesy *Fort Worth Star-Telegram* Collection, the University of Texas at Arlington Library.)

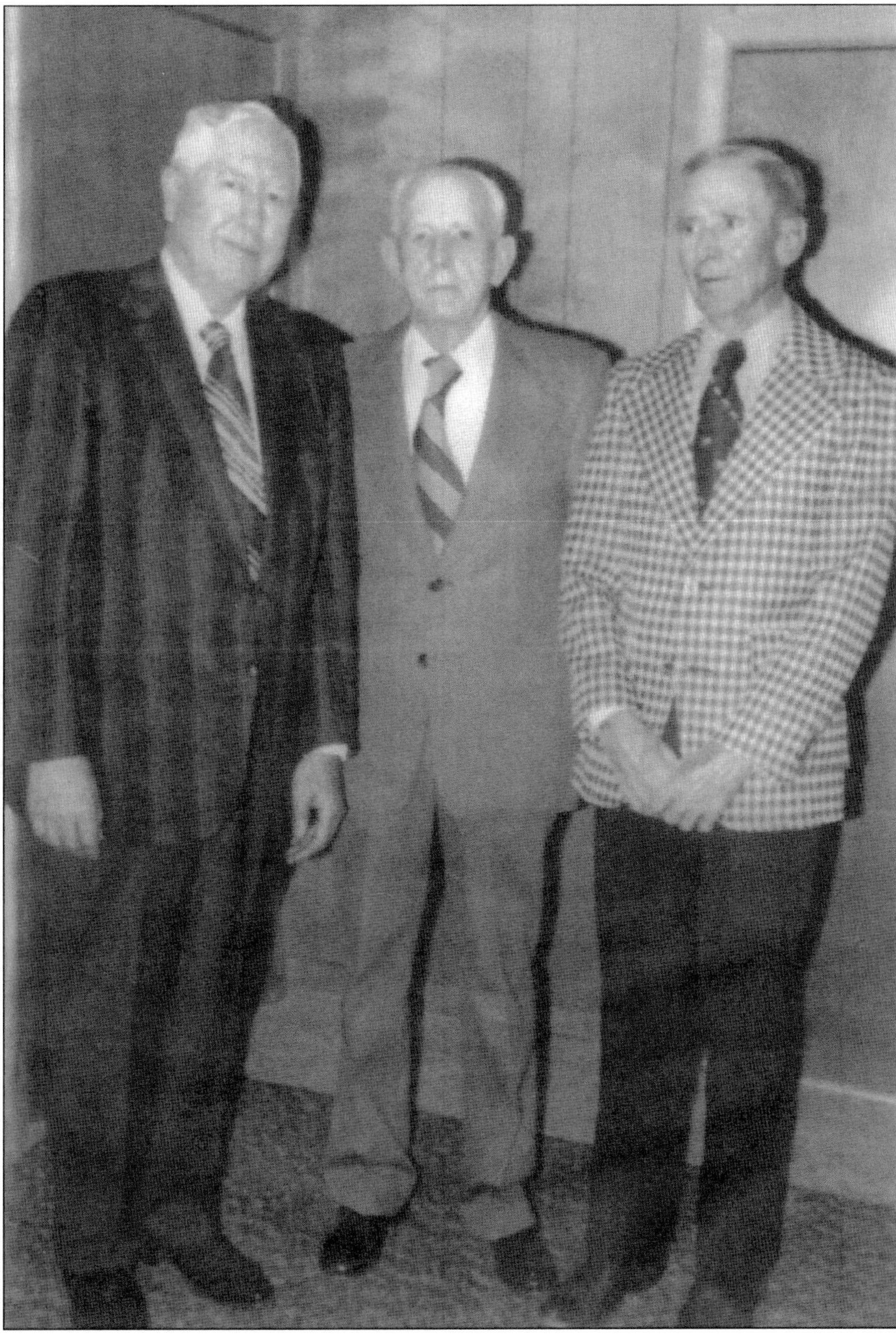

These bank men, pictured from left to right, are Cotton Cartwright, Jim Jarvies, and Ray White. On November 19, 1929, the Keller State Bank employed Robert L. "Cotton" Cartwright. Between 1942 and 1946, while Robert was in World War II, the Keller State Bank sold its notes at full value to Union Bank and Trust in Fort Worth, along with the deposits. James E. "Jim" Jarvies was given the position of vice president. The Keller State Bank's charter was later liquidated.

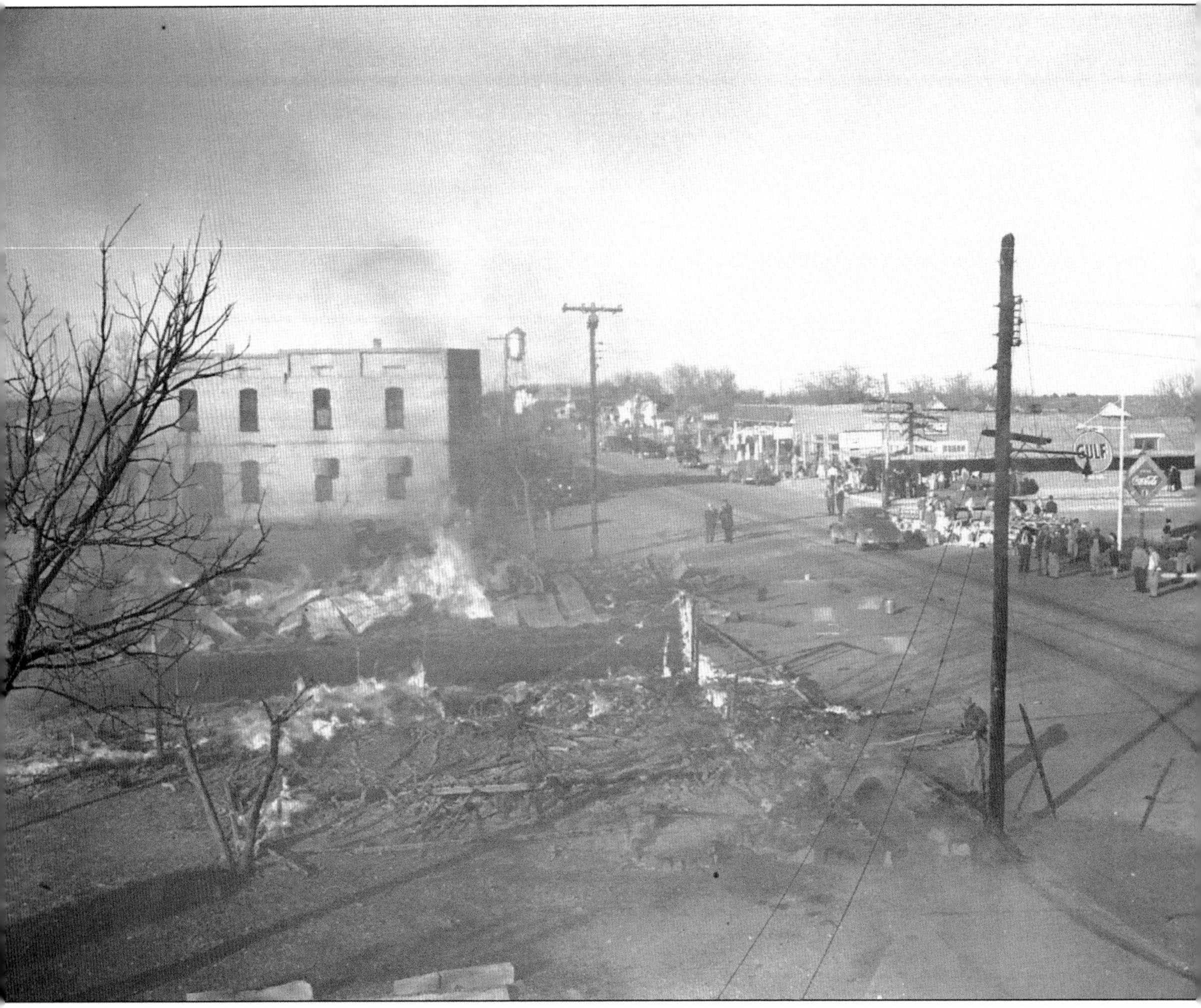

Flames swept through Keller in December 1941. Residents watched helplessly as a lumberyard, beauty parlor, and a hardware store burned to the ground on Main Street. Soon after this incident, a volunteer fire department was formed. (Courtesy *Fort Worth Star-Telegram* Collection, the University of Texas at Arlington Library.)

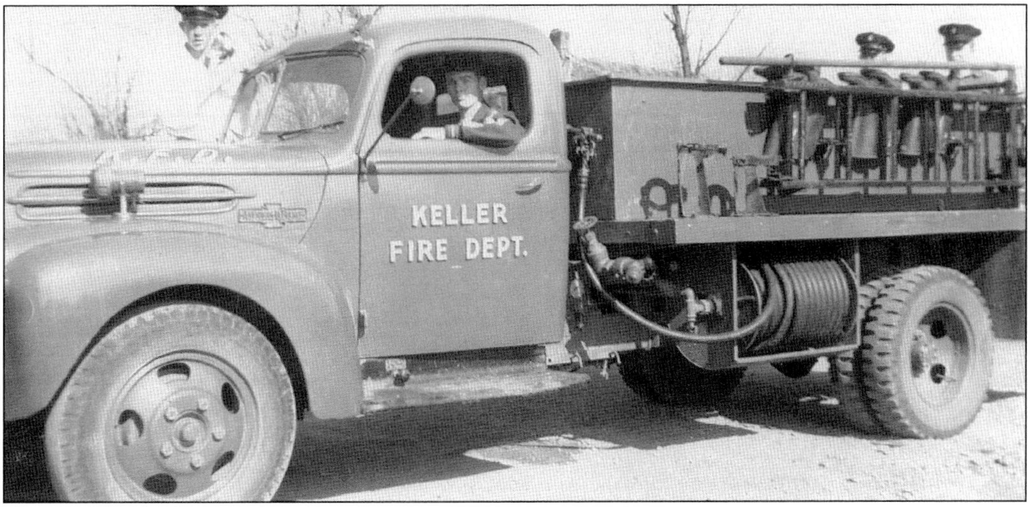

This 1951 photograph shows a Keller Fire Department truck. The driver is Larry Buchanan, standing on the passenger running board is Wendel Berry, and the men at the rear of the truck are unidentified. (Courtesy Keller Fire Department.)

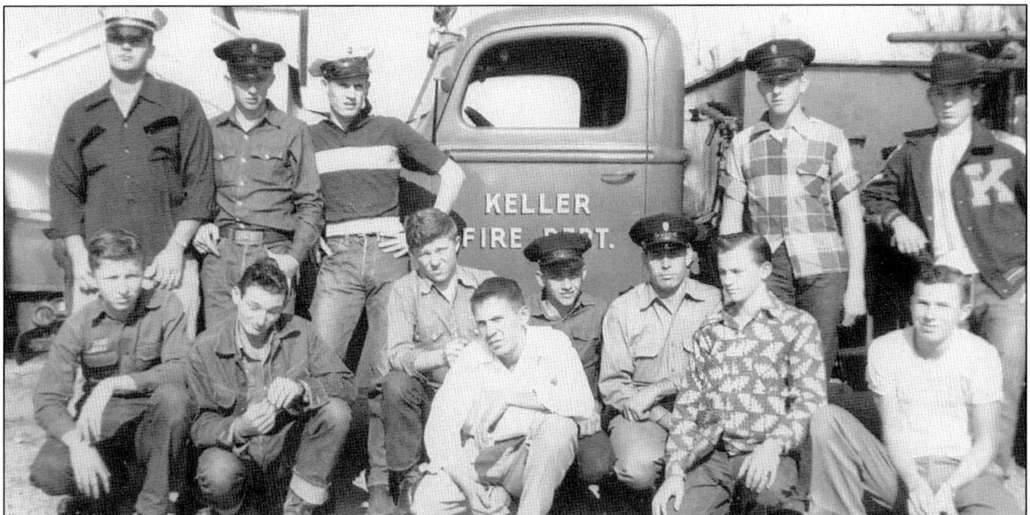

Members of the 1951 Keller volunteer fire department are, from left to right, (first row) Andy Armstrong, Gary Hughes, Billy Travis, Wendel Berry, John Wayne Oldham, James Marcum, Lanny Partin, and Dwayne Miller; (second row) Billy Johnson, Jimmy Oldham, Marlin Braddock, unidentified, and Larry Buchannan. (Courtesy Keller Fire Department.)

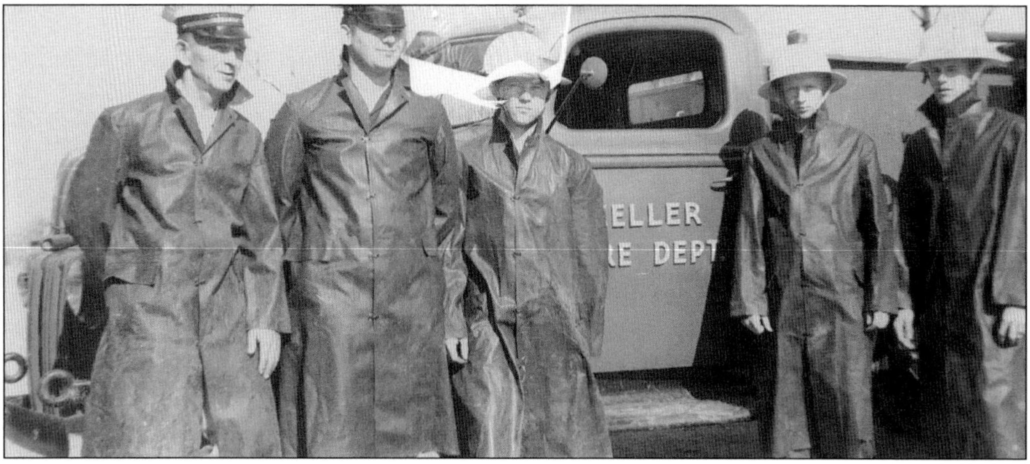

Pictured here from left to right are 1951 fire chief B. Stephenson (left), Billy Johnson, Billy Travis, Jimmy Oldham, and Marling Braddock. Current fire chief Chuck Blankenship is Stephenson's grandson. (Courtesy Keller Fire Department.)

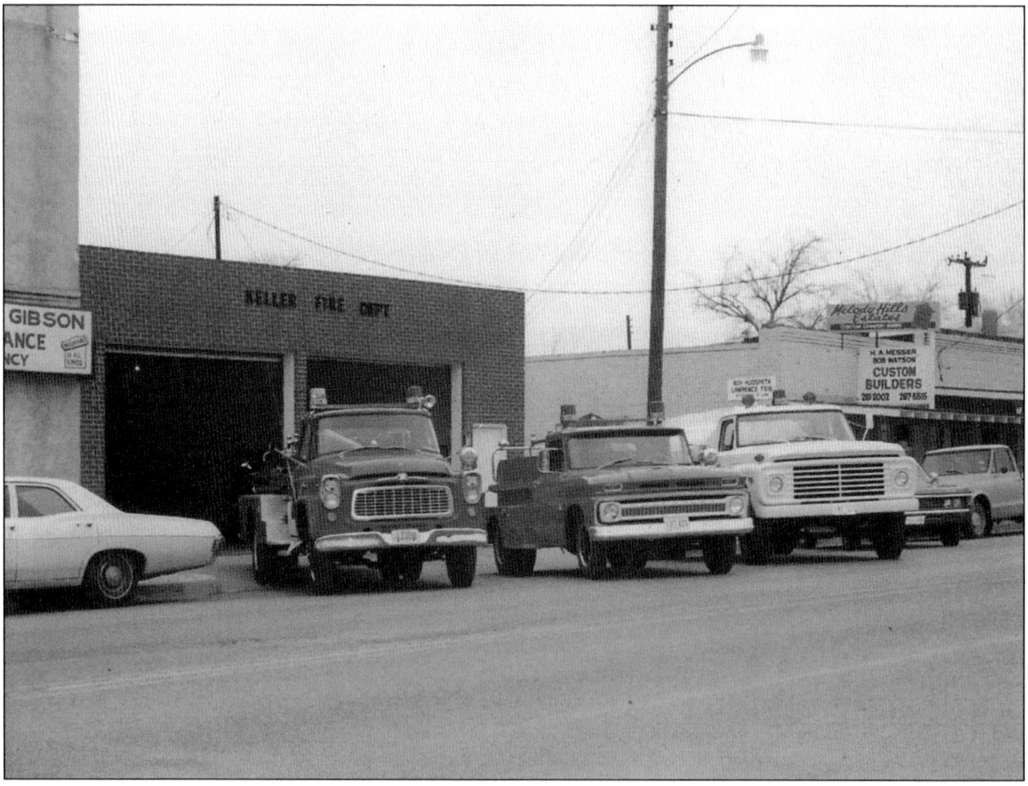

This mid-1960s photograph shows Keller Fire Hall, which was located on Main Street (U.S. Highway 377) next to Ann Gibson Insurance Agency. The Keller Fire Administration offices are currently located in the same place, however the building has been remodeled. (Courtesy Keller Fire Department.)

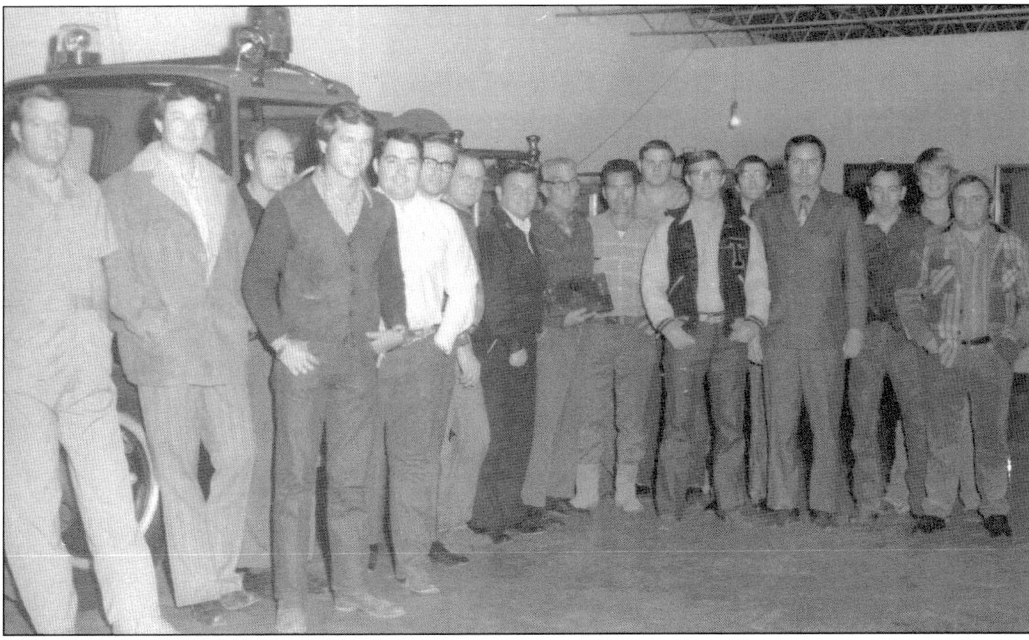

The Keller volunteer firemen in this *c.* 1965 photograph are, from left to right, Wilson Pipkin, Donald Blevins, Q. Marcum, Bob Watson, Bill Ford Blevins, J. B. Marcum, Joe Britt, Charles Elrod, unidentified, councilman Bob Dane, Dub Swanzy, Tim Price, unidentified, Robert Lee, Jeff Marcum, unidentified, and Johnny Cephus. (Courtesy Keller Fire Department.)

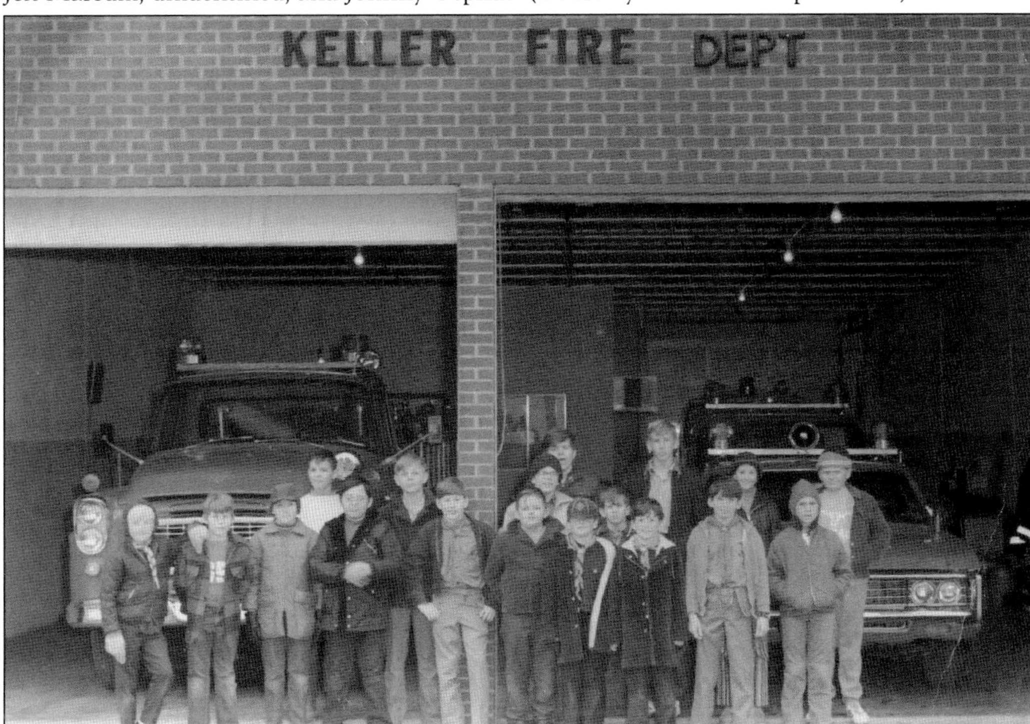

These Cub Scouts about are on a field trip to the Keller Fire Department around 1970.

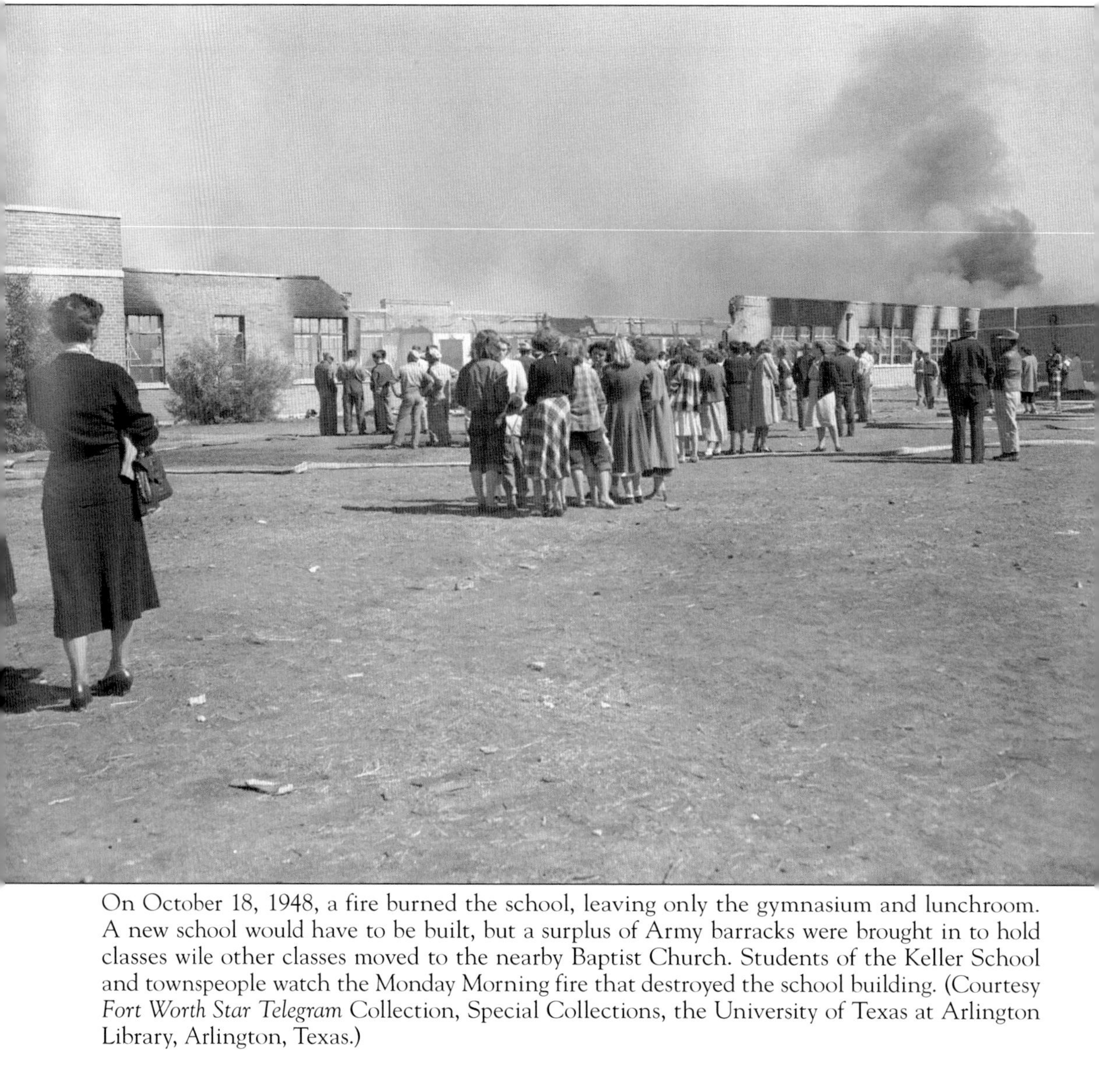

On October 18, 1948, a fire burned the school, leaving only the gymnasium and lunchroom. A new school would have to be built, but a surplus of Army barracks were brought in to hold classes wile other classes moved to the nearby Baptist Church. Students of the Keller School and townspeople watch the Monday Morning fire that destroyed the school building. (Courtesy *Fort Worth Star Telegram* Collection, Special Collections, the University of Texas at Arlington Library, Arlington, Texas.)

Keller Community Gloomy In Wake of School Blaze

KELLER, Oct. 19 (Spl).—The smoking ruins of the Keller School, which burned Monday morning a few minutes after a mysterious explosion in the attic of the building, cast an atmosphere of gloom over this Tarrant County farm community Tuesday morning as plans went forward to rebuild the structure.

Students, teachers and patrons alike were saddened by the loss of the school, built in 1938 at a cost of $76,000. Not even the smallest youngsters in the beginner grades appeared happy over the "no school" announcement.

Meanwhile, Superintendent Randell Simpson was in Austin arranging for a new supply of text books and securing information necessary to speed the financing of a new building. He will return here Tuesday in time for a meeting of the school board at 7 p. m. in the school gymnasium.

Principal Seaborn Jones was conferring Tuesday with pastors of six churches here with the idea that school classes might use space in Sunday school buildings temporarily. No effort will be made to resume classwork this week, Jones said, and it may not be possible to arrange for emergency classrooms until about Nov. 1.

Most of the 325 students might be housed temporarily in the school gymnasium and lunchroom buildings, Jones said, but it would require about a week to remodel them and install partitions.

Jones said Tuesday that the exact cause of the explosion and fire may never be known. School officials said Monday they believed it might have been caused by escaping gas in its butane system, since heat was being used in the building for the first time this year, but added that this theory had been discounted, and that faulty wiring might have set off the blast.

This is a 1948 *Fort Worth Star-Telegram* article about the school fire. (Courtesy Joyce Gibson Roach.)

KELLER FIRE

Continued From Page 1.

He expects to return Tuesday afternoon in time for another session with the school board at 7 p. m. in the gym building. Although most of the school's textbooks were destroyed in the fire, new supplies should be arriving here by next Monday, Simpson added.

A final estimate of the loss will be determined after E. M. Armitage of the Insurance Adjustment Bureau at Dallas concludes an examination of the site, Jake Isaac of the James H. Aldridge Insurance Company said Monday while talking with Simpson.

Simpson and Seaborn Jones, principal, praised the pupils' calmness during the fire and declared that orderly movement from the building prevented any injuries.

Marched Out Singing.

One class in the lower grades filed from the building while giving full voice to a marching song, Jones stated. Mrs. Dorothy Forrest, who was conducting a high school commercial class when she felt an explosion in the building, said her class kept typing until it became evident that the structure was burning.

Shortly before the flames reached full force, 13-year-old Dwayne Miller ripped a telephone from a threatened wall and hurried with the rescued instrument toward the downtown section of Keller—where his father is a telephone repairman and former owner of the Keller telephone exchange.

Coach Charles (Babe) Webb related that he and Simpson, assisted by Bill Barnes, 15, Roy Blankenship, Tom McPherson, 16, Don Jones, 15, and Bobby Jacobs, 15, were attempting to remove a desk from Simpson's office when it jammed in a door leading into another room.

"I never saw smoke move so fast—it came in just like a fog," Webb said. "We yelled to the boys to get out, since they were on the other side of the desk and could make a run for it, but when Simpson and I started out we couldn't get by the desk. Then Simpson opened a window—I had not thought of that—and we climbed out."

Saved Typewriters.

Blankenship, one of the larger boys who returned to the building in a successful effort to save the typewriters, related that when "I went back in to get a typewriter the second time, I was driven out by the smoke and one of the boys had to crawl on his hands and knees."

Accounts varied as to the number of explosions heard.

"I heard a sort of bump like bombs made at Pearl Harbor when they fell a long distance away," Webb said.

Jones said he heard two slight explosions but thought nothing of the noise until Jack Binion, agriculture teacher, called him into a classroom to look at some smoke issuing from the ceiling. Simpson reported that pieces of fiber board ceiling were falling and the ceiling was bulging downward when he went into one classroom.

Billowing smoke was the only outward sign of fire for several minutes after the alarm, Jones said, but with the first evidence of trouble the lines running from two butane tanks, approximately 50 yards from the building, were closed. The school's heating system had been turned on Monday morning for the first time this term.

Explosion in Attic.

The school officials agreed that the explosion occurred in the attic but by late Monday were unable to determine the cause.

"Some of the butane men said gas couldn't get up there," Jones explained. He added that electrical wiring in the shallow attic is encased in BX conduits.

A. L. Pitkin, school board member and assistant fire chief of Keller, said he was the first on the building's roof but could not detect any flames at first. Later, when a skylight was broken,, fire gushed from the roof, he said.

Some time later, a portion of the roof collapsed near Gaines Blevins, filling station operator, and he retreated from his place on the roof with difficulty.

During the course of the three-hour blaze, fire fighting equipment from Fort Worth, Roanoke and Grapevine came to the aid of the Keller force but were unable to control the flames because of water scarcity.

Simpson said he was able to save permanent files pertaining to students but practically all other papers were lost.

1949

This is a continuation of the 1949 *Fort Worth Star-Telegram* article about the school fire. (Courtesy Joyce Gibson Roach.)

The Brownings were early settlers of Keller, and their farm has carried on to the present day. The land originally belonged to Lawson Stateham, and his daughter Maude married Claude, which is how the Browning family dynasty began. The couple, parents to Guy and Jimmy Browning, stands in front of the family car. (Courtesy Homestead Farms.)

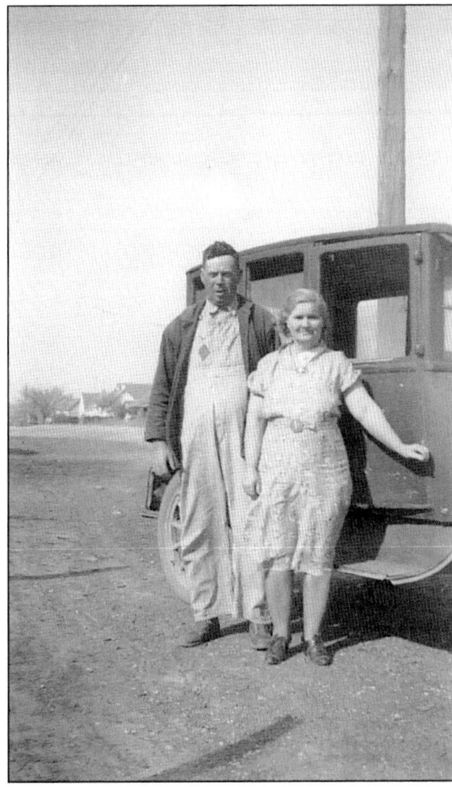

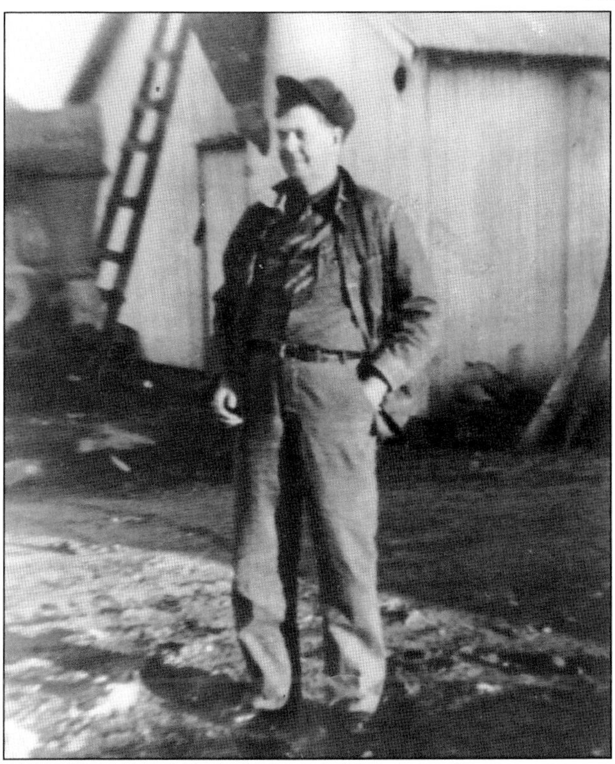

Claude Browning comes in from a hard day's work. His wife, Maude Browning, took this picture. (Courtesy Homestead Farms.)

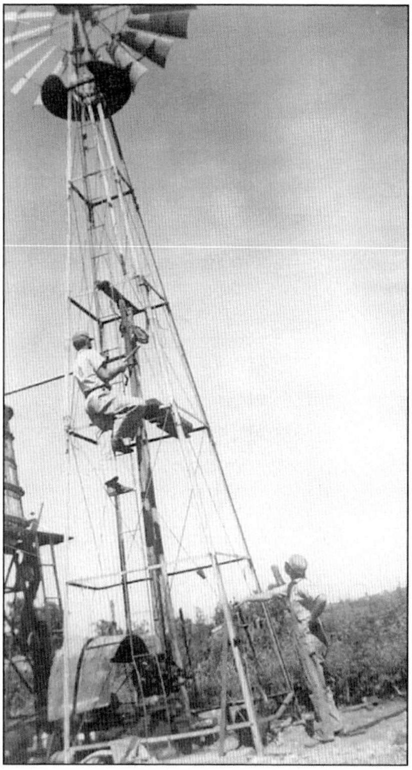

Guy Browning (top) repairs a water pump as Jimmy Lawson Browning assists with the mending of the family windmill. Their great-grandfather Benjamin N. Browning was a Civil War soldier who died in 1917 and is buried at the Bourland Cemetery. (Courtesy Homestead Farms.)

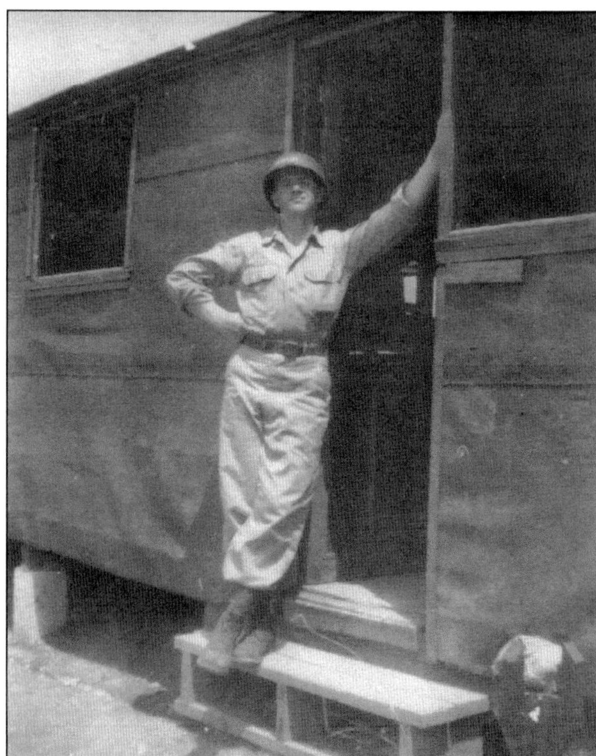

Jimmy Lawson Browning served in World War II and was sent to Japan after the bomb was dropped to assist in the rebuilding of Japan. Jimmy Browning later died from medical complications of increased exposure to radiation from his stay in Japan. (Courtesy Homestead Farms.)

Guy and Minnie Browning stand in front of their new car. They were later married and had two sons, Grover and Steve Browning. (Courtesy Homestead Farms.)

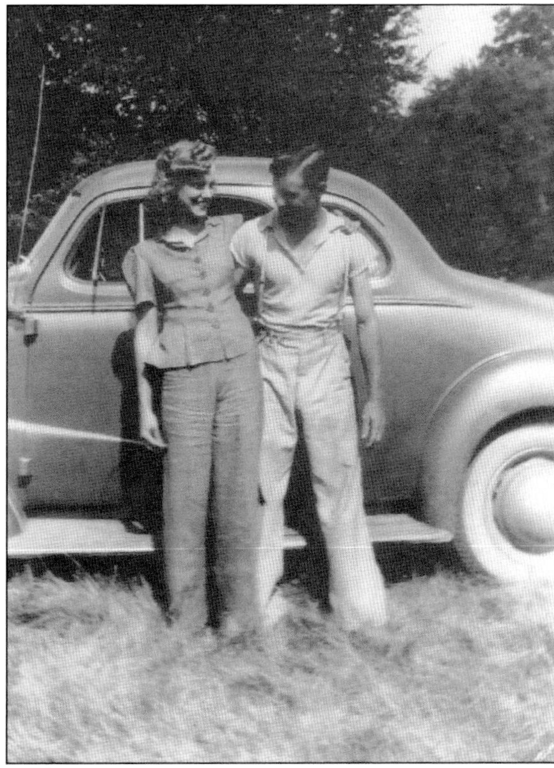

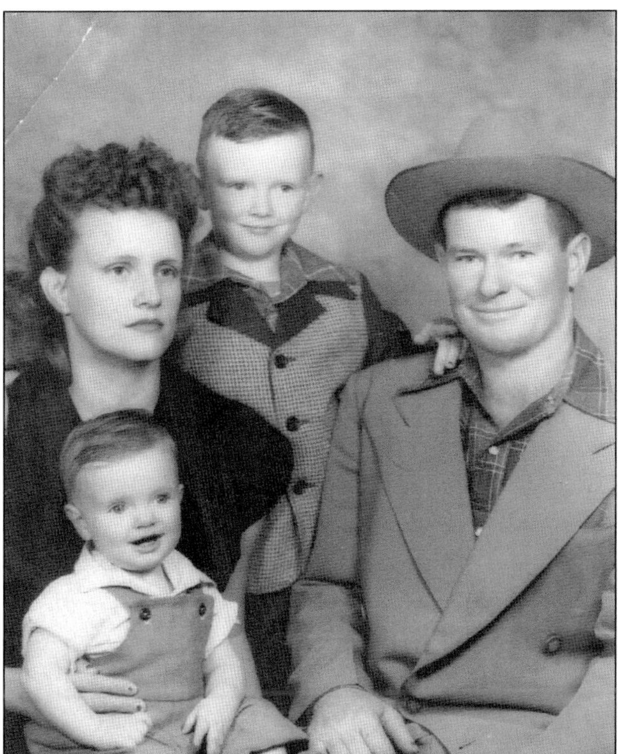

In this photograph of the Browning family are, from left to right, Minnie Browning, baby Steve Browning, Grover Browning, and Guy Browning. (Courtesy Homestead Farms.)

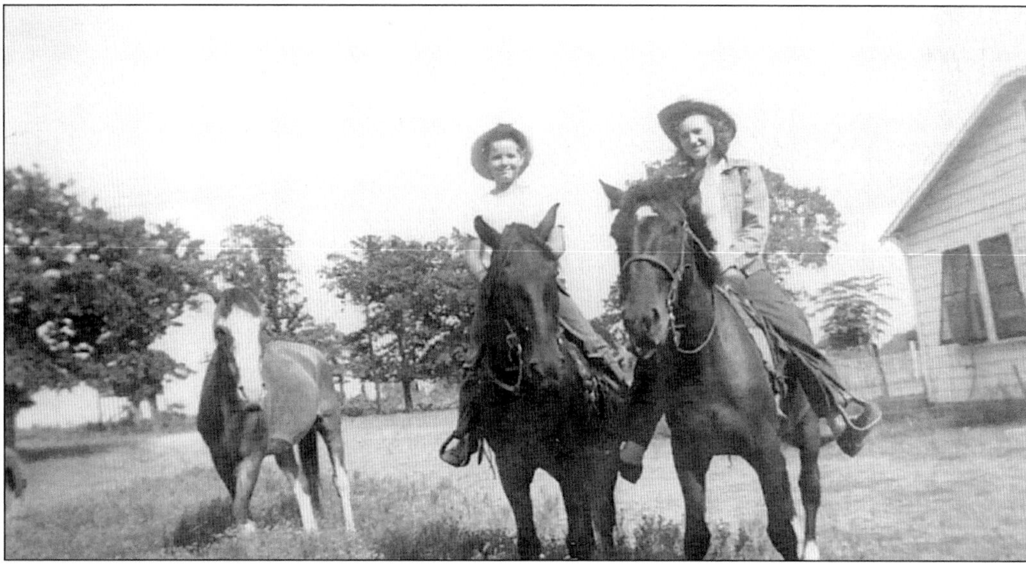

Eight-year-old Grover Browning and his mother, Minnie Browning, enjoy a fine Texas day on horseback on their farm in Keller. (Courtesy Homestead Farms.)

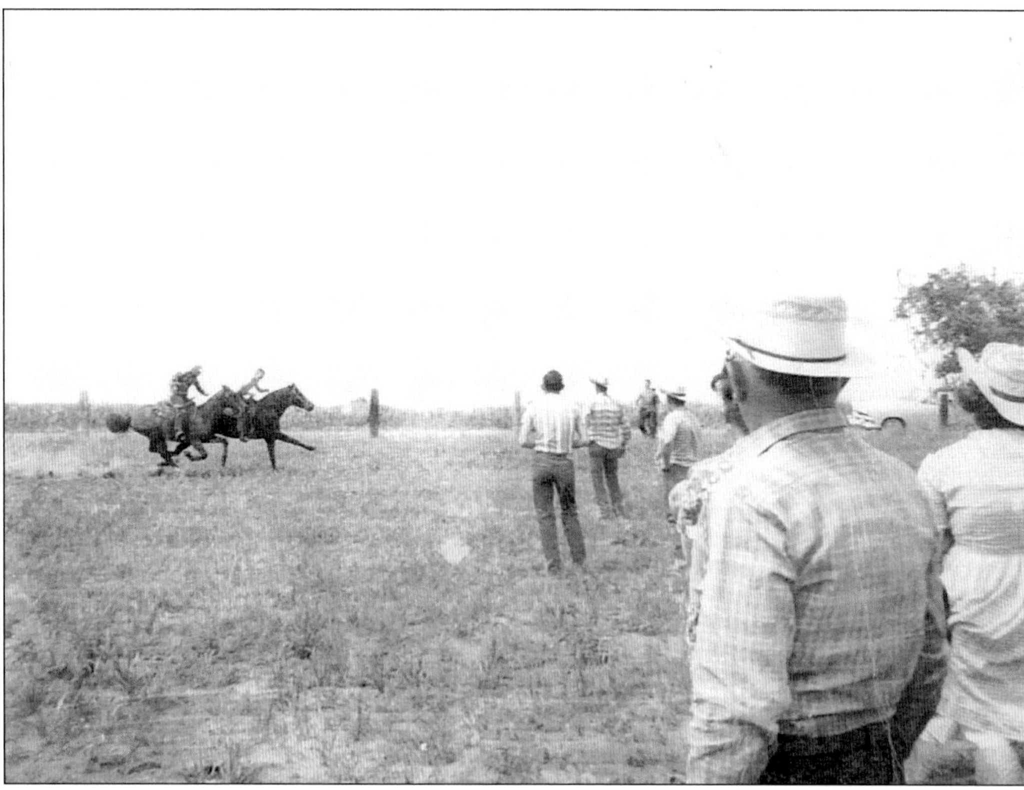

It was a fun day on the Browning farm when horse races broke out between neighbors. (Courtesy Homestead Farms.)

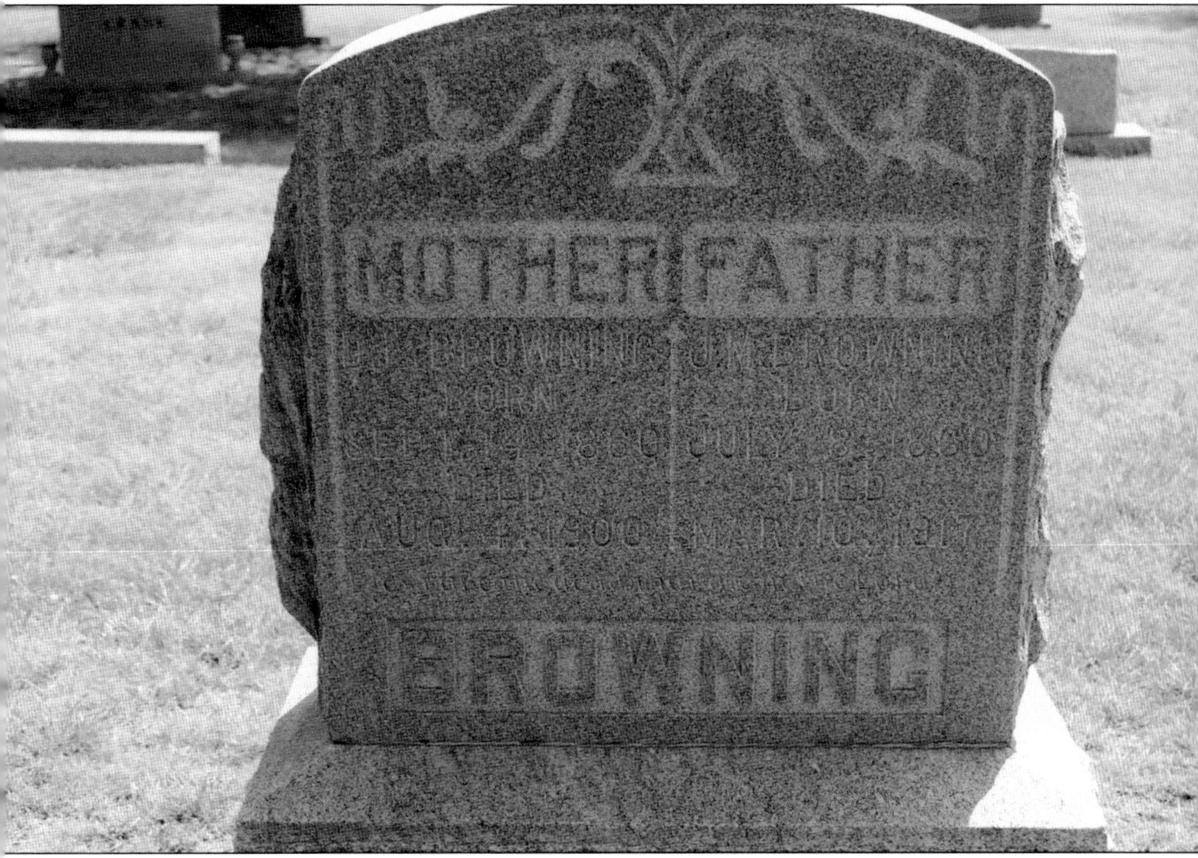

This grave marker at Bourland Cemetery is for Claude's parents, Debbie L. Browning and J. M. Browning. Debbie died in 1900 and J. M. later remarried Lizzie Allen. The Allens were some of the original settlers of Keller. (Courtesy Jennifer Featherston.)

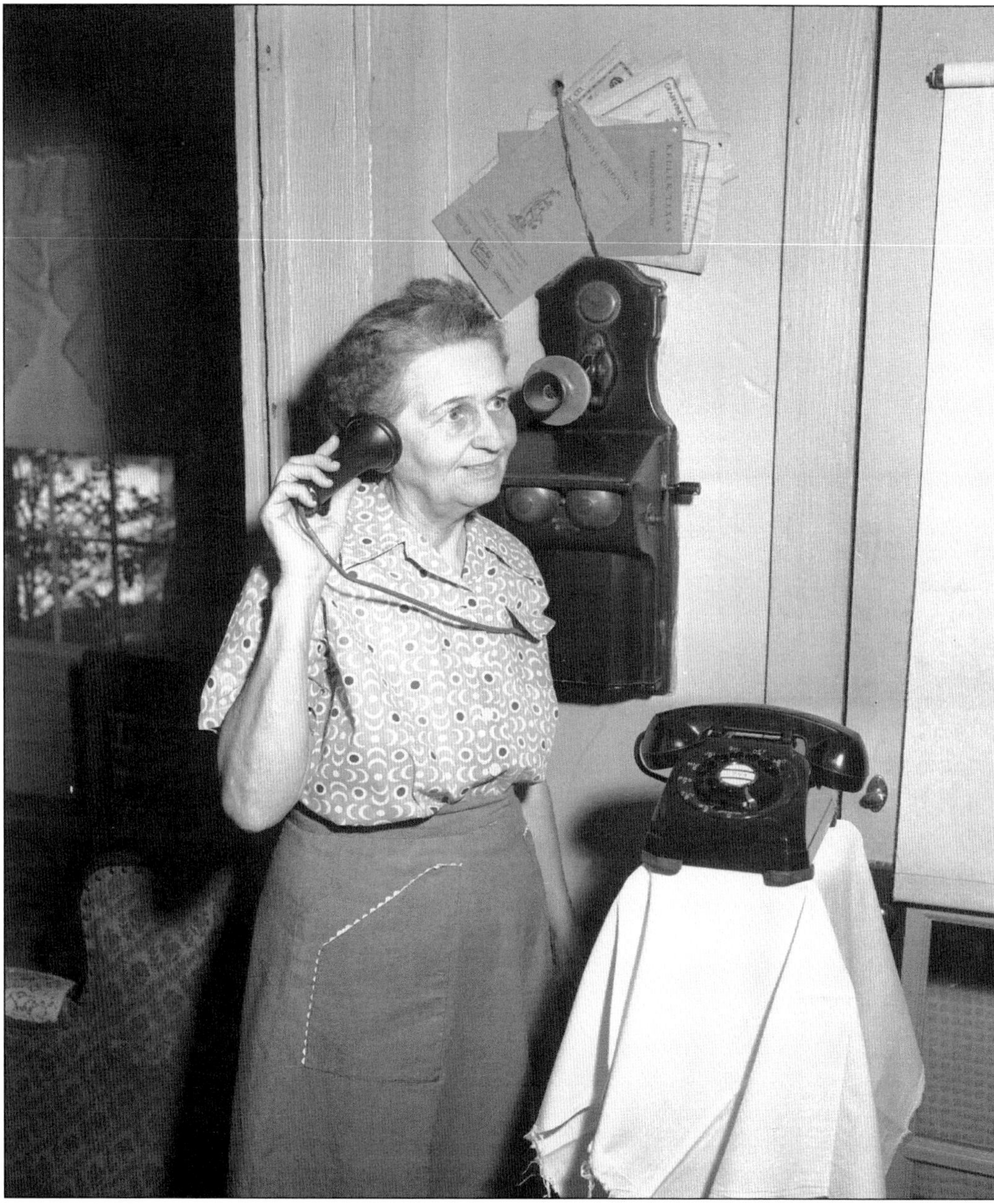

Progress beckons as Mabel Scott of Keller makes a call on the old-time Magneto wall telephone in her home the Thursday before the new dial phone beside it was hooked up. (Courtesy *Fort Worth Star-Telegram* Collection, Special Collections, the University of Texas at Arlington Library.)

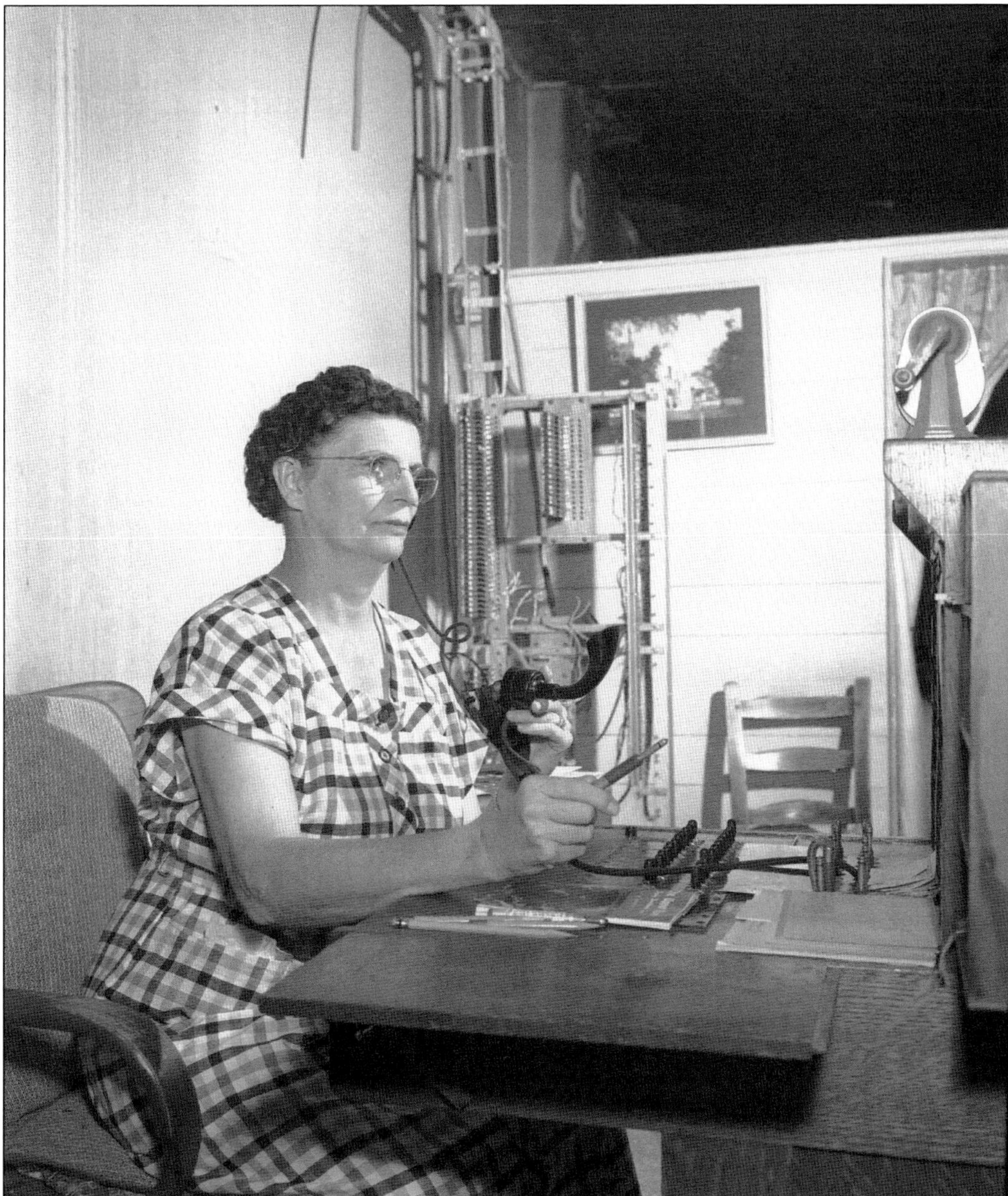

Going out with the old phone system is the job of Mrs. C. A. Kelley, the chief operator at Keller for a dozen years. The old switchboard is on the way out as well.

Keller Telephone Company

SERVING KELLER & COPPELL

COPPELL GENERAL INFORMATION

EMERGENCY CALLS

POLICE:	County Sheriff's Office, Dallas ....RI 7-8641
F.B.I.:	Dial Operator
FIRE:	Dial GE 6-2442
NUMBERS NOT LISTED:	Dial Operator ..ask for COPPELL INFORMATION
Business matters such as installations, moves, etc.:	Dial GE 6-2222 ......if no answer Dial GE 6-2231
To report a telephone out of order:	Dial GE 6-2222 ......if no answer Dial GE 6-2231

How to Use Your Dial Telephone

Suppose you want to call GE 6-3099. To make the call:

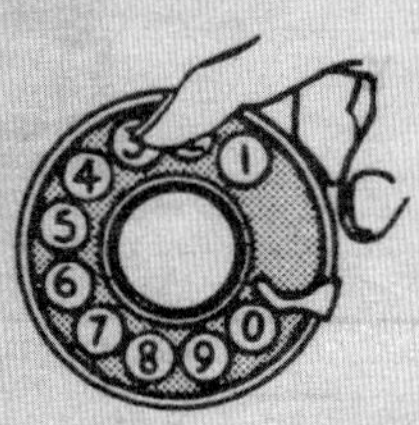

1. Lift the receiver to your ear and wait until you hear a humming sound. This is the signal to go ahead.
2. Place your finger in opening where you see the letter "G."
3. Pull dial around until your finger strikes the stop. Remove finger and let dial spin back freely.
4. Do the same thing with letter "E" and numbers "6," "3," "0," "9," and "9." You will hear the other telephone ring (a burr-r-ing sound) or the busy signal (a buzz-buzz).

DON'T HURRY ! ! TAKE TIME TO DIAL CORRECTLY!

Calls to another party on your line:

The telephone number of all parties on your line is the same except for the last digit. For example, if your number is GE 6-2122, the other parties on your line will have one or another of the following numbers: GE 6-2121, GE 6-2123, GE 6-2124, GE 6-2126, GE 6-2127, or GE 6-2128. To call another party on your line, DO NOT dial the directory number as listed. Instead you dial 66, then dial the last digit of your number and then the last digit of the number you wish to call. For example; if your number is GE 6-2122 and you wish to call GE 6-2128 you should dial 6628, then hang up your receiver. Your phone as well as the called party's phone will ring. When the called party answers, your phone will cease to ring. You can then pick up your handset and start your conversation. If the called party does not answer, the ringing will cease automatically after 2 to 4 minutes. If you wish to stop the ringing yourself, simply lift the receiver momentarily.

A 1965 Keller phone book instructs users on how to use their dial phone. (Courtesy Joyce Gibson Roach.)

Three

Boomtown

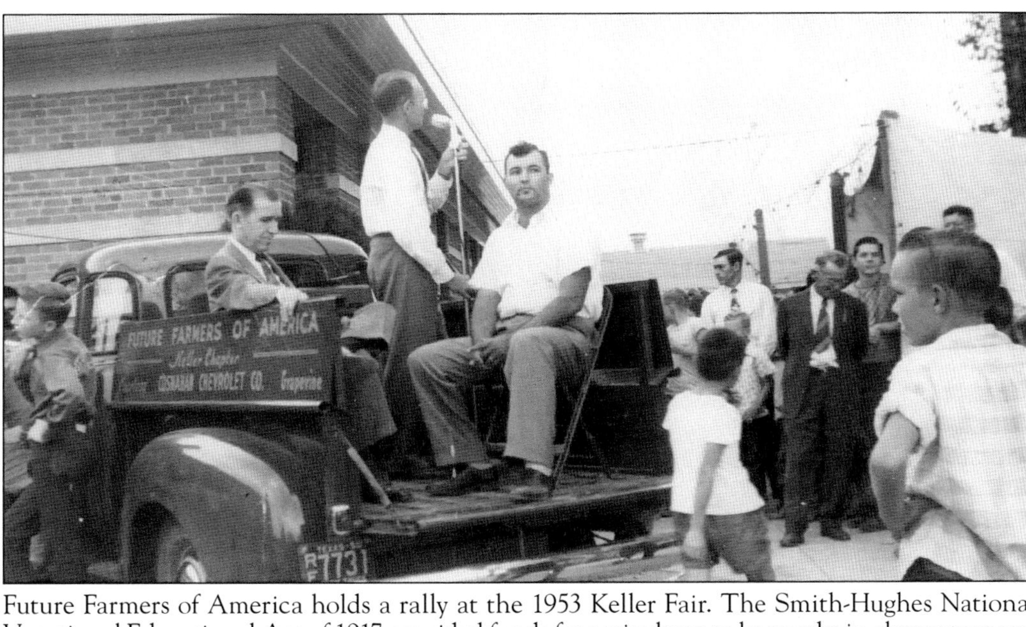

Future Farmers of America holds a rally at the 1953 Keller Fair. The Smith-Hughes National Vocational Educational Act of 1917 provided funds for agriculture to be taught in elementary and secondary schools. However, the Texas Legislature preceded this; all schools in the Texas were required to offer elementary agriculture classes as early as 1907. Teacher training was implemented in 1909 and required at certain colleges. The first FFA Texas chapter was organized in 1928, and the first meeting was held at College Station in April 1929.

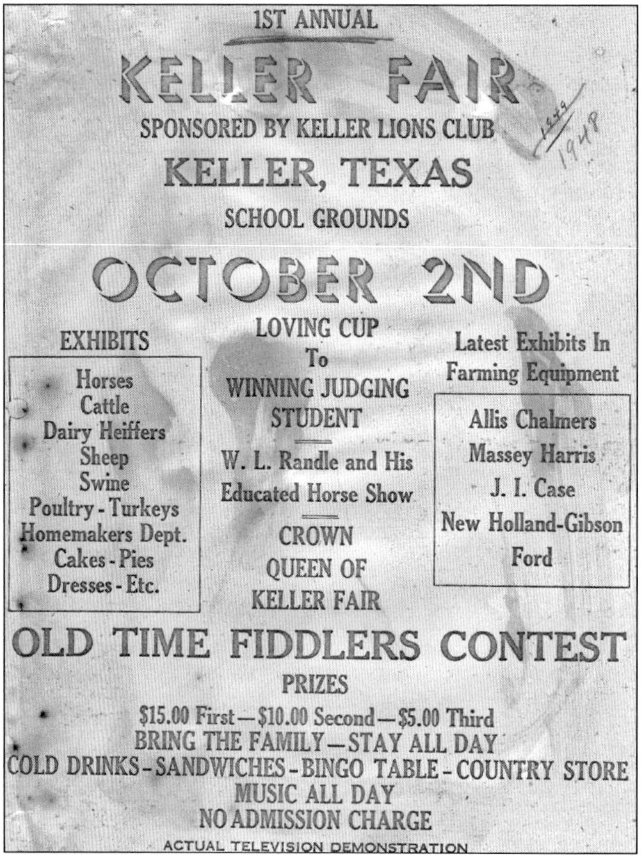

The First Annual Keller Fair, held on the Keller school grounds in 1948, was sponsored by the Lions Club and held numerous activities, both night and day. The fair also provided businesses the opportunity to have booths to promote their products and services.

The 1950 Keller Lions Club caravan came together to promote the Keller Fair. The little boy in the first row with the cowboy hat (third from the right) is 10-year-old Donald Blevins, who would become president of the Lions Club in 1969. His sister, eight-year-old Dianne Blevins, is in the second row with a cowboy hat (fourth from the right). She sang with the band that played at this fair.

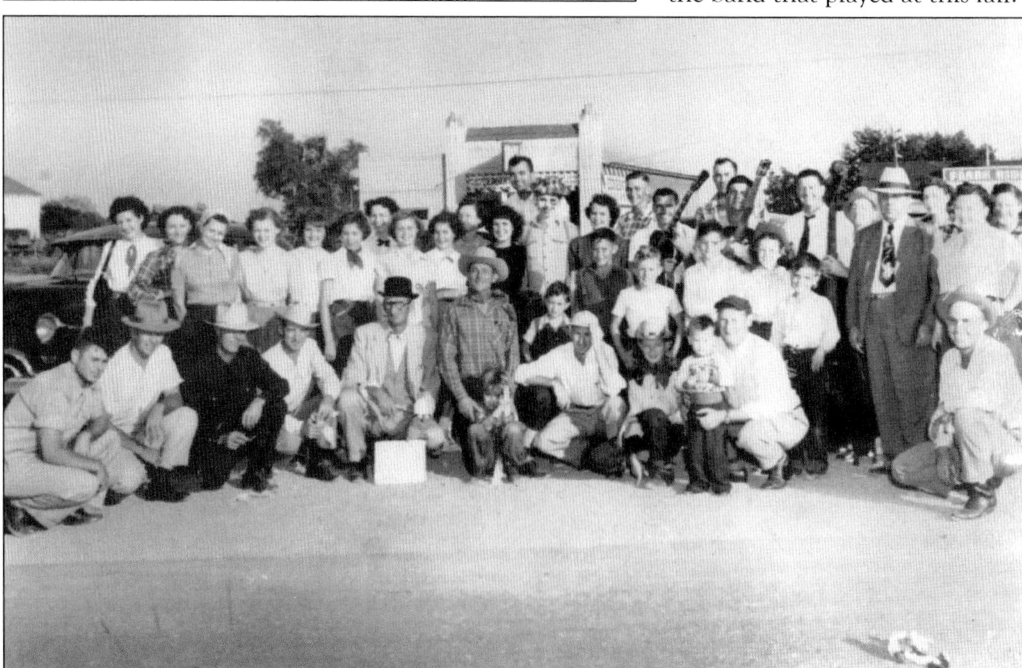

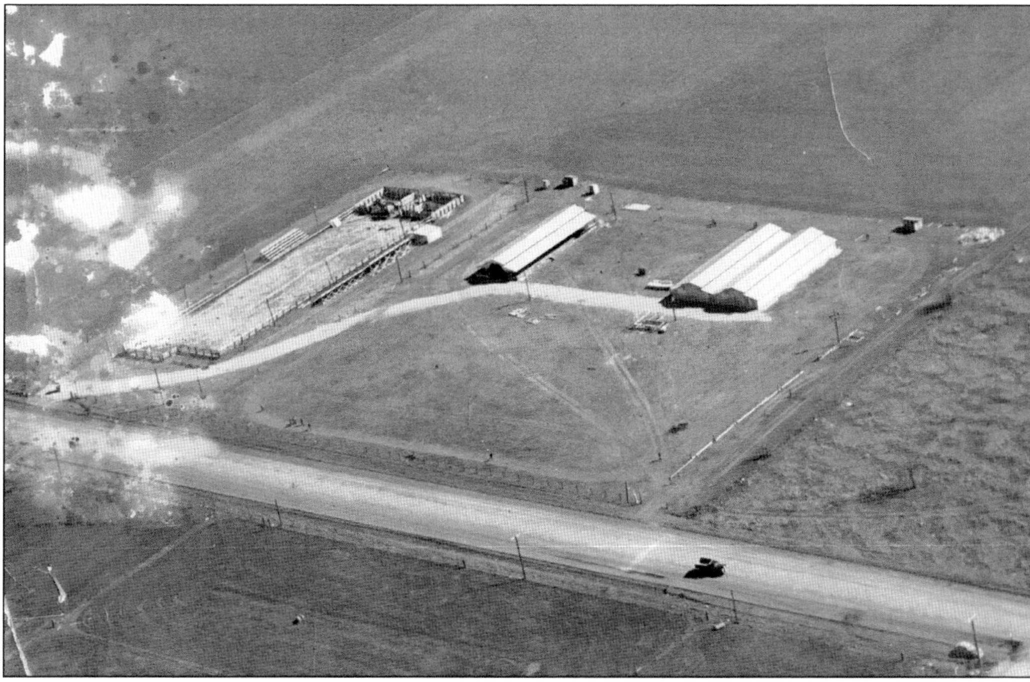

This 1953 aerial view of FM 1709 (Keller Parkway) is going east to west. The Keller Lions Club moved to this new location on the corner of Keller Parkway and Cindy Street, where the Lions Club is still located today.

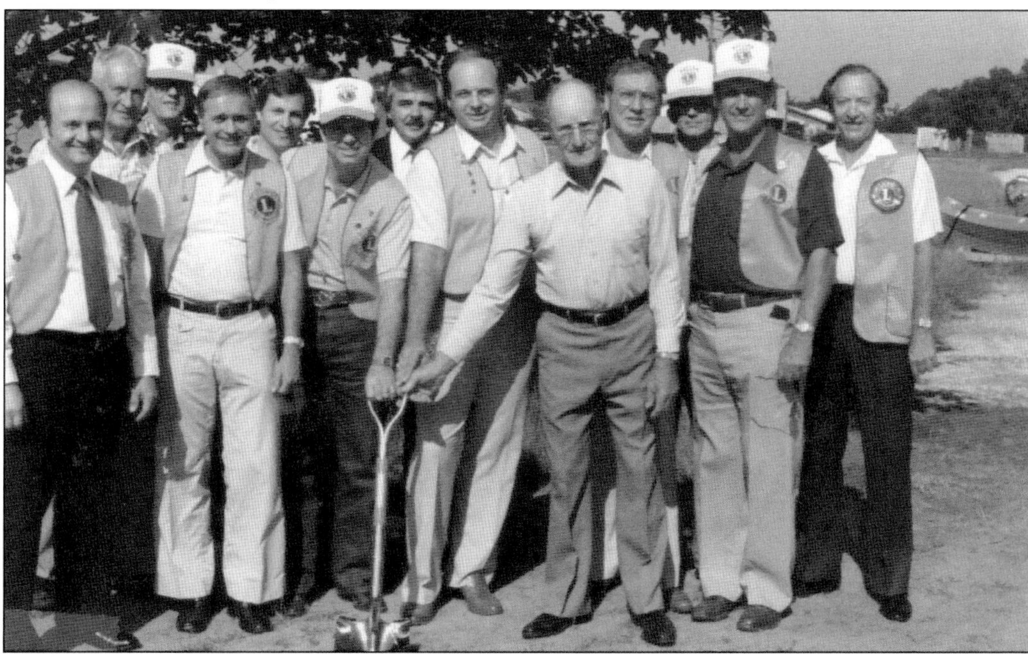

This is the ground-breaking of the new Keller Lions Club and fairgrounds. The attendees are from left to right (first row) Del Fast, Harold Pipes, Ike Sauzge, Robert Garner, Bob Holder, and unidentified; (second row) Jay Sharp, Bud Feaster, Bob Martin, Paul Meine, Tommy Knox, Terry Craig, and unidentified.

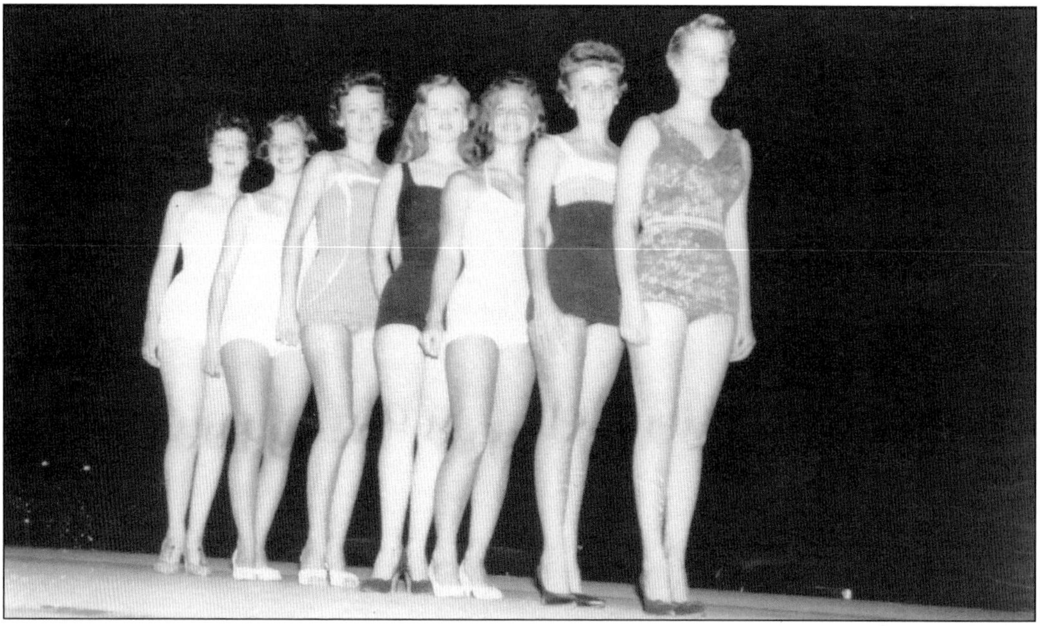

The beauty contest held annually at the Keller Fair featured some of area's most beautiful girls, as young women from different cities would compete to become the Keller Fair Queen. The beauty contest rules were as follows: All contestants must be 15 to 21 years of age and unmarried; she may participate in the parade on Tuesday afternoon (must have a sponsor and convertible to be in the parade); she must wear either a formal or semiformal dress in the parade; each contestant will be required to appear in one-piece swimsuit and formal or semiformal dress for judging; the winner will be required to attend on Saturday night to be introduced as the Keller Fair Queen. Pictured from left to right, these Keller beauty contestants are Charlotte Warner, two unidentified, Sandra Neeper, Beth Austin, Sandra Keller, and Mary Orr.

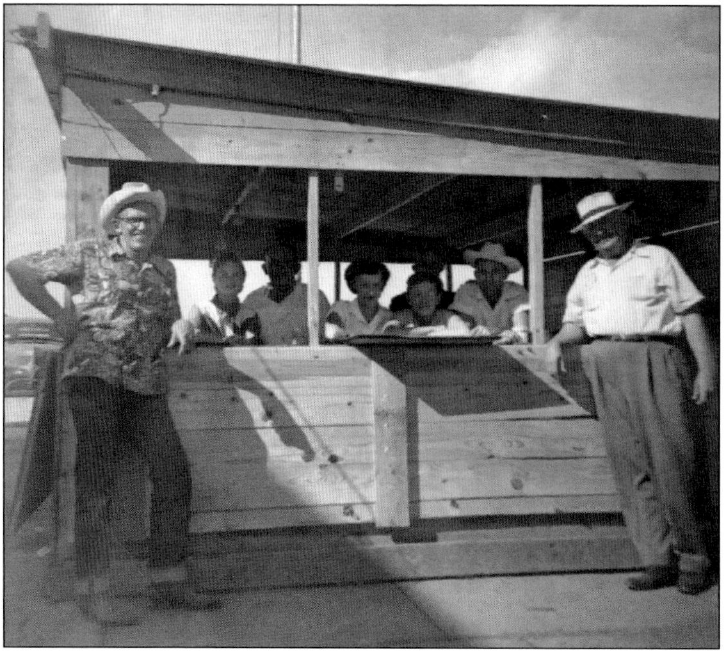

These Keller Lions members are enjoying a day at the 1952 Keller Fair as they staff a booth and prepare for the day's festivities.

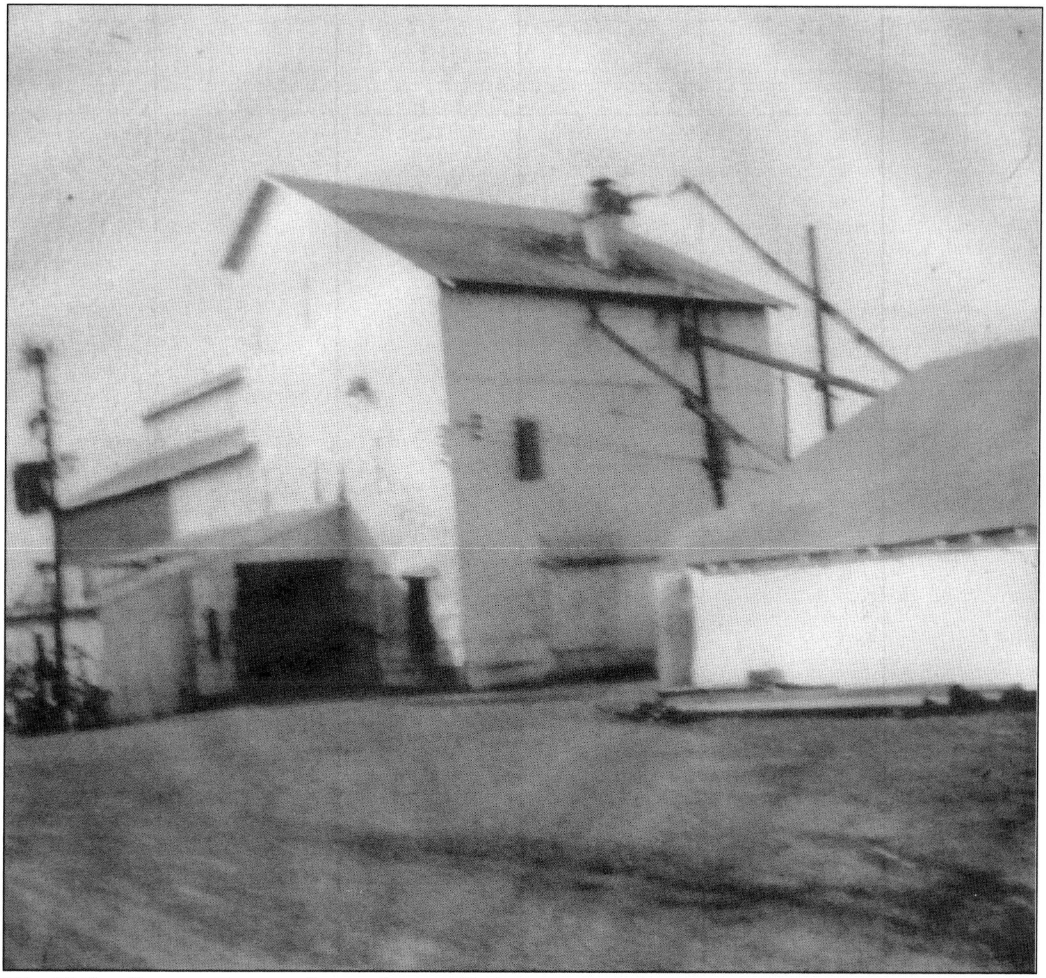

The Keller Cotton Gin was located just off of Katy Road. (Courtesy Joyce Gibson Roach.)

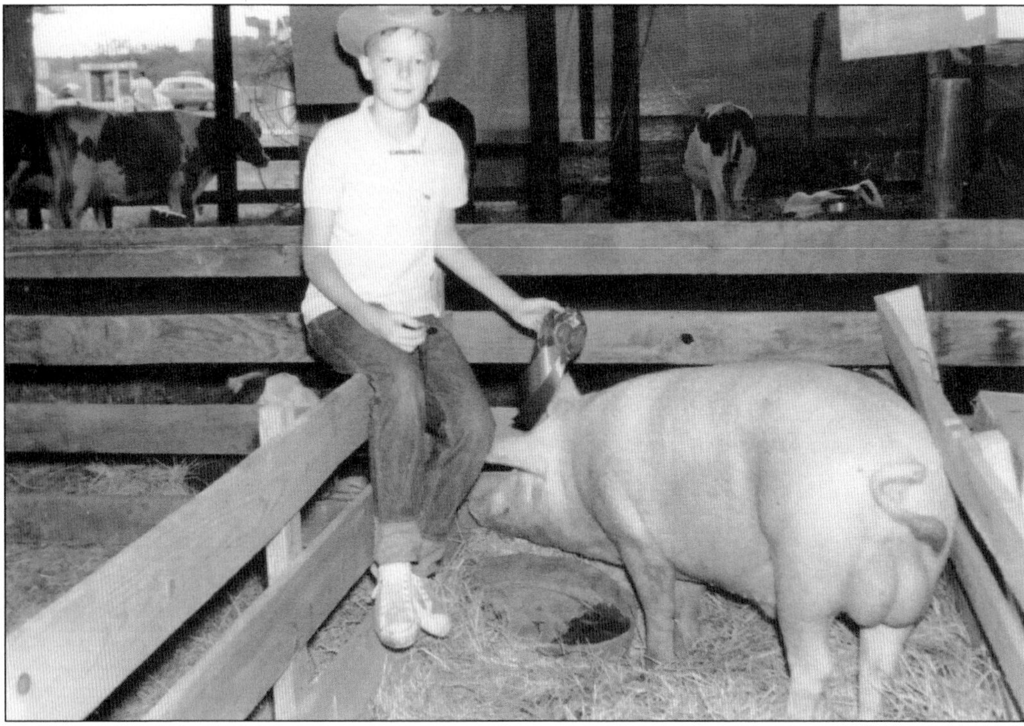

This young boy shows off his prize-winning pig. According to the program rules and regulations of the Livestock Department, the livestock show was open to any boy or girl who was a member of any FFA, 4-H, or Future Homemakers of America (FHA) chapter ages 9 to 20. An exhibitor could enter as many classes he or she wished but could only place twice in any one class. The entry fee was 75¢ for cattle and 25¢ sheep and swine. The livestock shows were popular, and bringing home a blue ribbon was quite an honor. The image, along with those on the following pages, is from the 1960s.

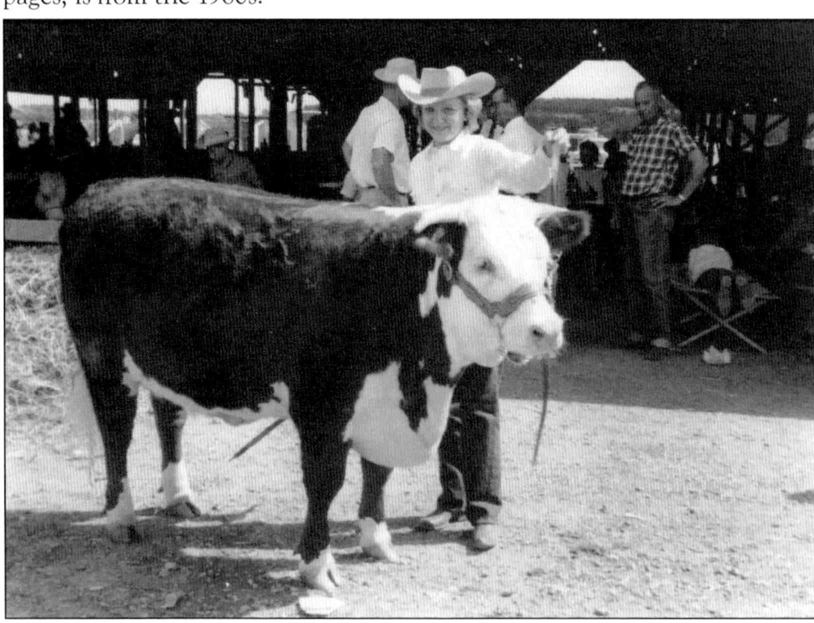

Here is a girl with a prize steer.

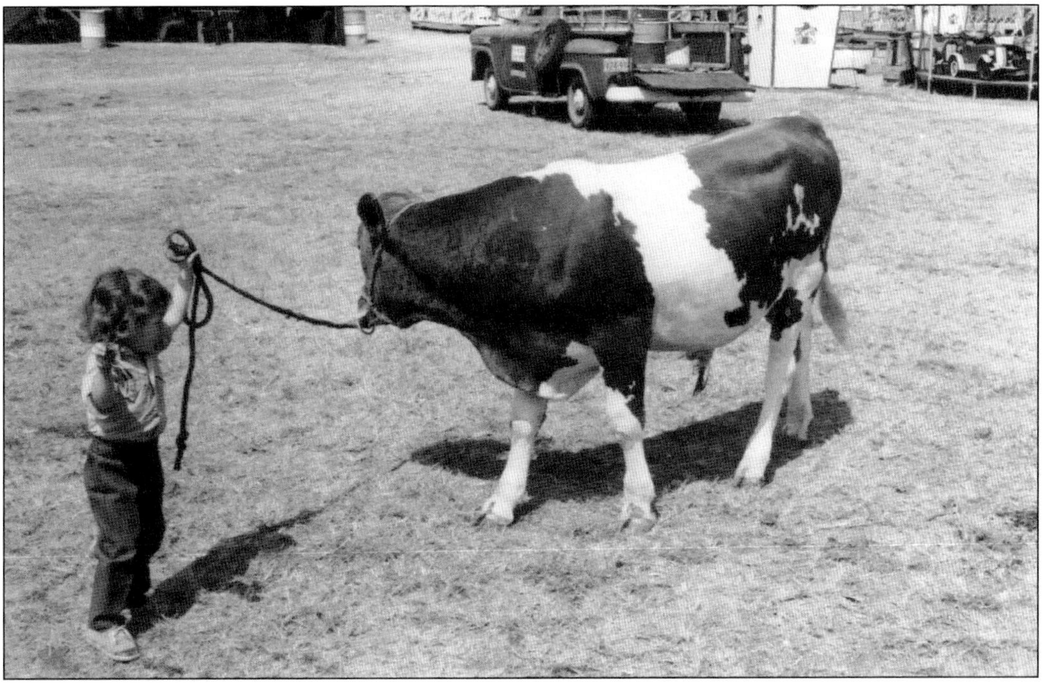

This little girl, about three years of age, poses with her steer.

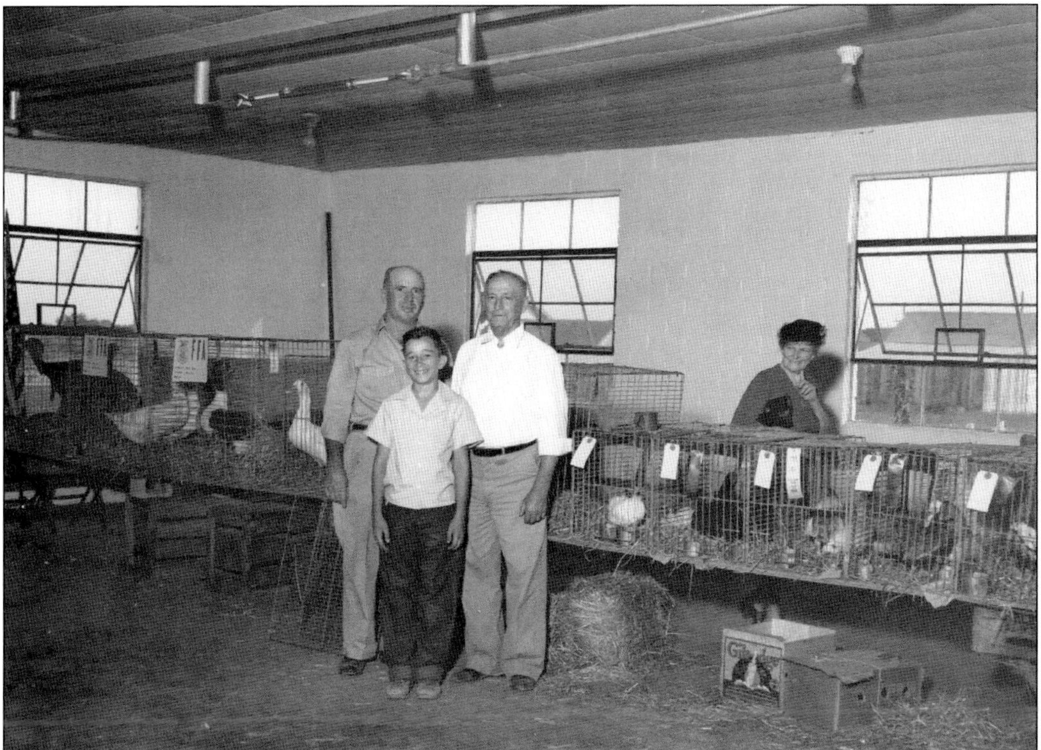

A boy poses with his prize-winning chickens.

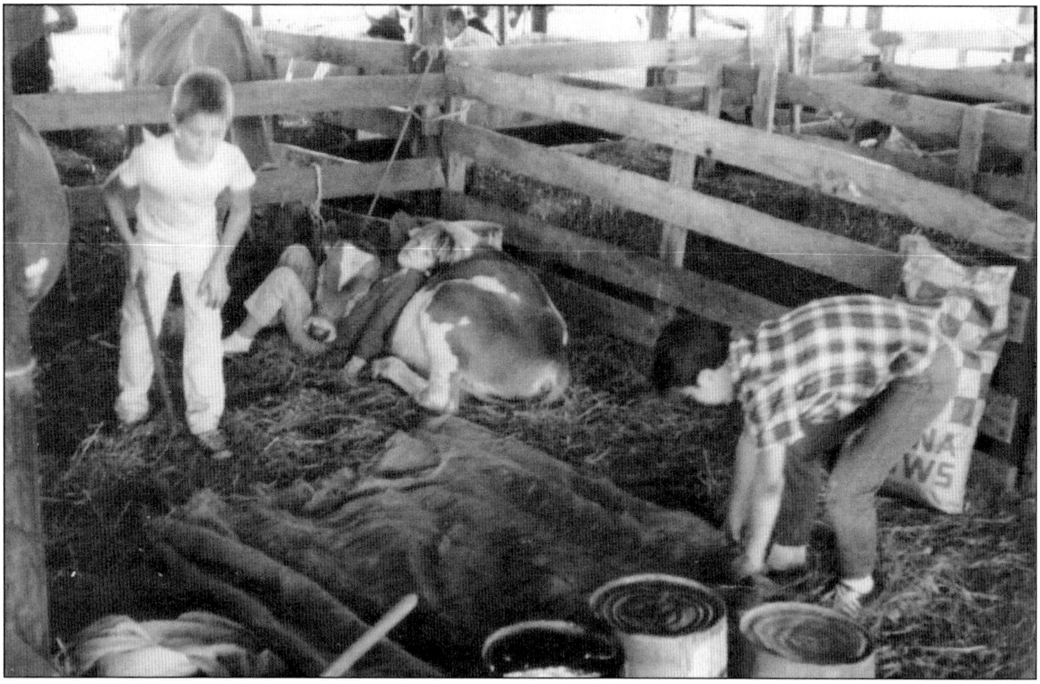

Children are pictured here with their cows.

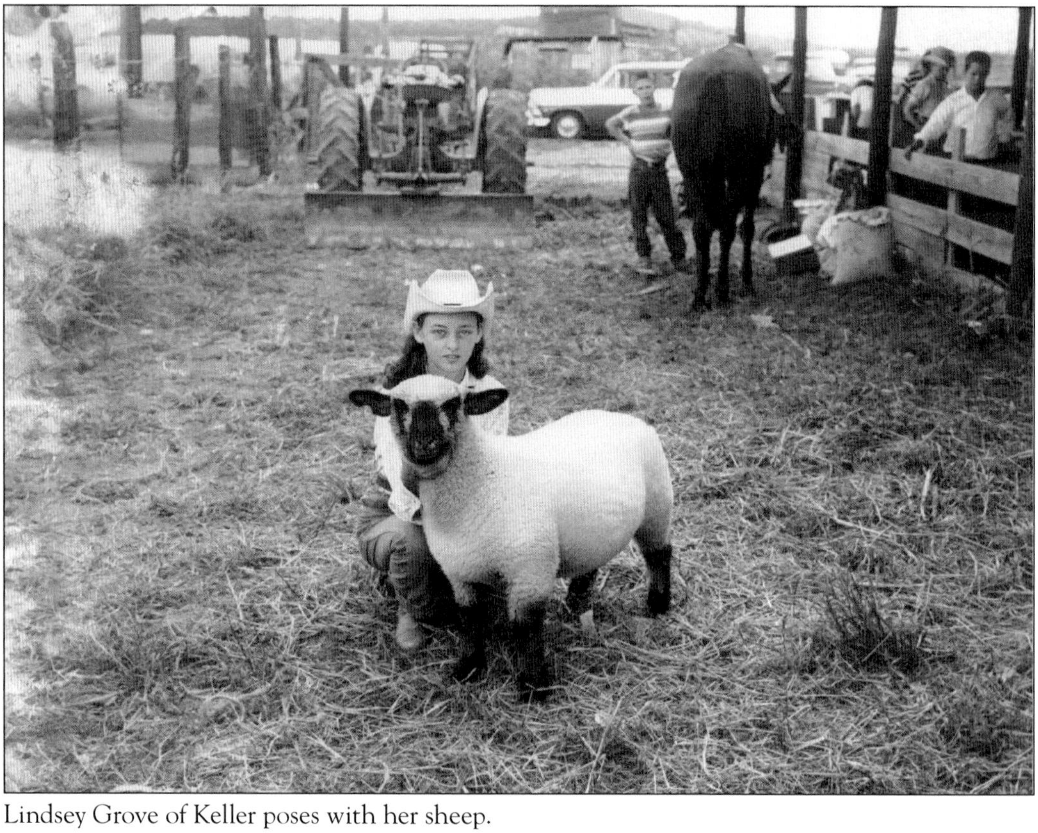

Lindsey Grove of Keller poses with her sheep.

This 4-H booth informed attendees of the many activities 4-H provided for kids and their families.

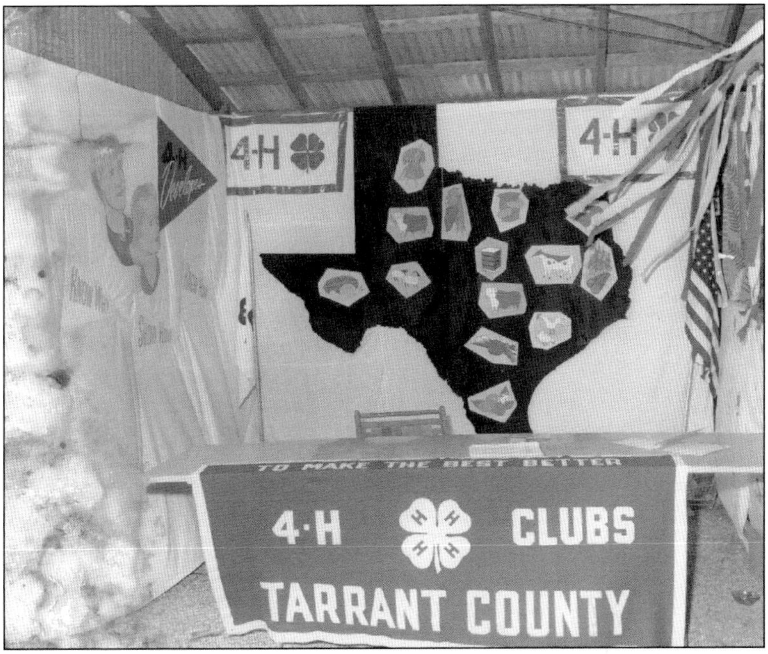

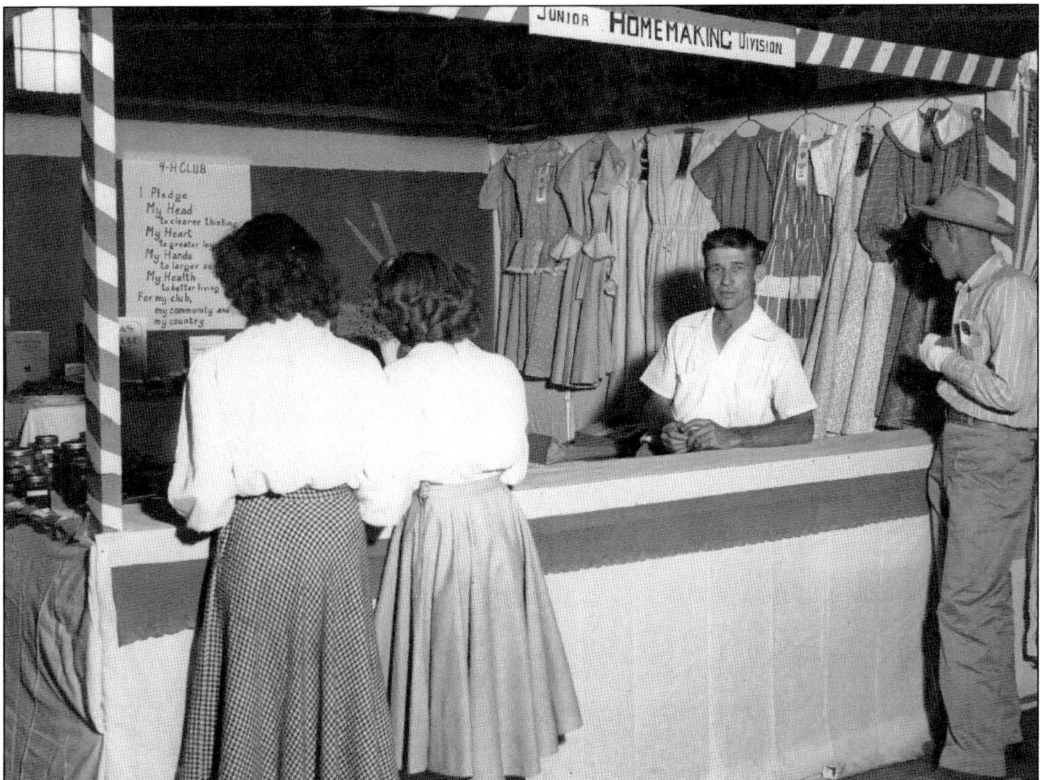

Young ladies observe the many items made by the FHA at the Junior Homemaking Booth. The sign in the back reads, "I Pledge: My Head to clearer thinking. My Heart, to greater loyalty. My Hands to larger services. My Health to better living. For my club, my community and my country."

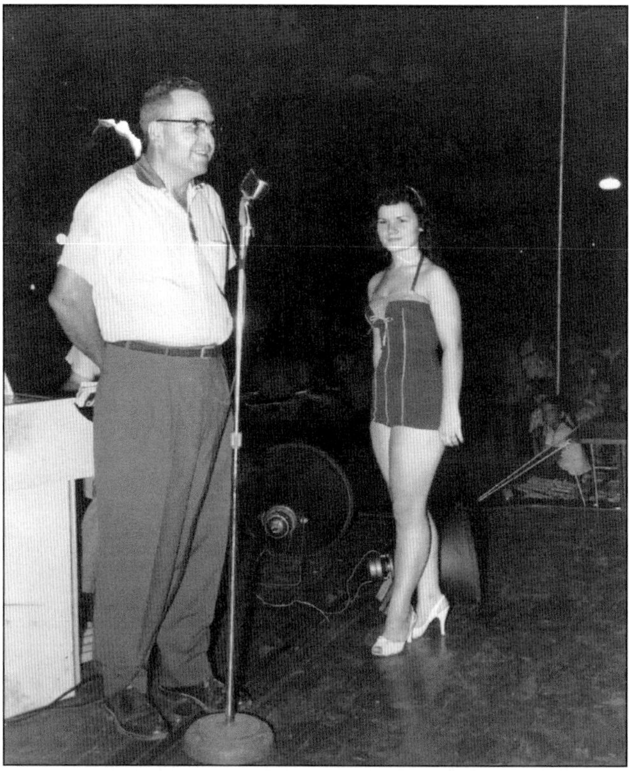

Mary Jobe, a teenage Keller High freshman, wins the 1958 beauty pageant. The announcer is Ross Harvel, the Keller High School vocational and agriculture teacher and Lions Club member. Keller-Harvel Elementary was named after Ross Harvel, and the school is located where the Harvel property once stood.

Many spectators watch the show and cheer on their favorite riders at a Saturday night rodeo at the Keller arena.

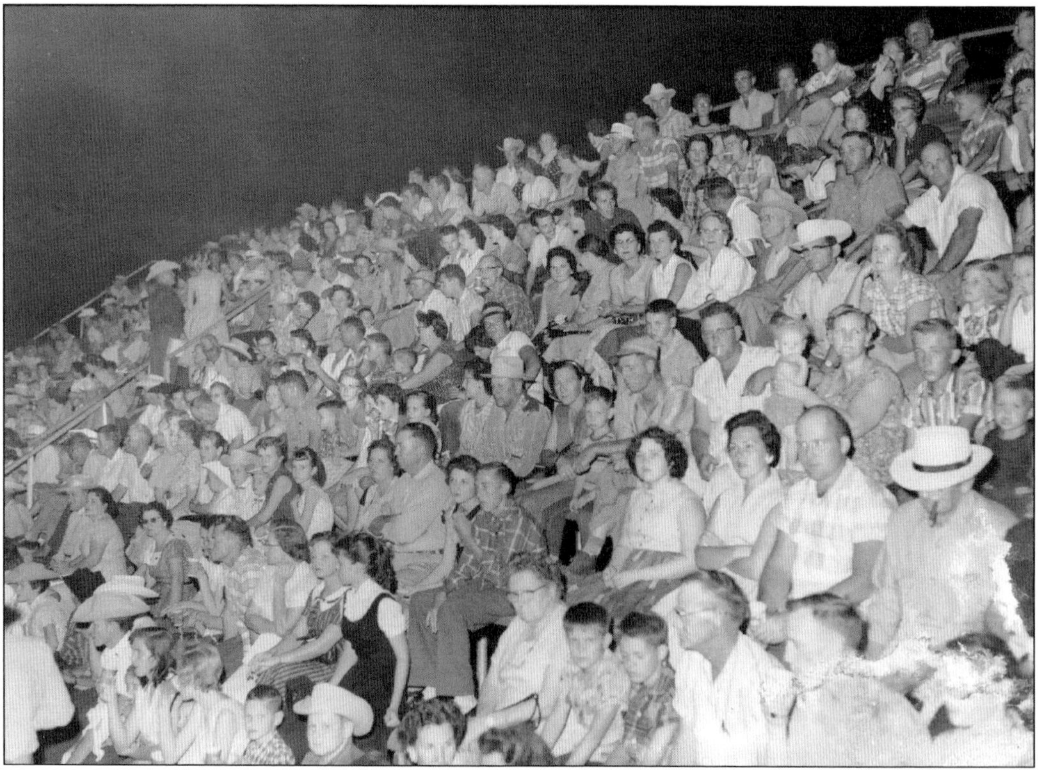

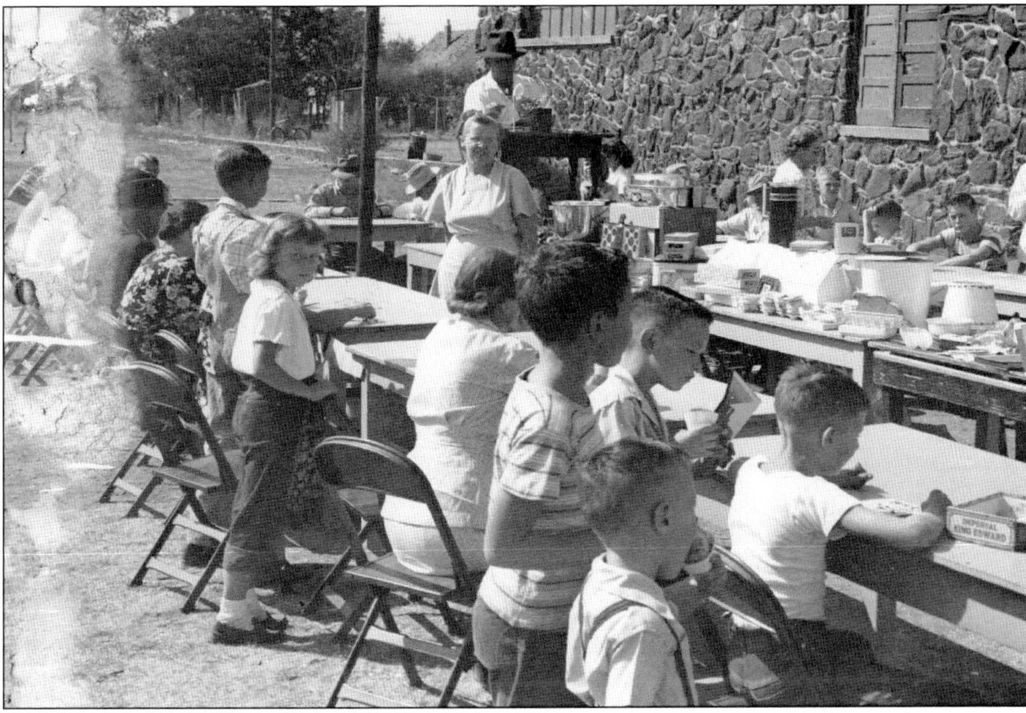

Kids play bingo outside of the Rock Gym.

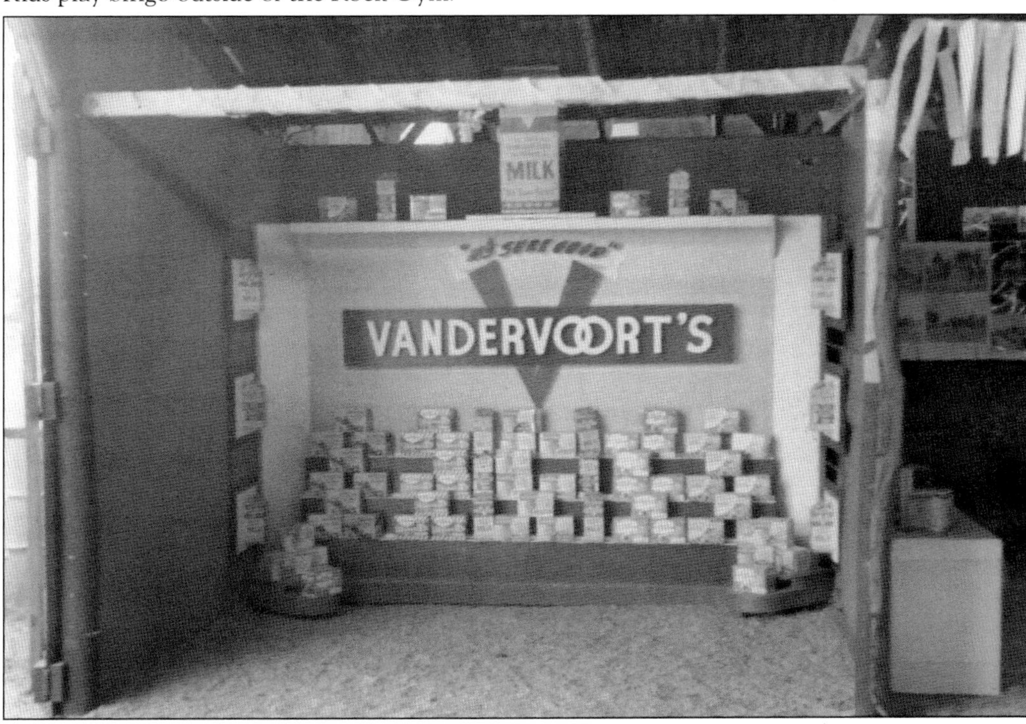

Vandervoort's Dairy proudly displays its products. Vandervoort's was a popular dairy facility in the late 1950s in Fort Worth, producing a wide variety of products such as milk and ice cream. It is currently operating today under a parent company, Kroger Foods.

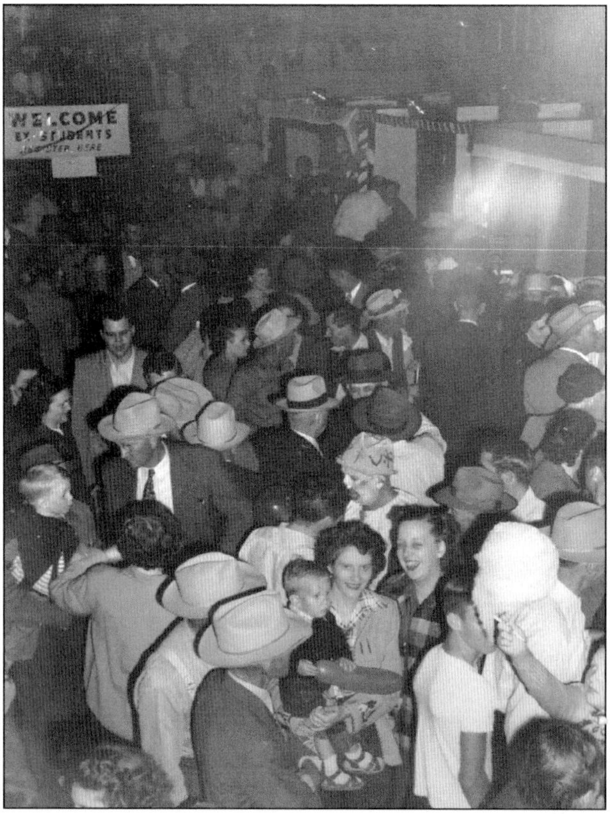

Vendors at the Keller Fair have put up display booths inside the Rock Gymnasium, where locals could beat the heat and enjoy some indoor festivities.

Spectators from the Keller Fair continue to support the many vendors inside the Rock Gym.

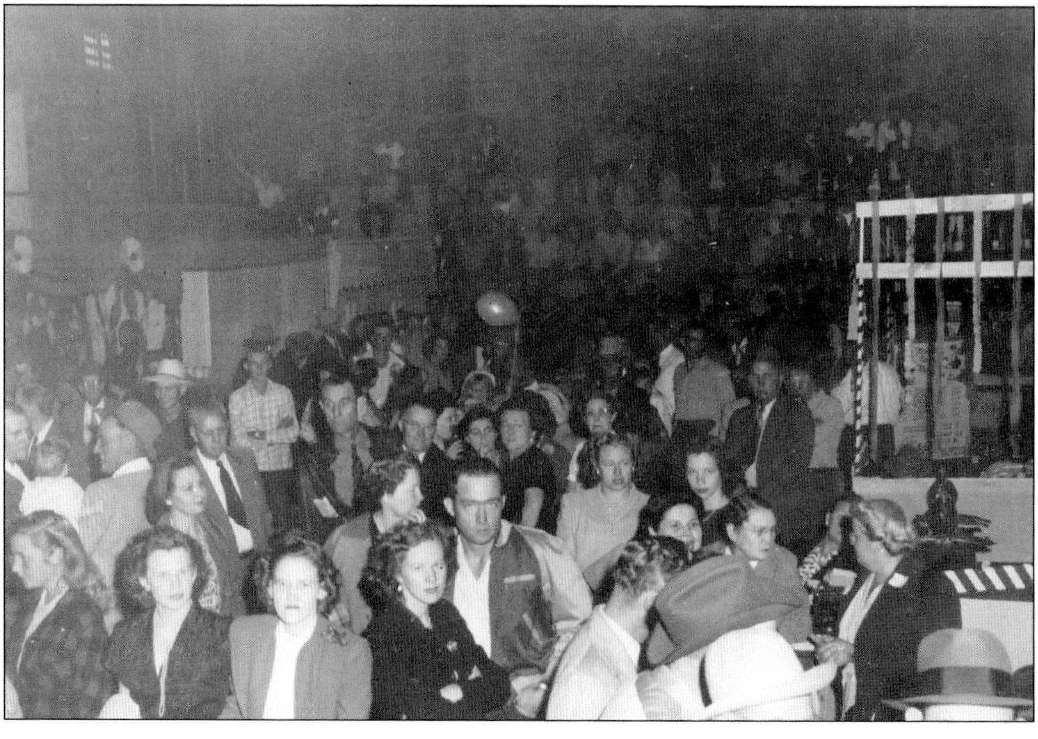

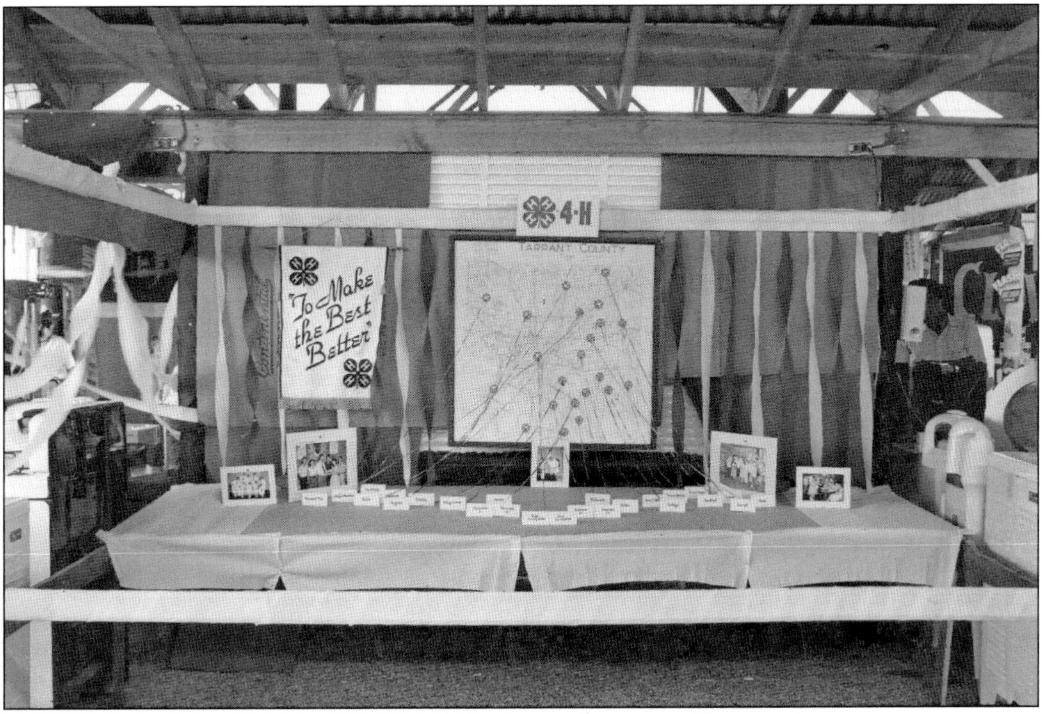

A 4-H booth display shows a wall map of the many chapters in Tarrant County.

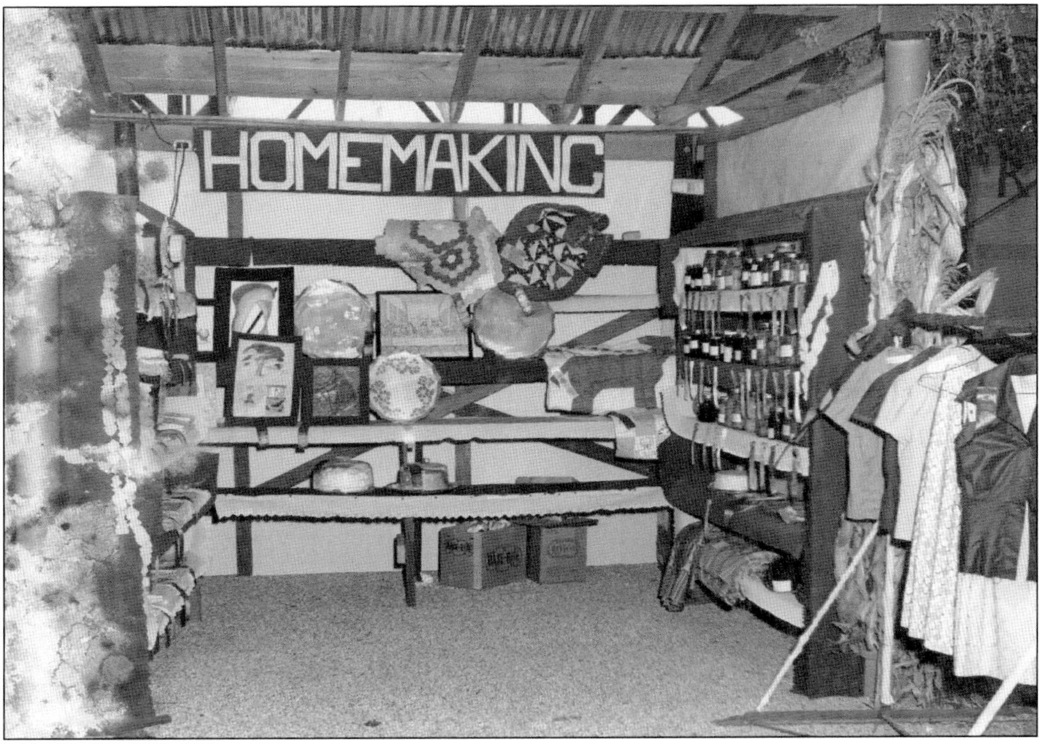

Prize-winning homemaking items are displayed from Future Homemakers of America. Items include dresses, quilts, artwork, photography, cakes, and jams and other canned food items.

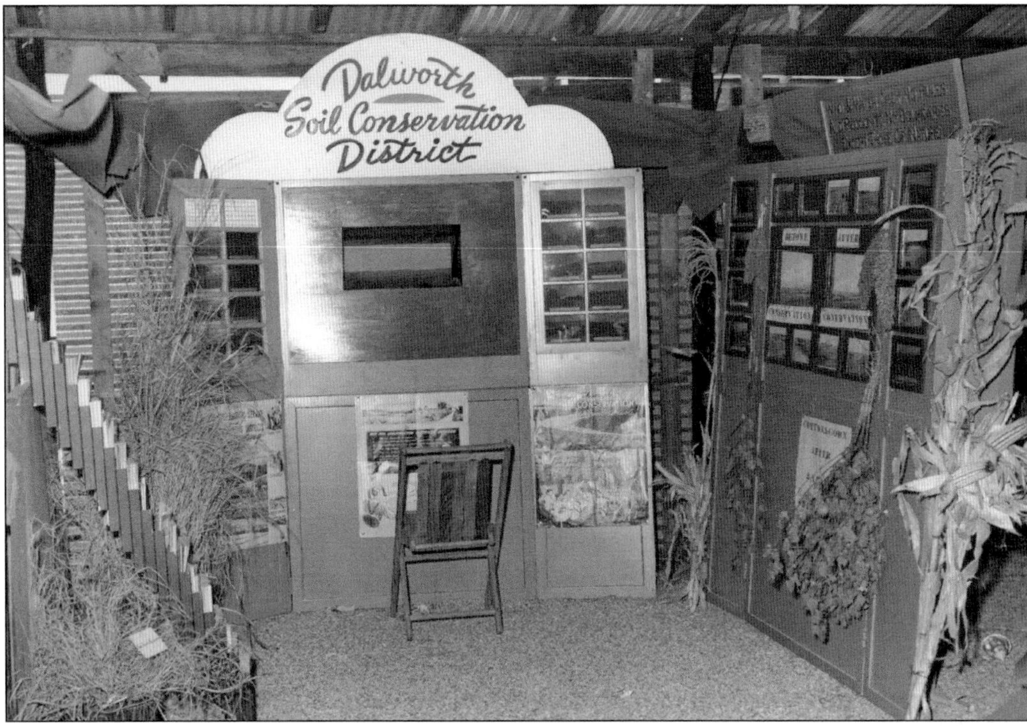

The Dalworth Soil booth displays the many crops grown in Texas, which include, cotton, corn, and hay among many others. This booth shows the positive effects soil and water conservation has on the crops and land.

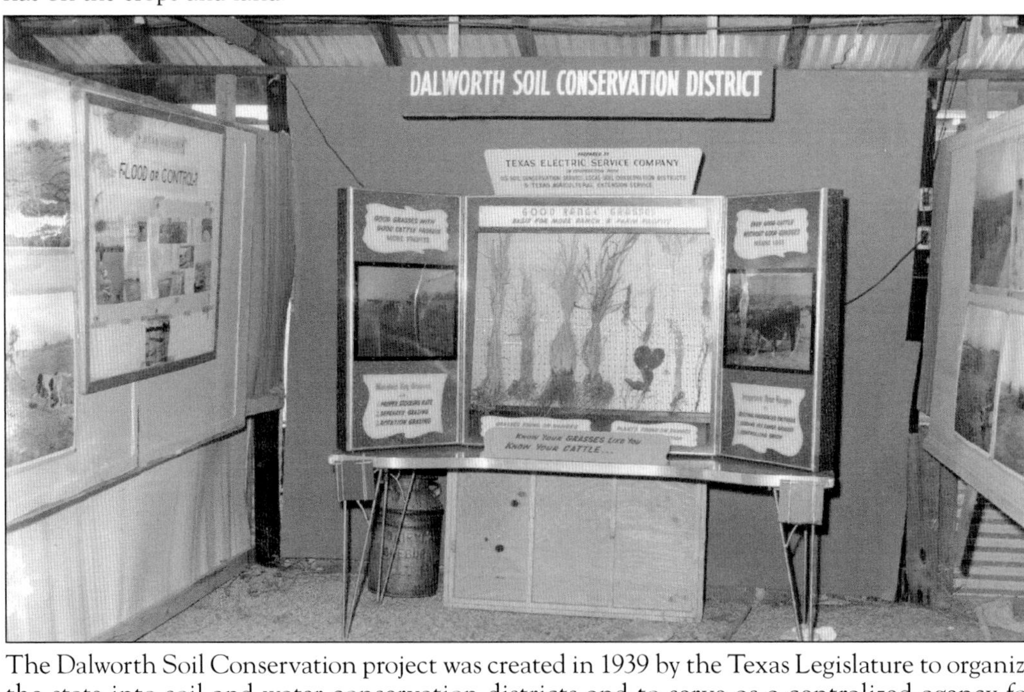

The Dalworth Soil Conservation project was created in 1939 by the Texas Legislature to organize the state into soil and water conservation districts and to serve as a centralized agency for communicating with the Texas Legislature as well as other state and federal entities.

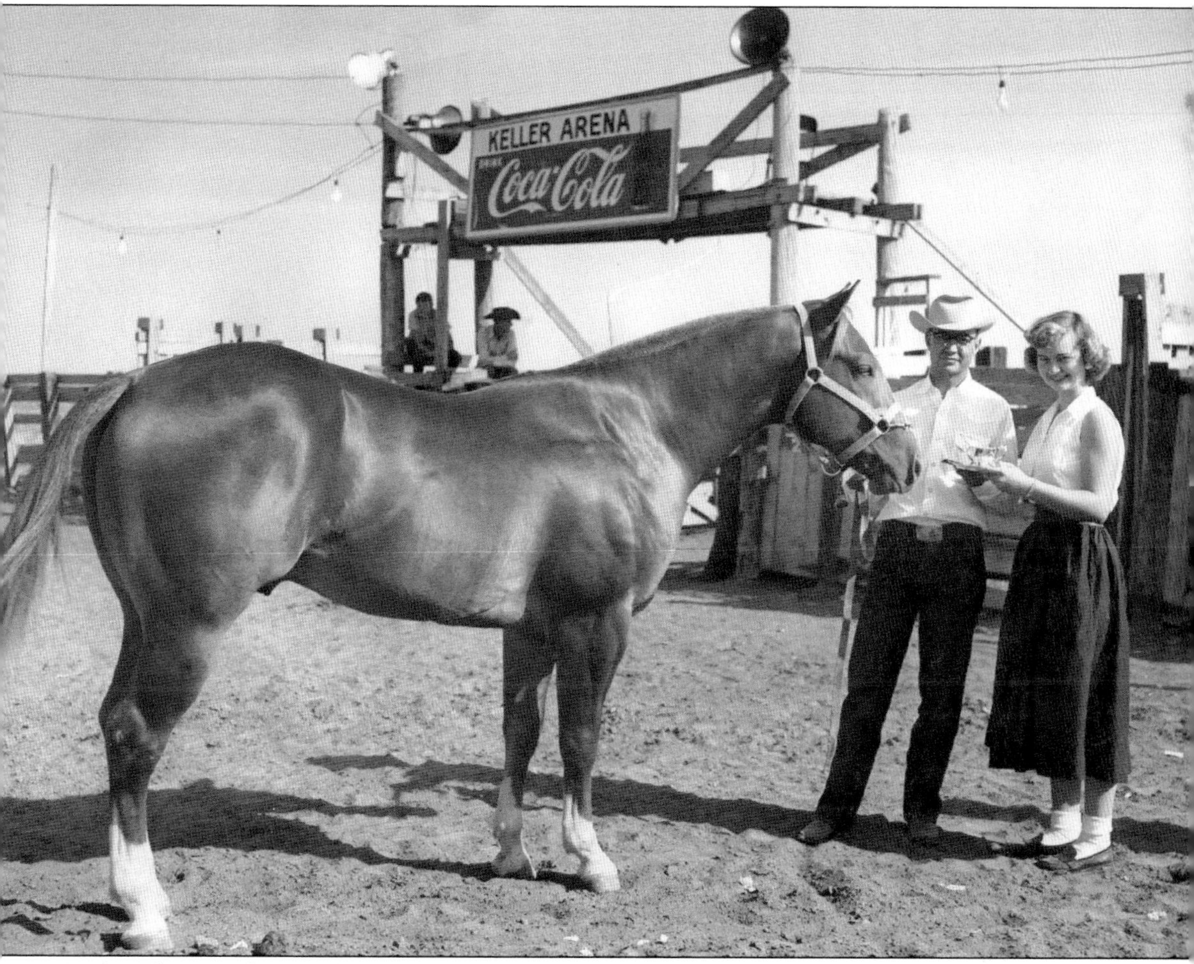

Martha Thorton, from Keller, Texas, presents an award to Paul Curtner, from Jacksboro, Texas, for his horse Town Cry in front of the Keller Arena.

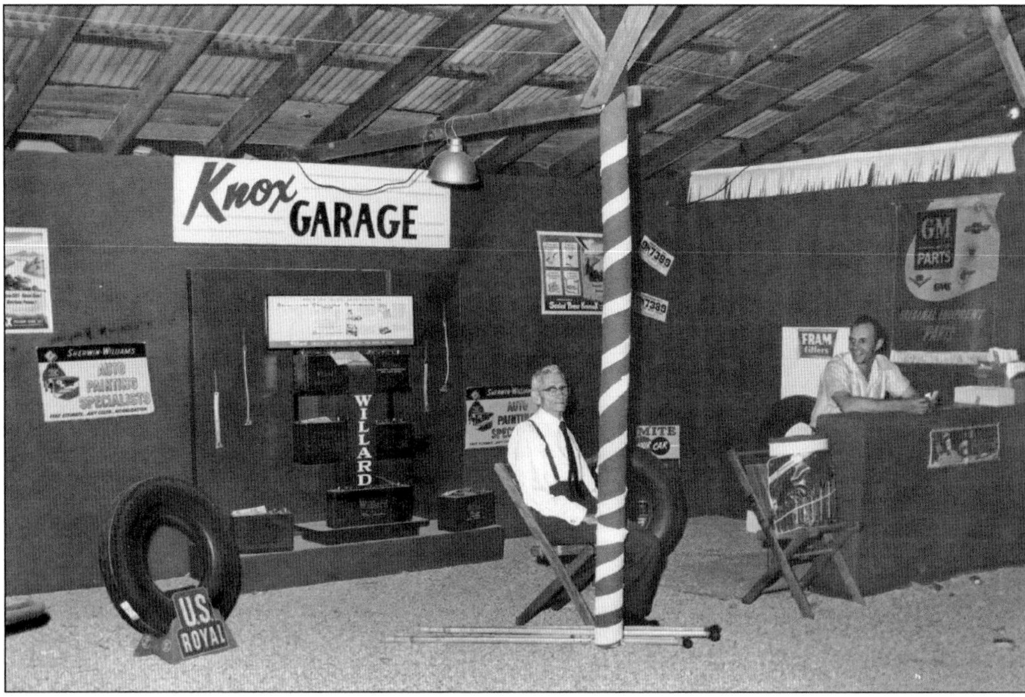

This is Knox Garage's booth. The garage was located on Main and Bates Streets and was originally started by Jasper Knox in 1913. Pictured here are Newton Knox (left) and Joe Knox.

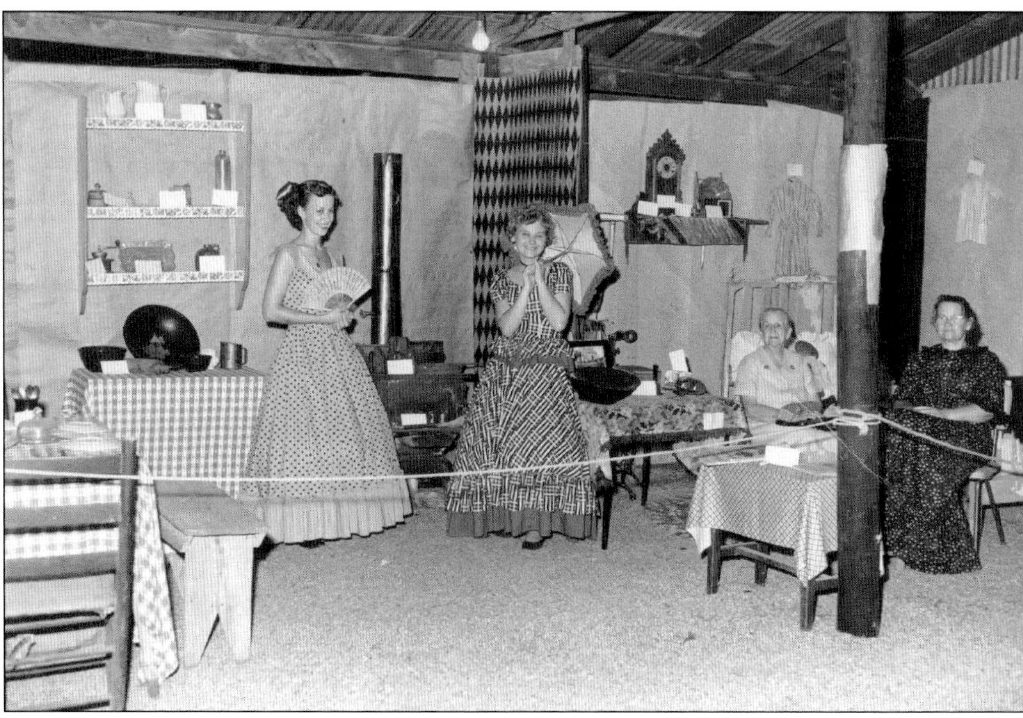

Lady Lions Jonnie Lee Berry (left) and Laura Ann Berry (right) have dressed up as settlers from the past as they have fun in their booth at the Keller Fair.

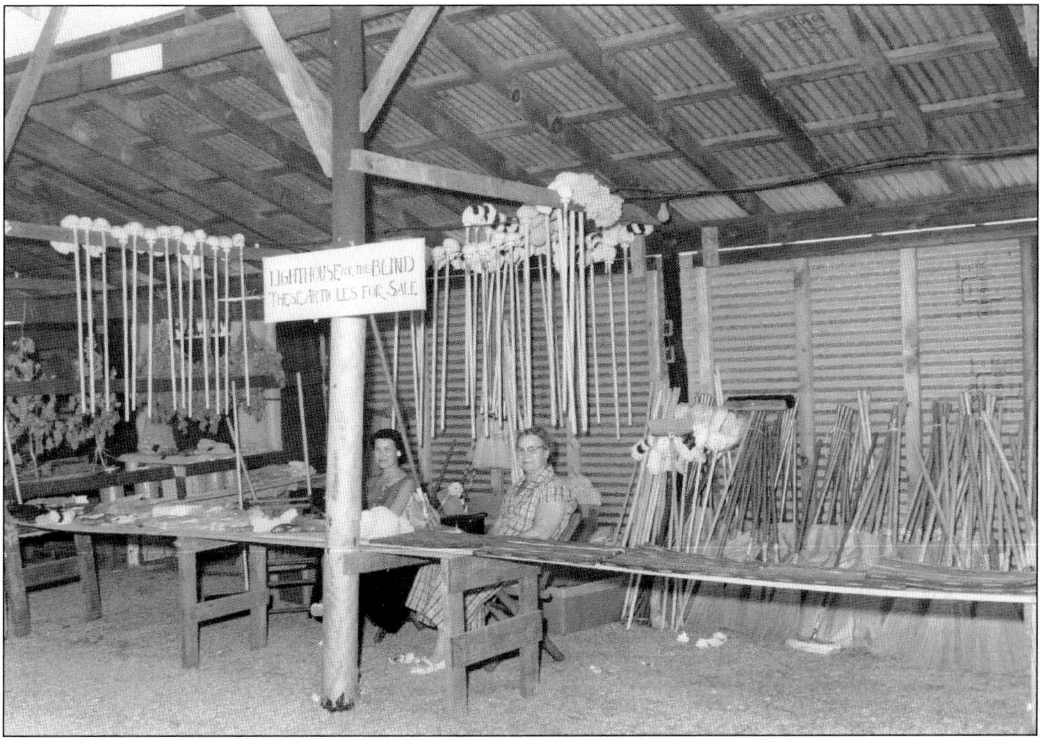

Seen here are mops made by the blind for sale at the Keller Fair. The Lighthouse for the Blind of Fort Worth was founded in 1935 by Willie Fay Lewis, a blind woman who was sent to Fort Worth, according to the organization's Web site, "To find a handful of blind people and see what she could do to help them." The Lighthouse has helped the visually impaired for the last 70 years and now has an 80,000-square-foot location in downtown Fort Worth.

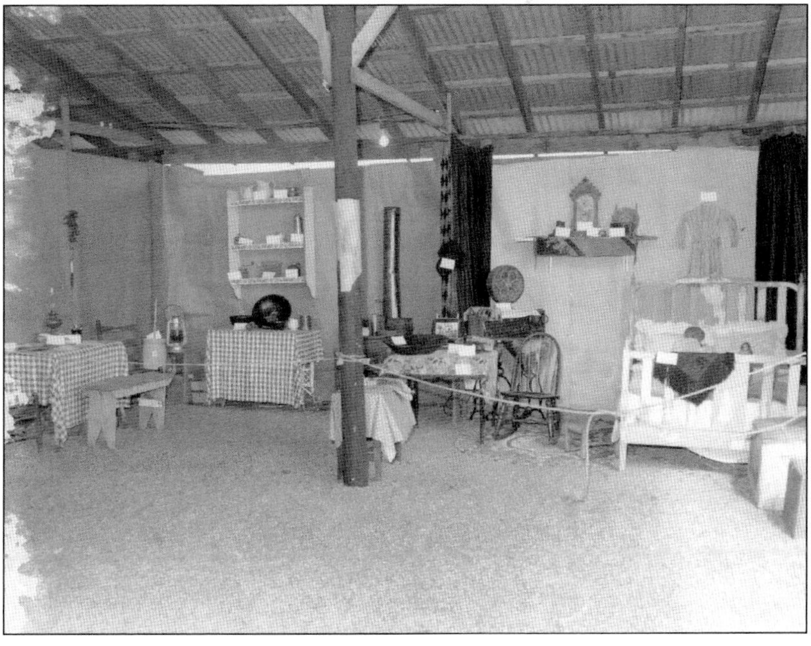

A fair booth displays items used by early settlers.

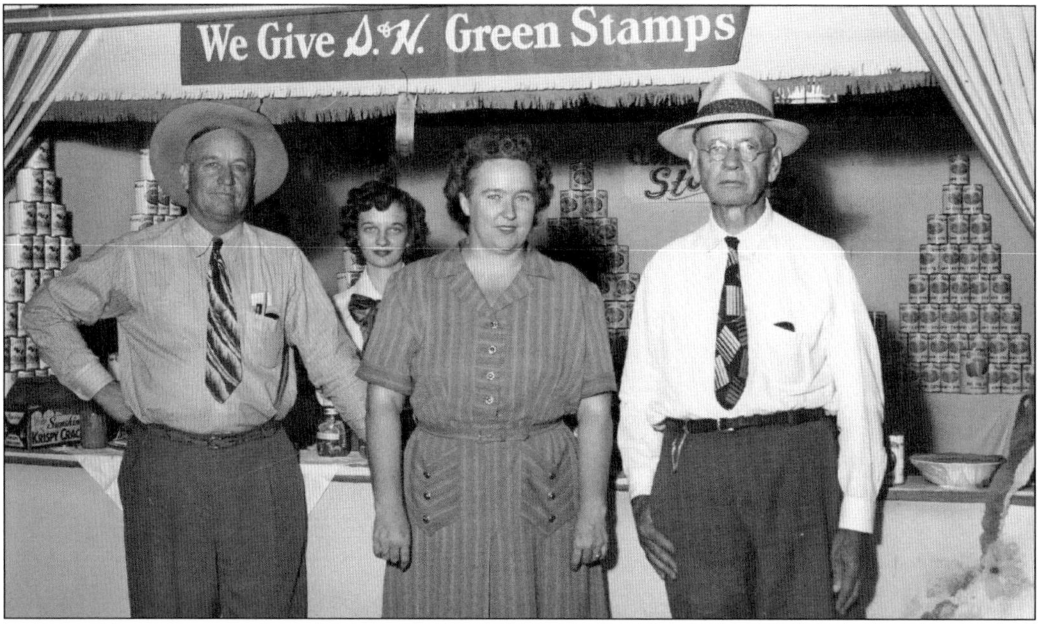

S&H Green Stamps became a popular retailer rewards program in the 1960s that was operated by the Sperry and Hutchinson Company. It became the largest publication in the United States during the 1960s; the company issued more stamps than the U.S. Postal Service. Customers would collect stamps at local grocery, gasoline, and department stores, as well as other retailers, and redeemed them for items and vacations.

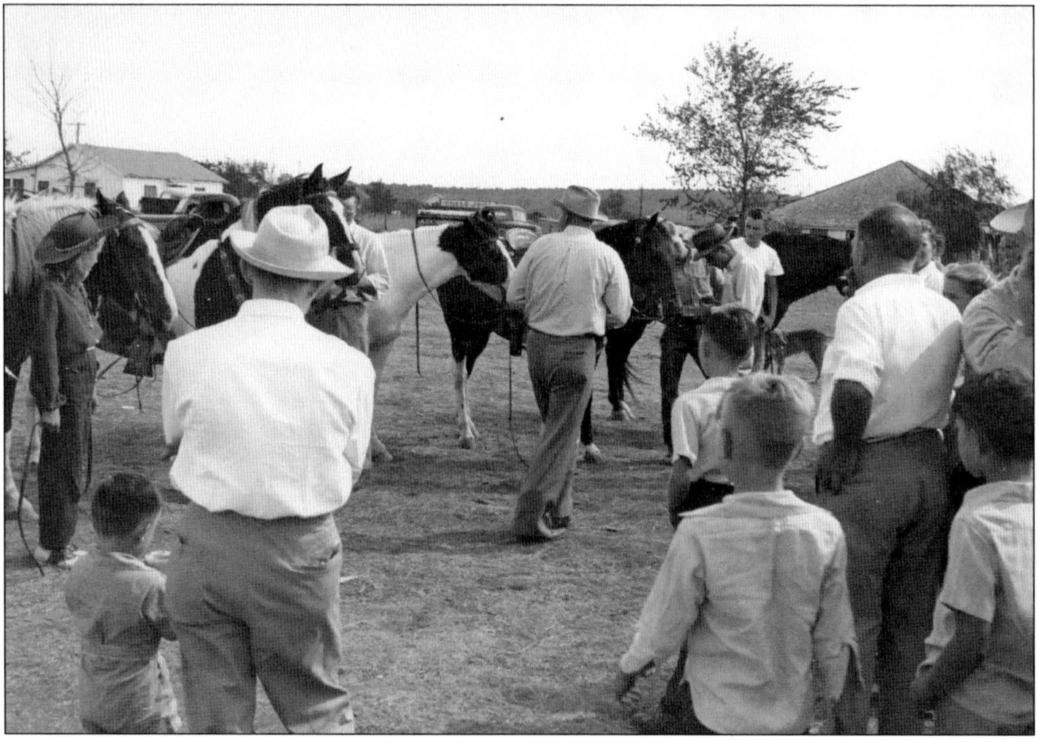

Horses are being judged at the Keller Arena as fairgoers look on.

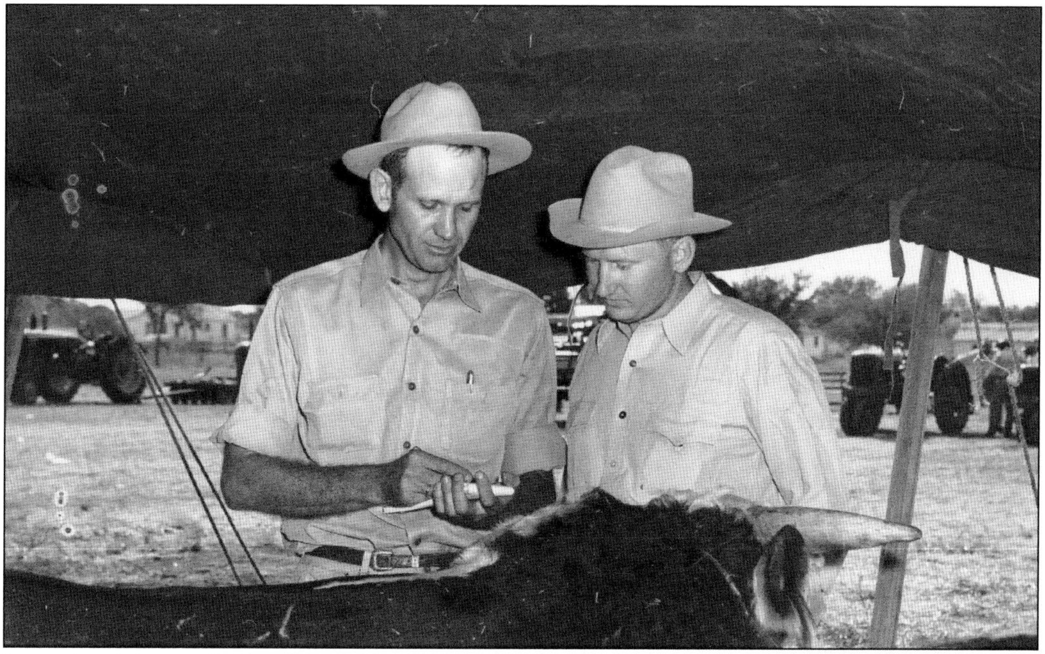

Lion Tom Hinton (left) judges livestock at the Keller Fair.

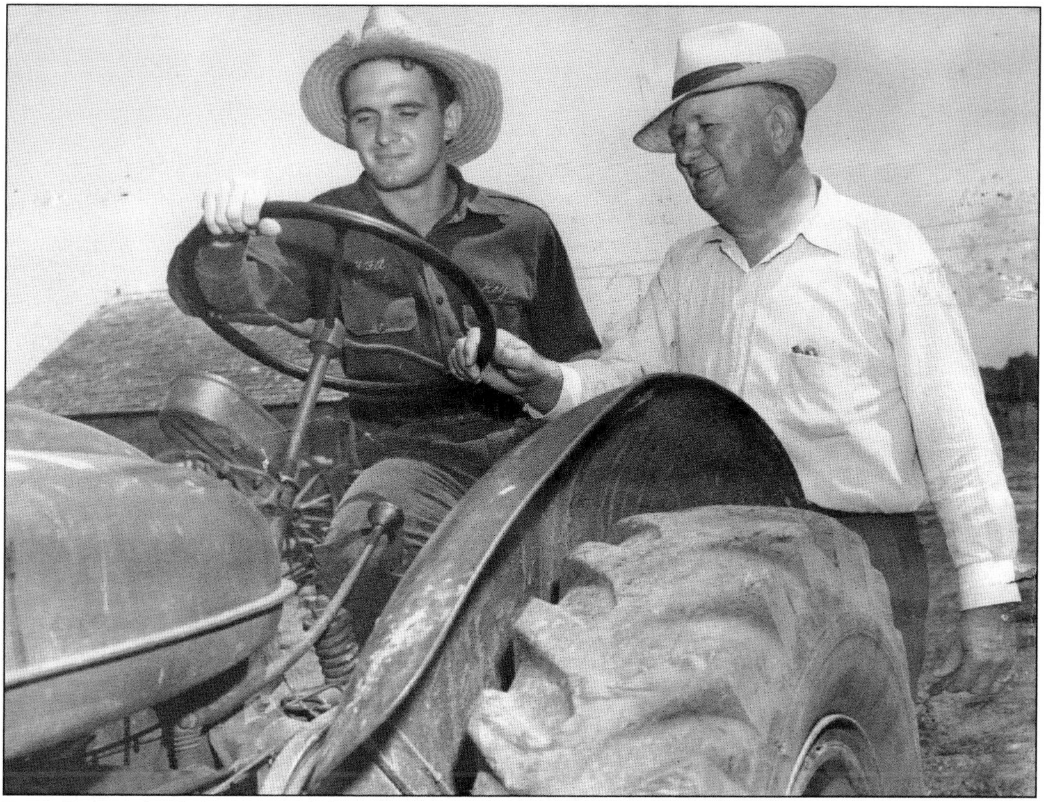

Burt Owens (right), Lions Club president in 1948, is demonstrating the features of a new tractor featured at the Keller Fair.

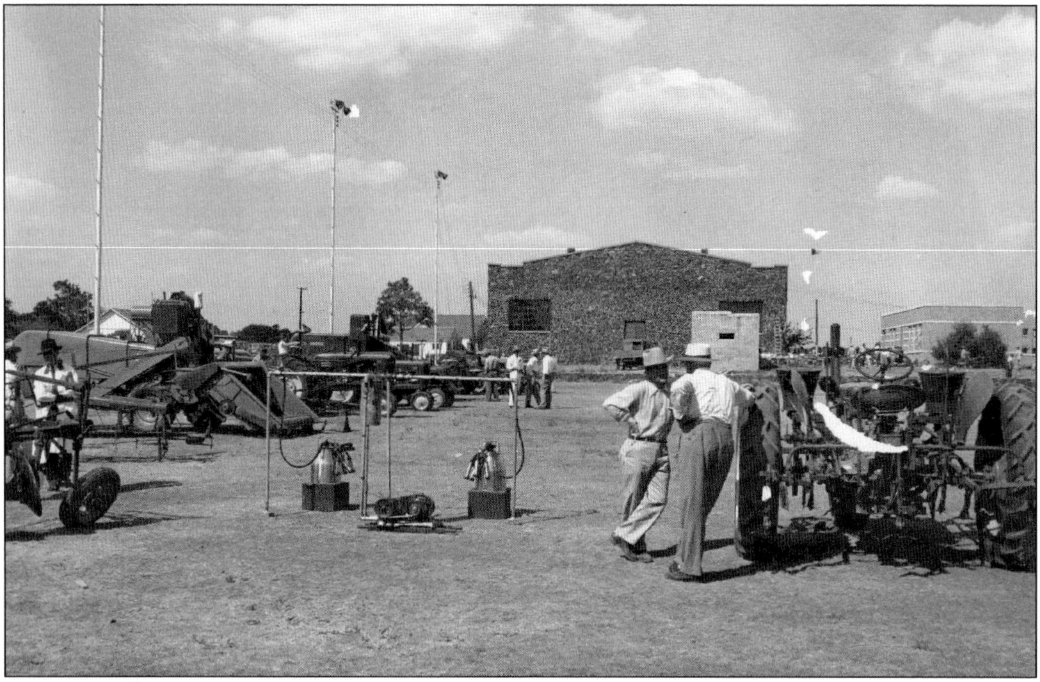

At a farm show in the rear of the Keller Rock Gymnasium, Burt Owens (left) leans on a tractor having a chat with a visiting fairgoer.

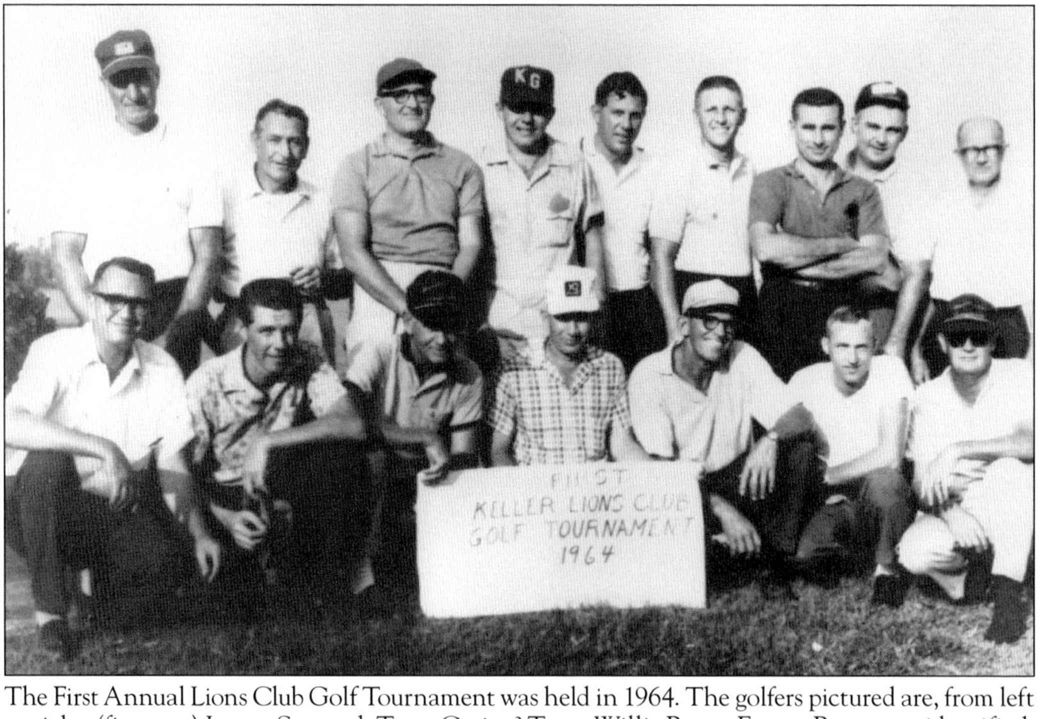

The First Annual Lions Club Golf Tournament was held in 1964. The golfers pictured are, from left to right, (first row) Lester Steward, Terry Craig, ? Tony, Willis Berry, Ernest Bursey, unidentified, and ? Hinton; (second row) Harold Pipes, Jim Grove, unidentified, Bob Raspberry, Wendell Barry, Orrie Harris, Billy "Mack" Blevins, Jerrell Newton, and Dr. Randall Simpson.

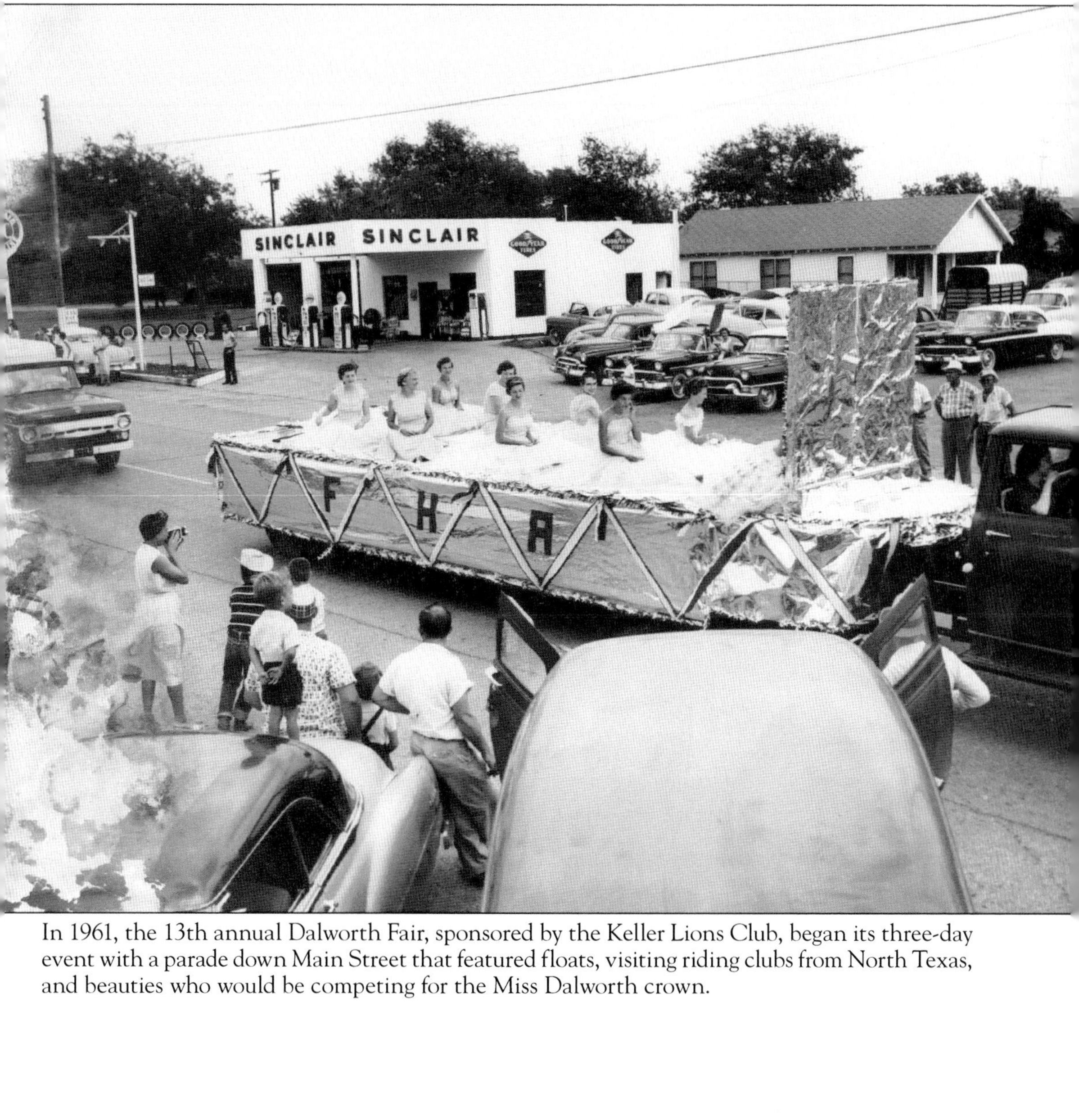

In 1961, the 13th annual Dalworth Fair, sponsored by the Keller Lions Club, began its three-day event with a parade down Main Street that featured floats, visiting riding clubs from North Texas, and beauties who would be competing for the Miss Dalworth crown.

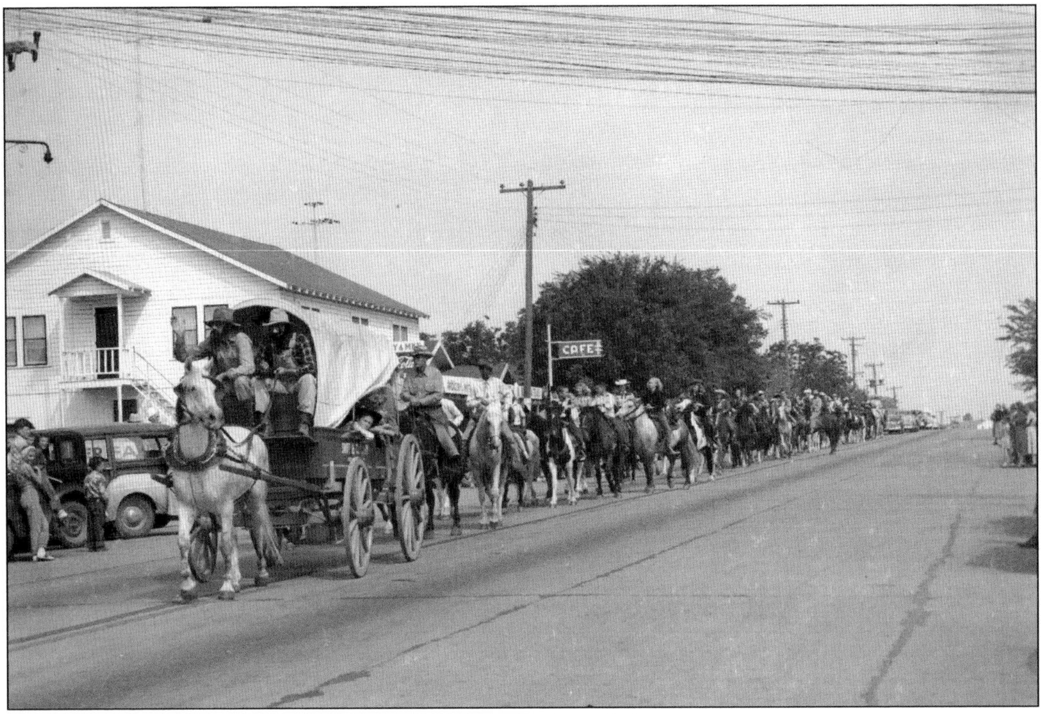

Pictured here is the opening-day parade for the Dalworth Fair.

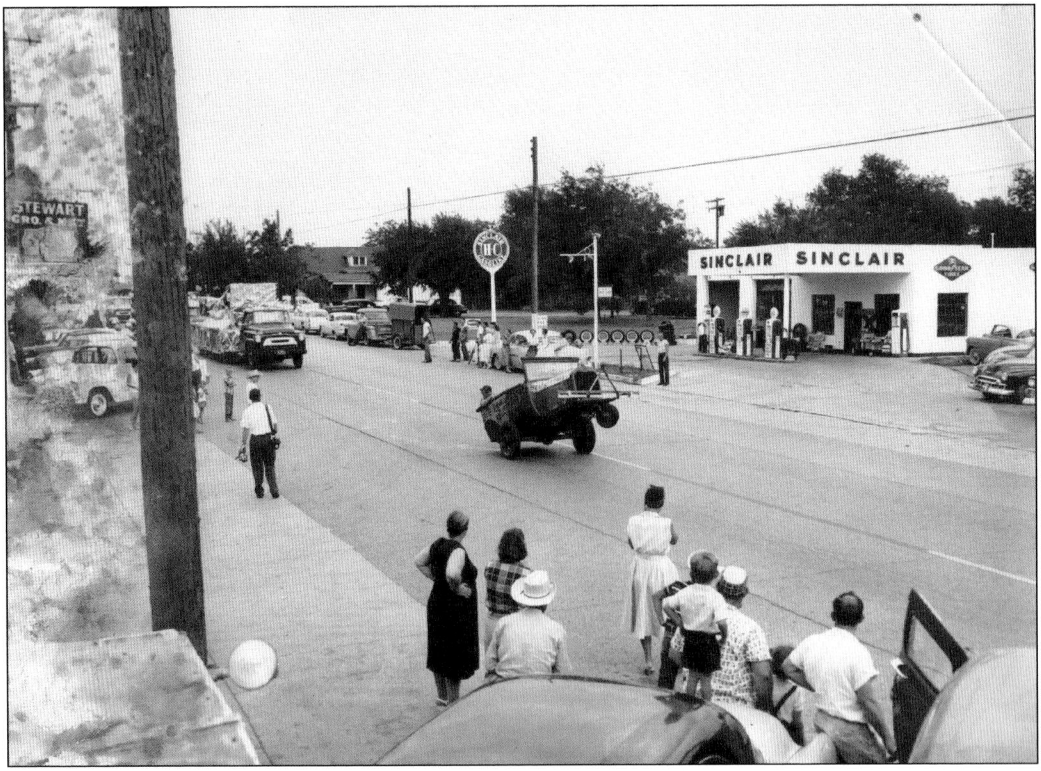

The Keller parade continues with cars on two wheels coming down Main Street.

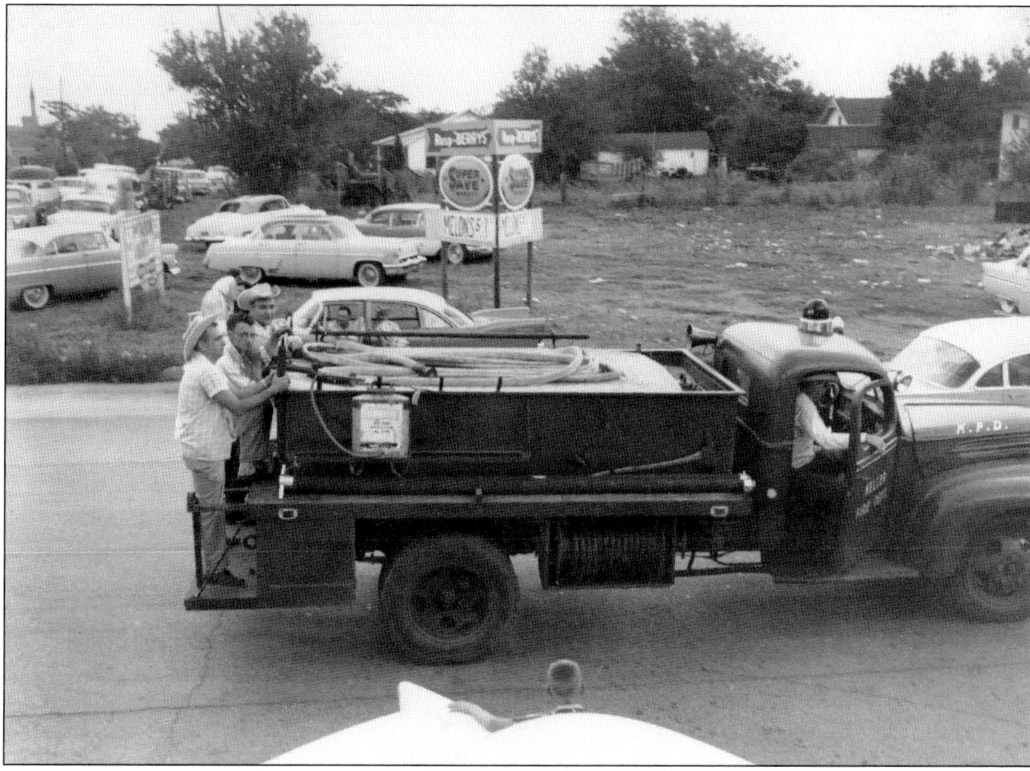

Men are pictured riding on the back of the fire truck in the Keller parade. The fun was only beginning, as the Dalworth Fair was about to get underway.

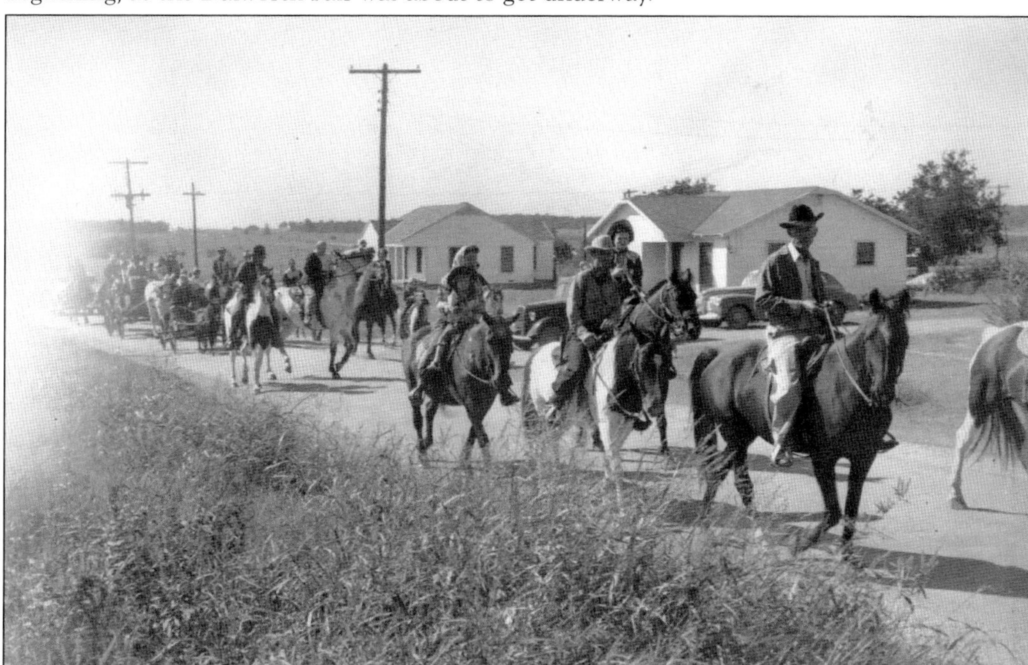

Keller residents and friends are riding on horseback in the parade.

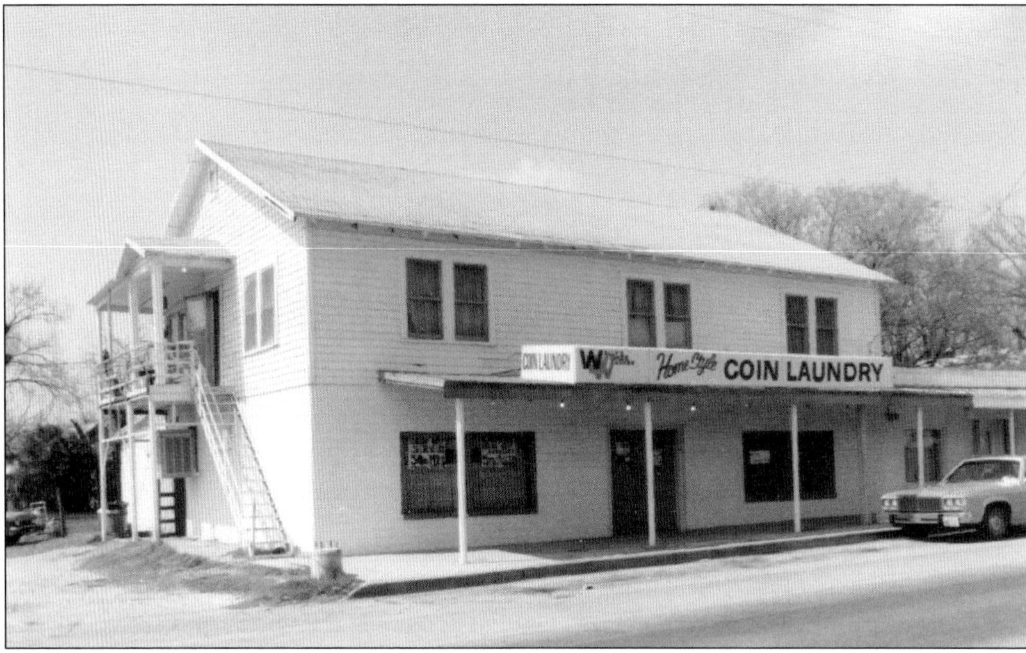

This mid-1960s photograph shows Coin Laundry on Main Street (U.S. Highway 377), where the Up 'N Smoke Restaurant is currently located. The sign in the left window states, "Drop off Service 50 cents per pound." The Coin Laundry eventually featured a café, where many locals discussed plans of their growing town. (Courtesy Joyce Gibson Roach.)

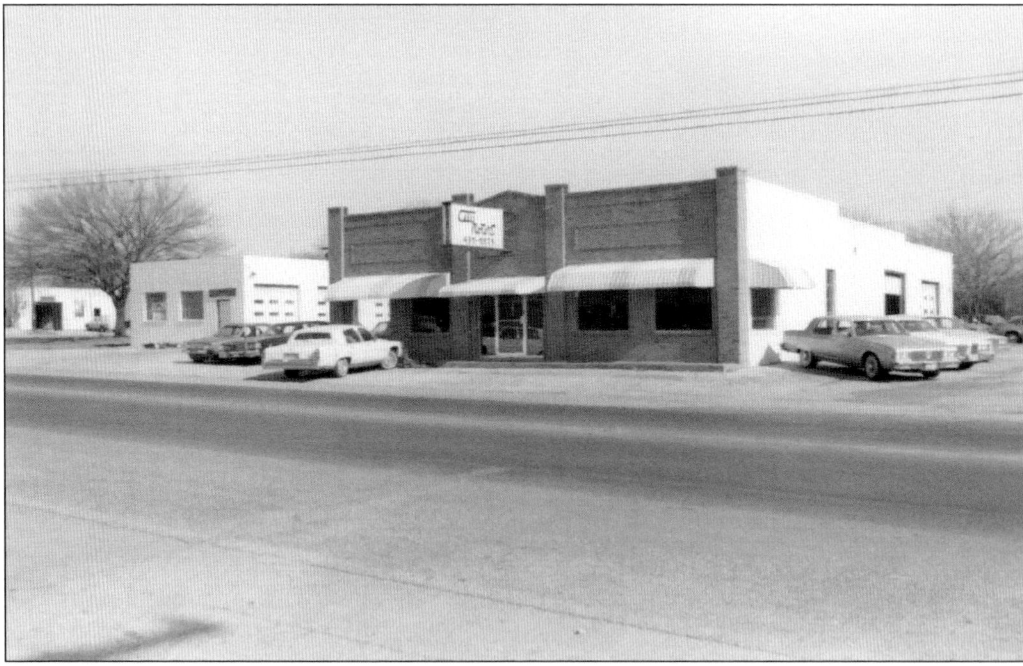

City Motors Car Garage was located across the street from the Coin Laundry. (Courtesy Joyce Gibson Roach.)

Four

Keller Today

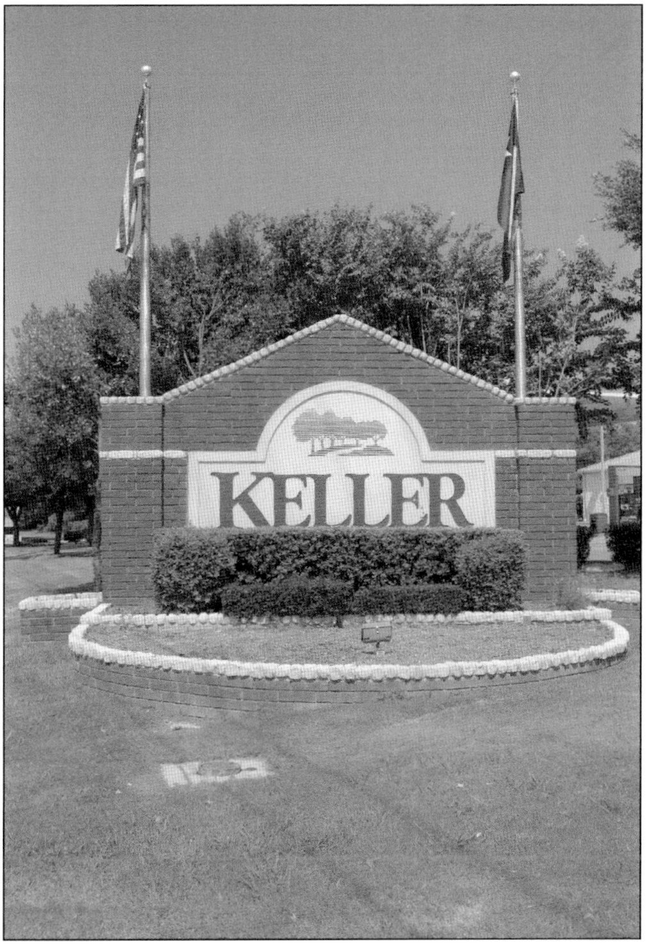

The Keller sign at Pearson Lane is considered the entrance to Keller. Located on the corner of Keller Parkway (FM 1709) and Pearson Lane, it greets residents and guests coming to the city for business or pleasure. (Courtesy Jennifer Featherston.)

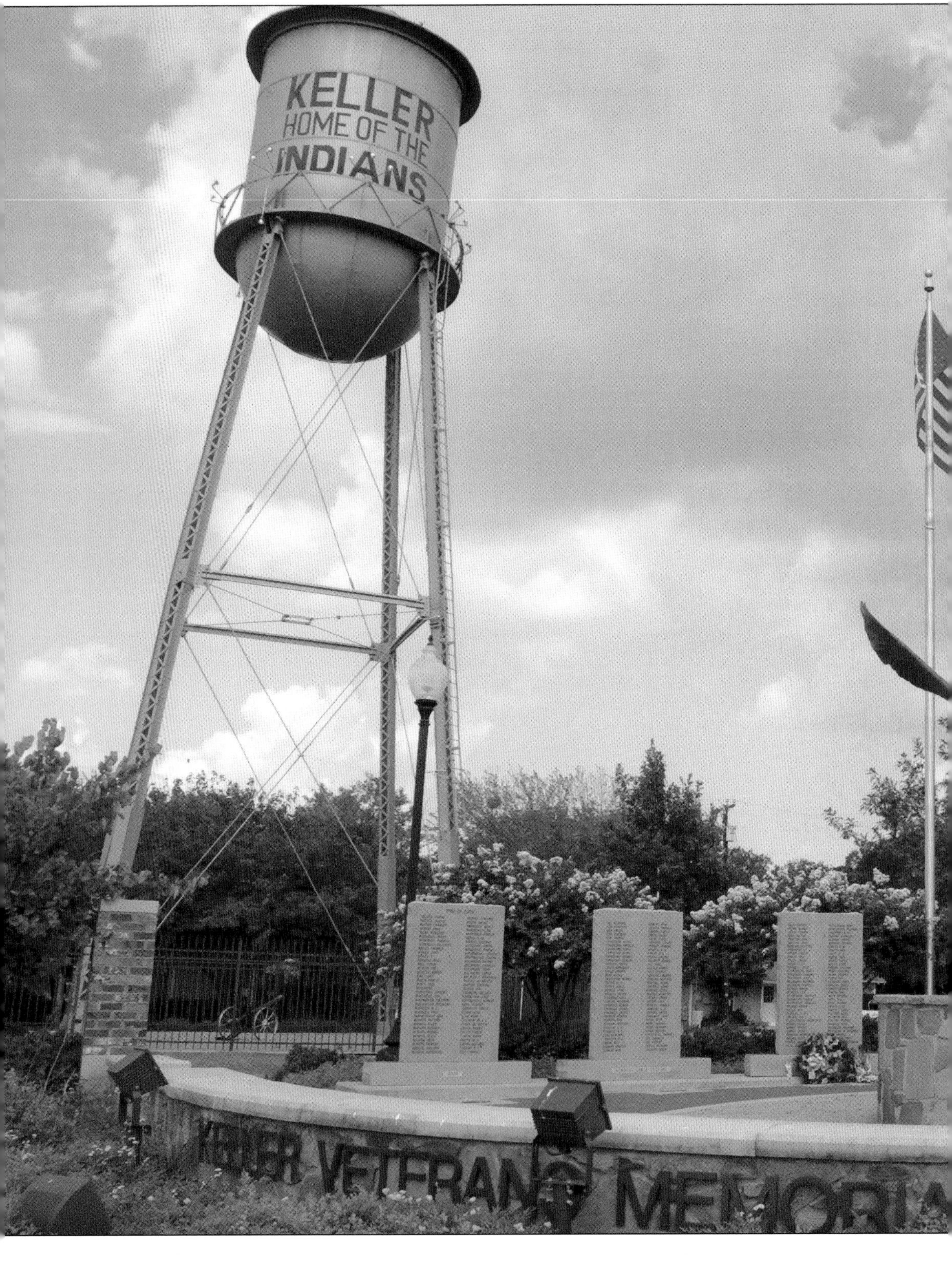
KELLER
HOME OF THE
INDIANS

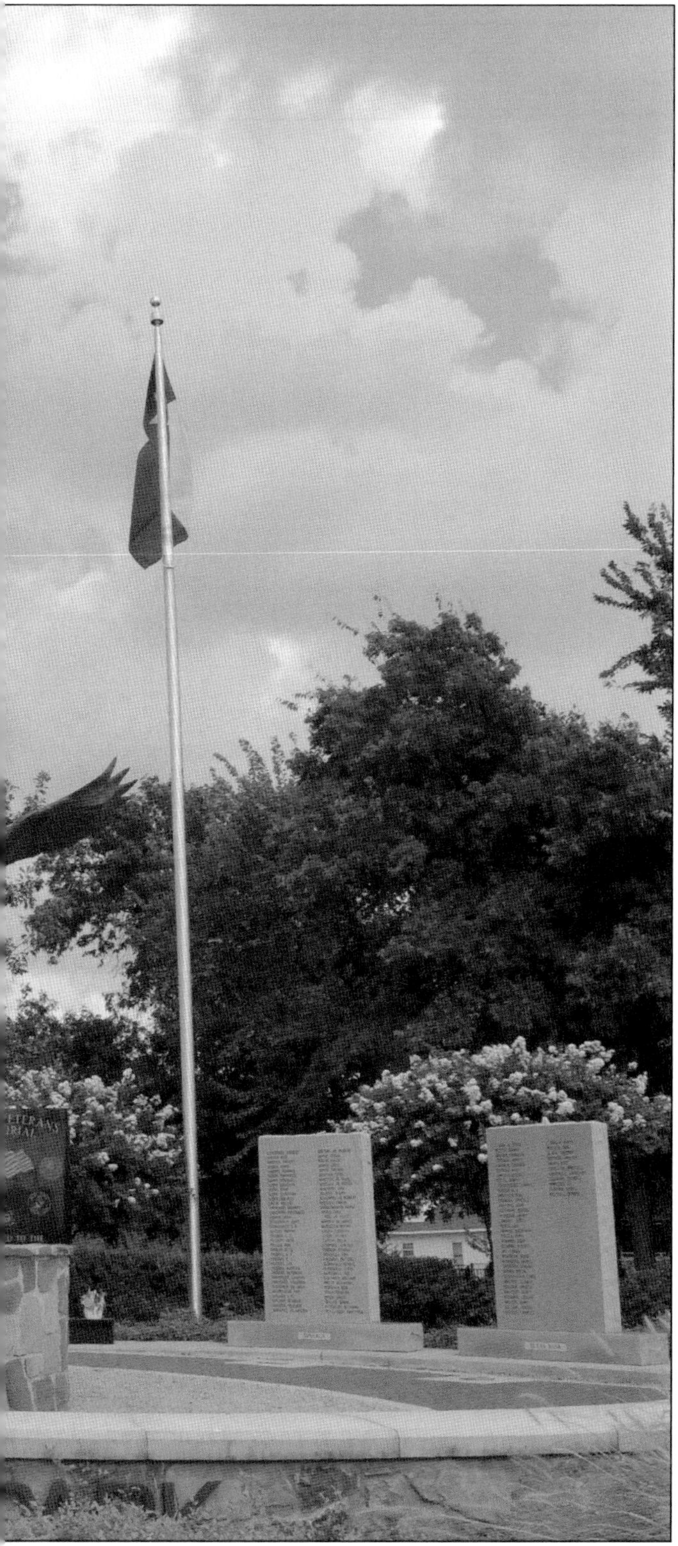

In conjunction with the City of Keller and Keller Rotary, the Keller Veterans Memorial Park was created in 2008. It honors its local veterans and Keller-area residents who actively served in the armed forces. Located at the corner of North Main Street (U.S. Highway 377) and Keller Parkway (FM 1709), the memorial rests near the historic water tower. The park is centered around seven granite pillars, including a monument to Keller veterans with names engraved on those pillars. (Courtesy Jennifer Featherston.)

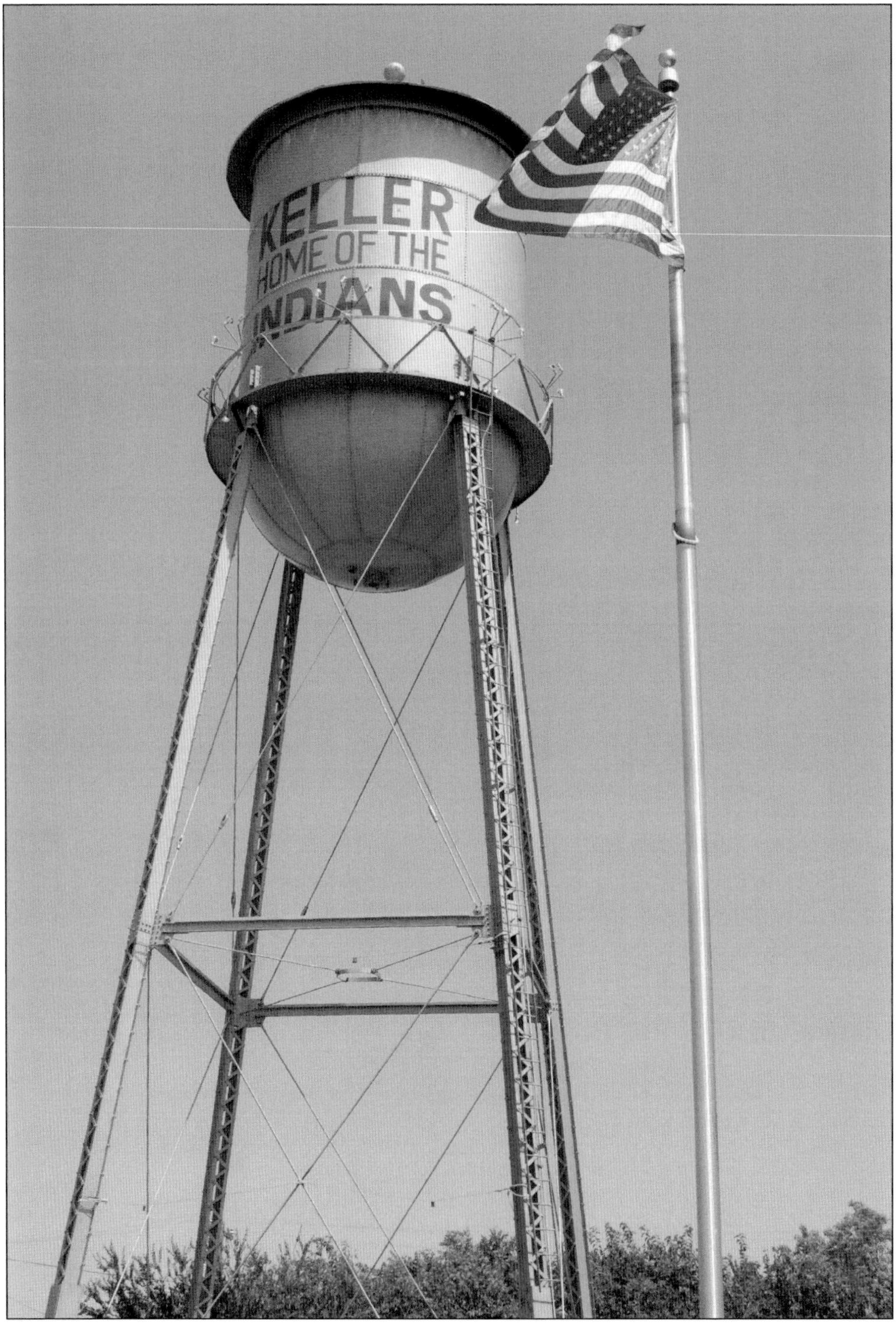

Keller Water Tower was built in 1906 and remained in service until 1960. A special feature of the water tower is the lights surrounding it. Once the Keller Indians football team wins a game, blue lights announce the win to the town; just another way Keller shows its community spirit. (Courtesy Jennifer Featherston.)

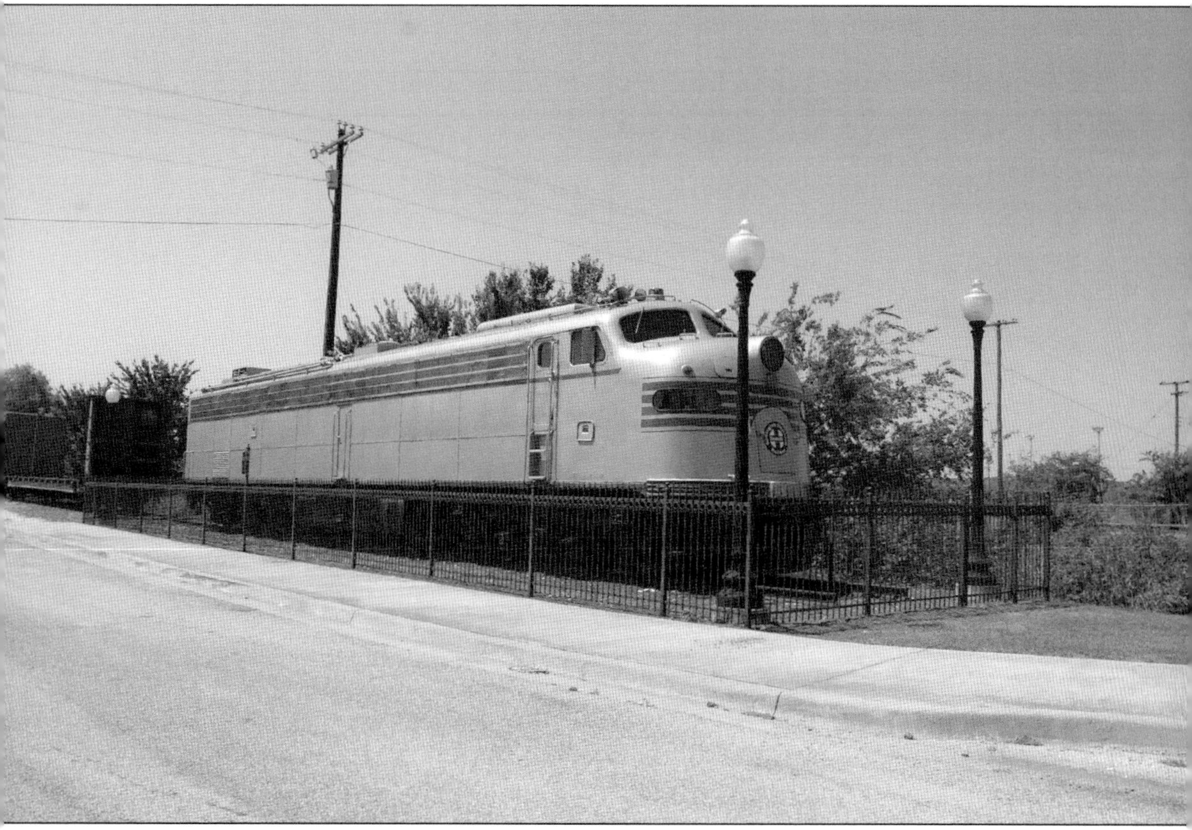

Whistle Stop Spur is a reminder of Keller's railroad origins. Locomotive no. 9920 sits at the site of the original Keller Train Depot, located on U.S. Highway 377 behind Up 'N Smoke Restaurant. (Courtesy Jennifer Featherston.)

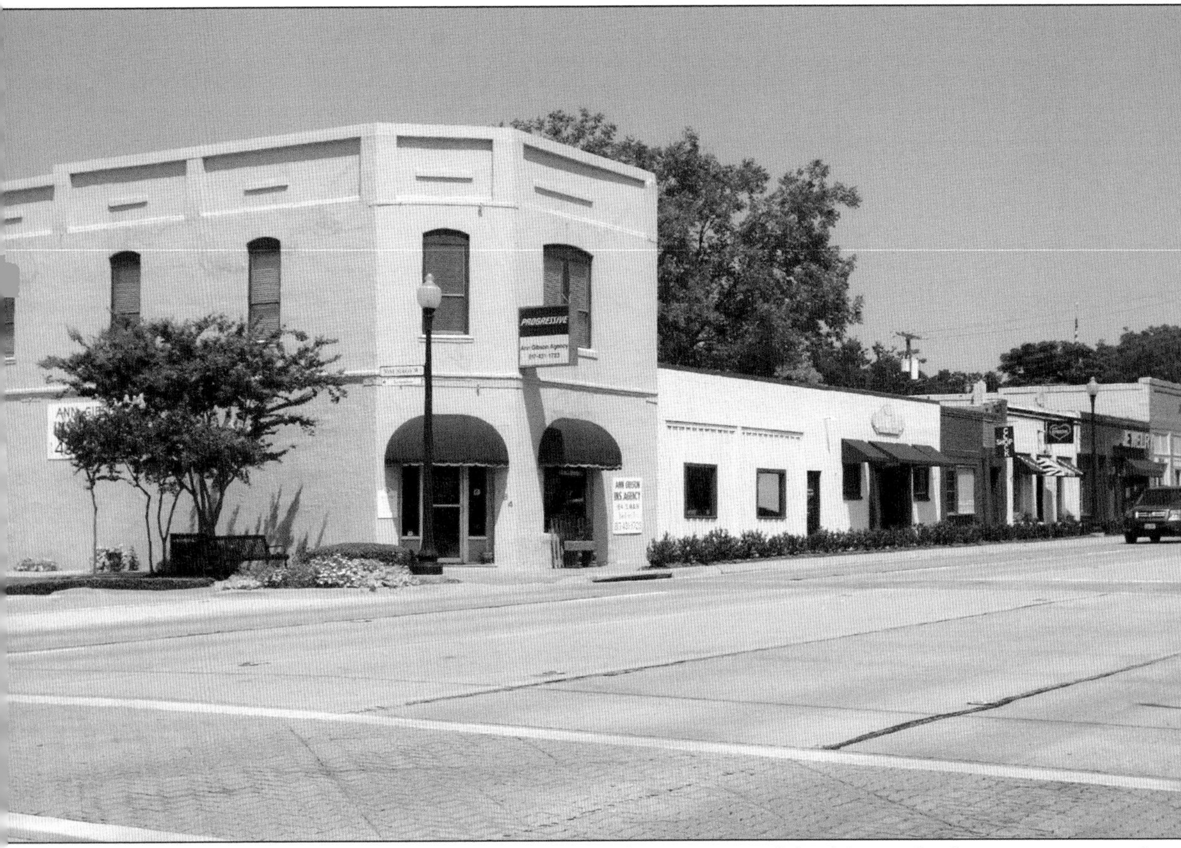

Ann Gibson Insurance is housed in the original Citizens Bank building, which was constructed in the late 1800s. Ann Gibson's daughter is renowned author and Texas historian Joyce Gibson Roach, who still resides in Keller. (Courtesy Jennifer Featherston.)

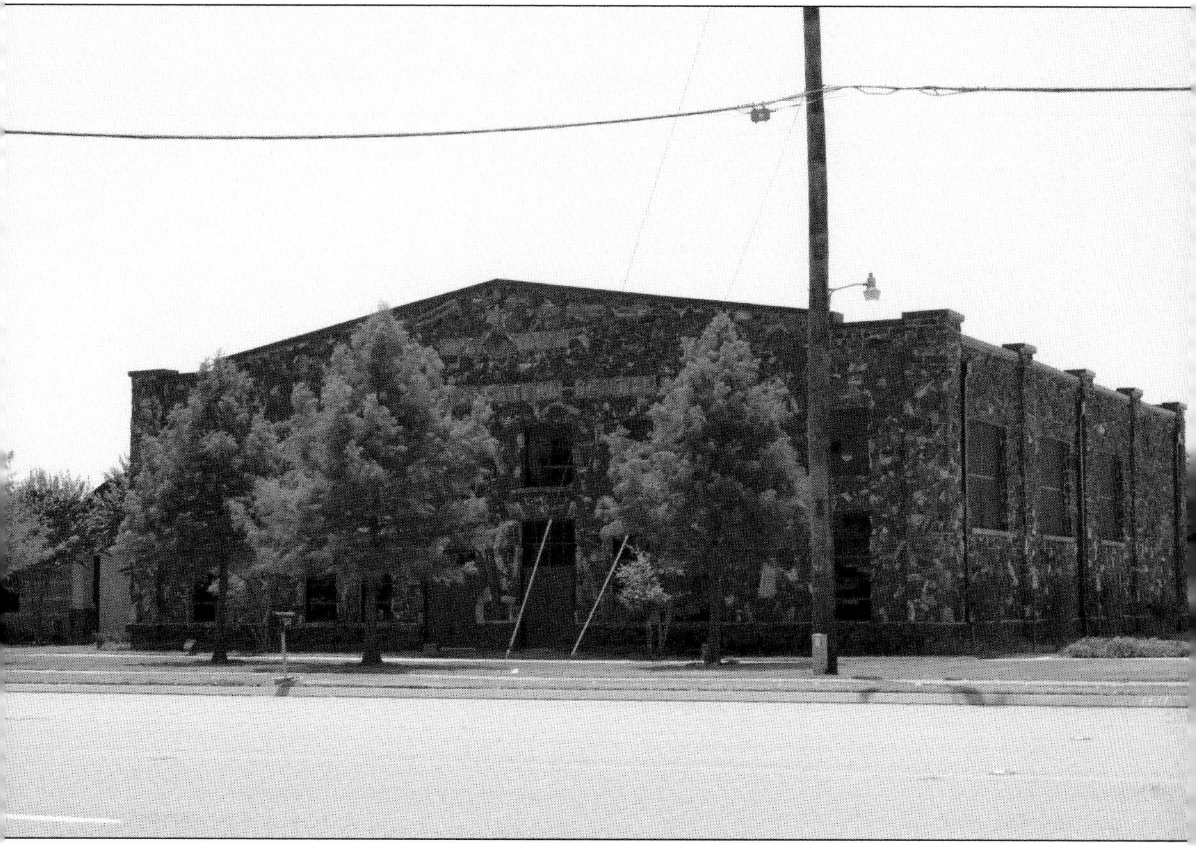

Rock Gym currently serves as a boardroom for Keller Independent School District's (KISD) trustees and adjoins the KISD's central administration and teacher training center. (Courtesy Jennifer Featherston.)

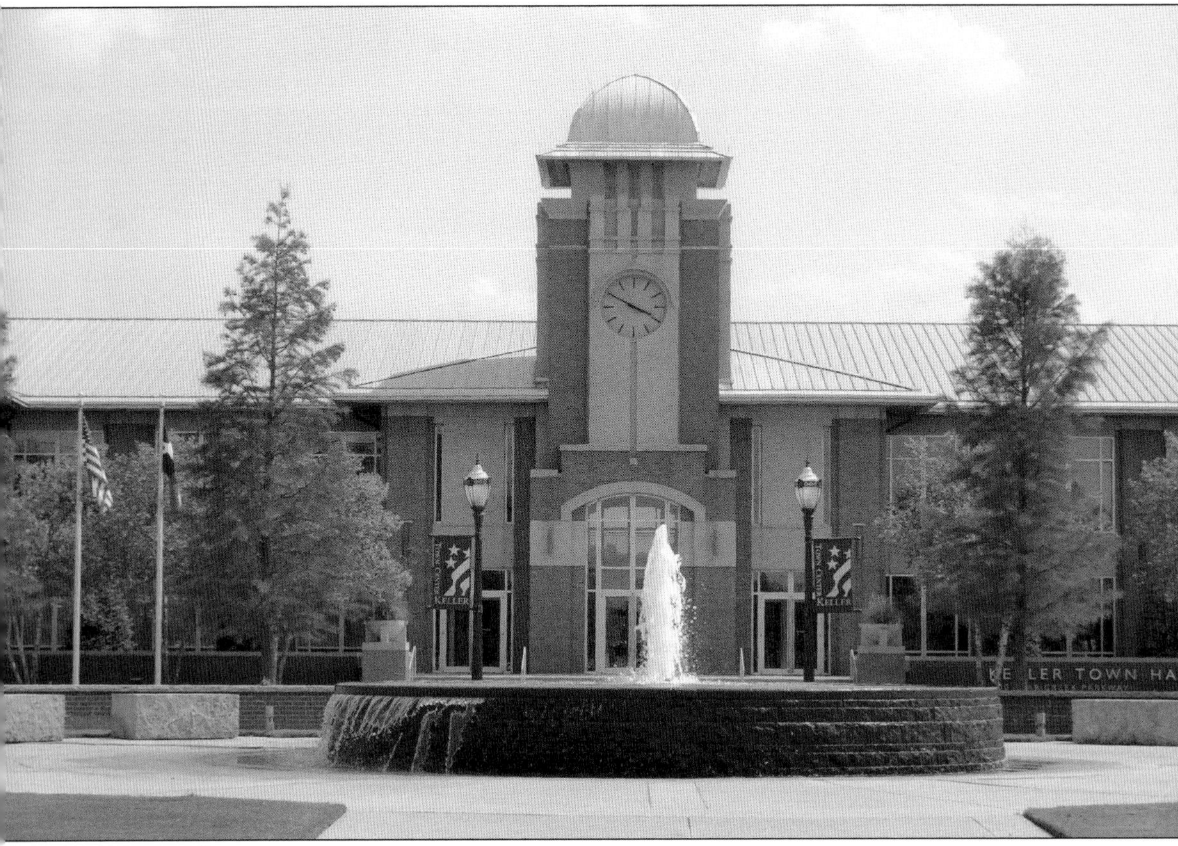

Keller Town Hall, located at 1100 Bear Creek Parkway, houses the City of Keller administration offices and is part of a 340-acre development known as the Keller Town Center. The Keller Town Center features pedestrian trails, greenbelts, lakes, and water displays. It incorporates municipal services and public gathering places with private use in the form of detached villas, luxury housing, ground-floor retail with office lofts above, restaurants, and entertainment venues to create a sense of community. (Courtesy Jennifer Featherston.)

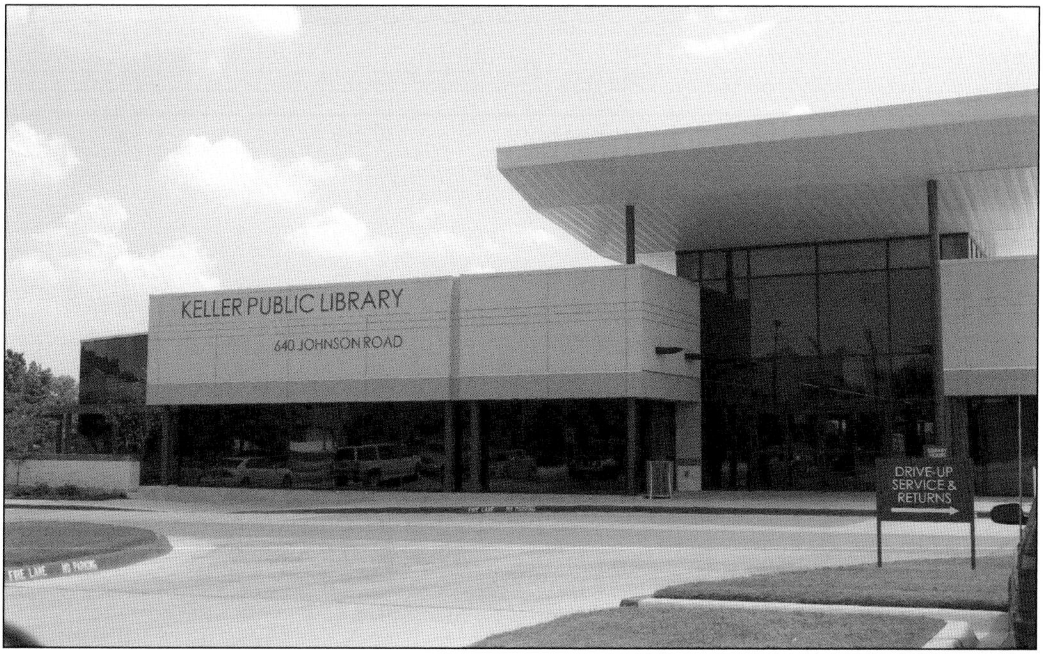

The Keller Public Library has newly renovated and expanded facilities now located at 640 Johnson Road. The library supports lifelong learning and fun through books, programs, and media. It features books, music and books on CD, DVDs, large-print books, and magazines available for checkout. (Courtesy Jennifer Featherston.)

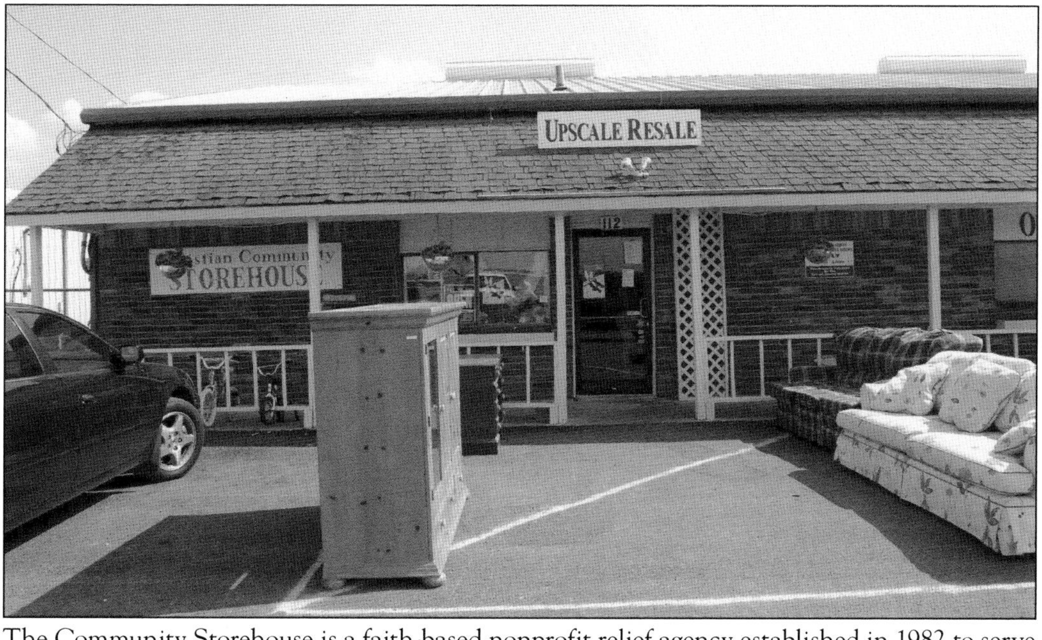

The Community Storehouse is a faith-based nonprofit relief agency established in 1982 to serve the children in Keller and Northwest Independent School Districts. Focused on providing basic needs, the Community Storehouse provides medical and dental care, eye care, prescriptions, school supplies, food, clothing, shelter, and counseling for children. In 2009, the Community Storehouse helped over 9,000 families, individuals, and children. (Courtesy Jennifer Featherston.)

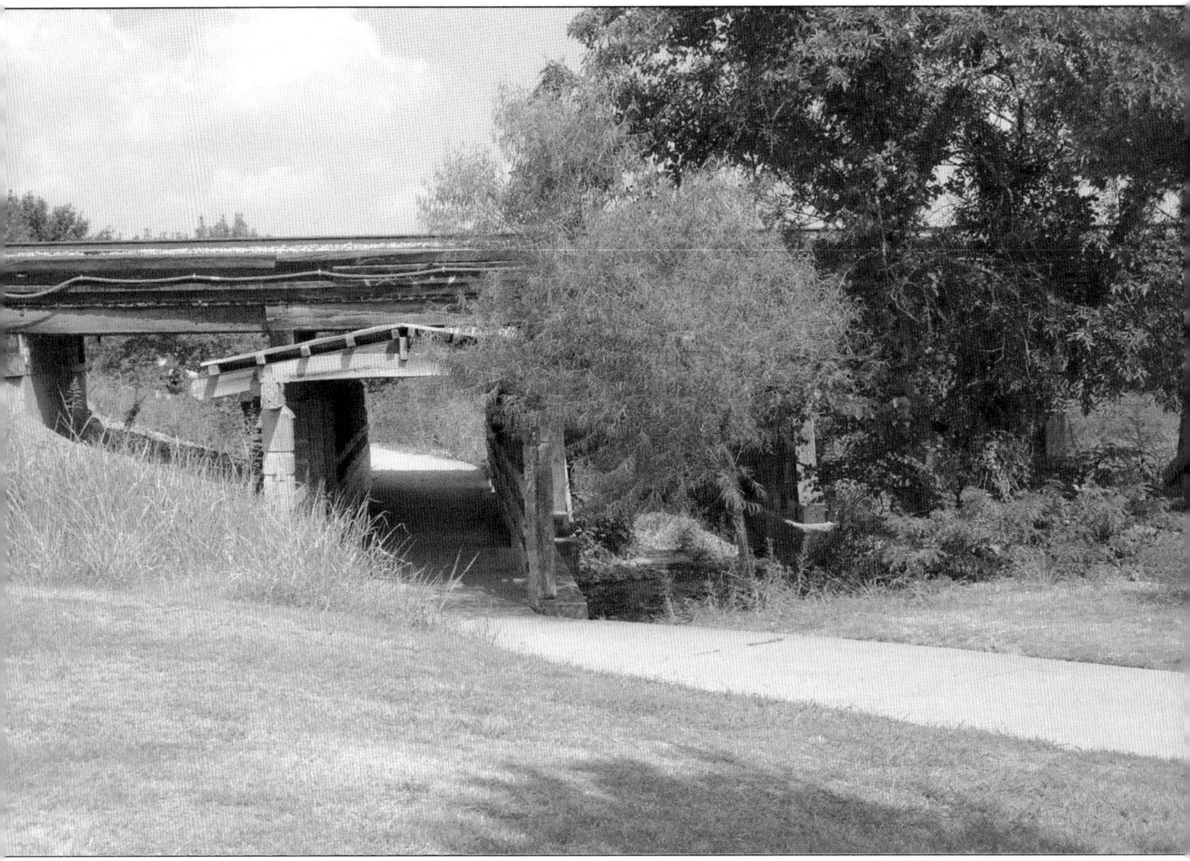

Bear Creek Beltway, located near Keller Sports complex off of Golden Triangle Boulevard, features walking trails, picnic pavilions, and creeks. The City of Keller has 426 acres of parkland and boasts 11 park sites, with more in development. (Courtesy Jennifer Featherston.)

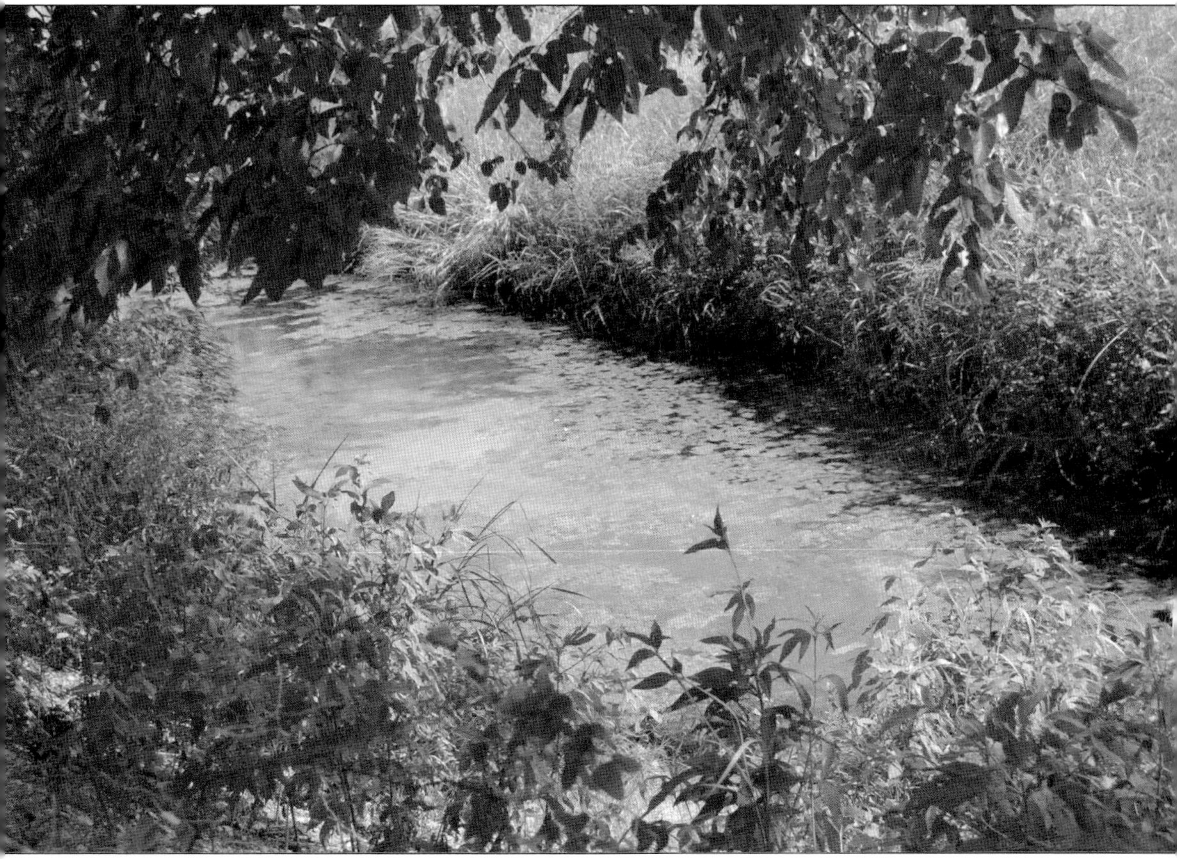

Bear Creek Park includes 44 acres and includes amenities such as playgrounds, a large and small pavilion, hiking and biking trails, gazebos, and a garden with a waterfall. (Courtesy Jennifer Featherston.)

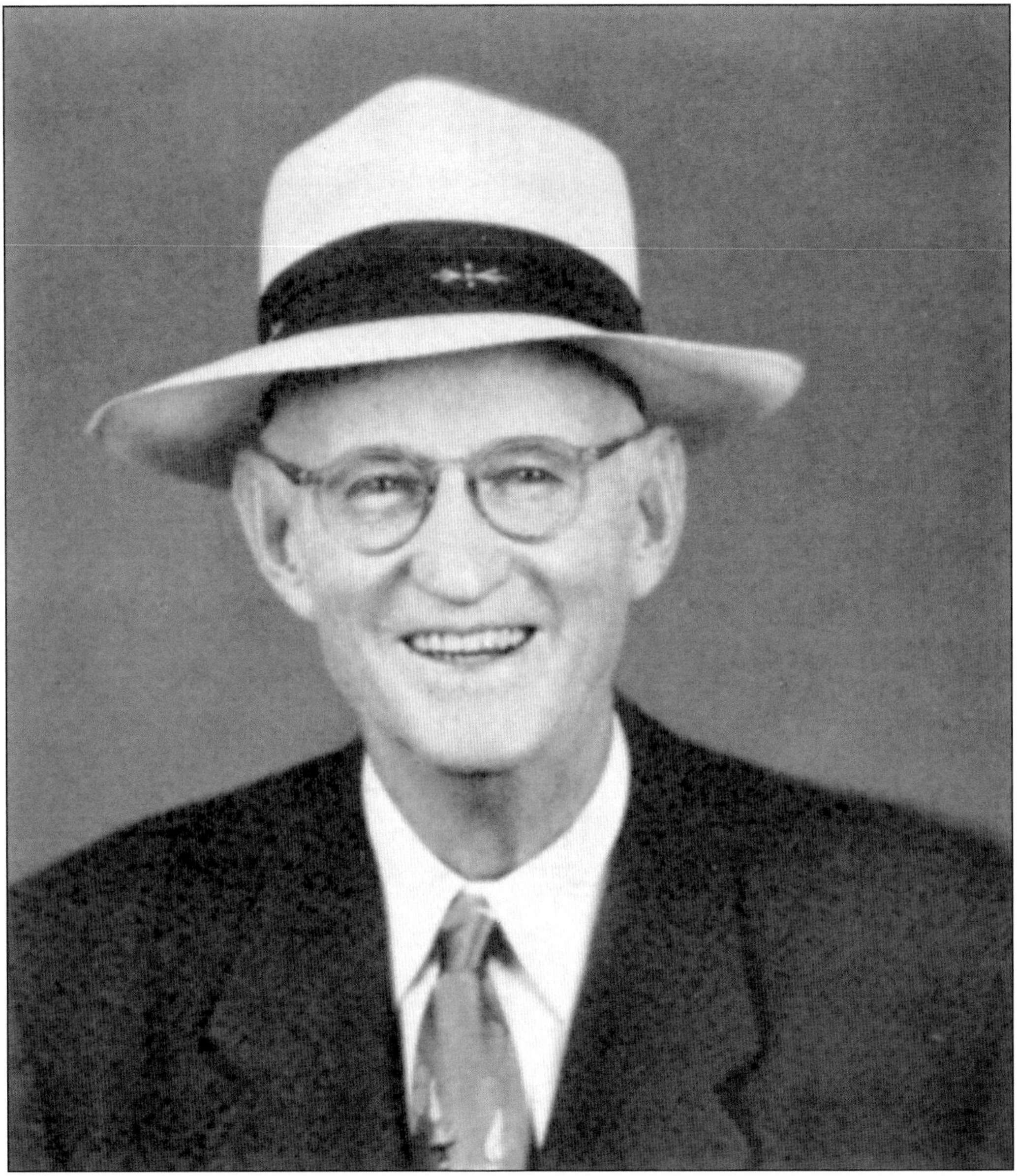

Edward Everett Dale, born in 1879, encapsulated his boyhood in the Keller area in the book *Cross Timbers: Memories of a North Texas Boyhood*, published in 1966. He became a professor at the University of Oklahoma, where Dale Hall is historically named after him. Dale wrote, "The fact that most persons worked hard made periods of leisure more dear. School, church, socials, play parties, literary society meetings, and visiting with friends and neighbors and picnics or fishing trips were all a part of the social life of our community. The opportunity to relax for an hour or two with a good book or magazine is a greater joy than any social function." Edward Everett Dale died in 1972. (Courtesy *Fort Worth Star-Telegram* Collection, the University of Texas at Arlington Library.)

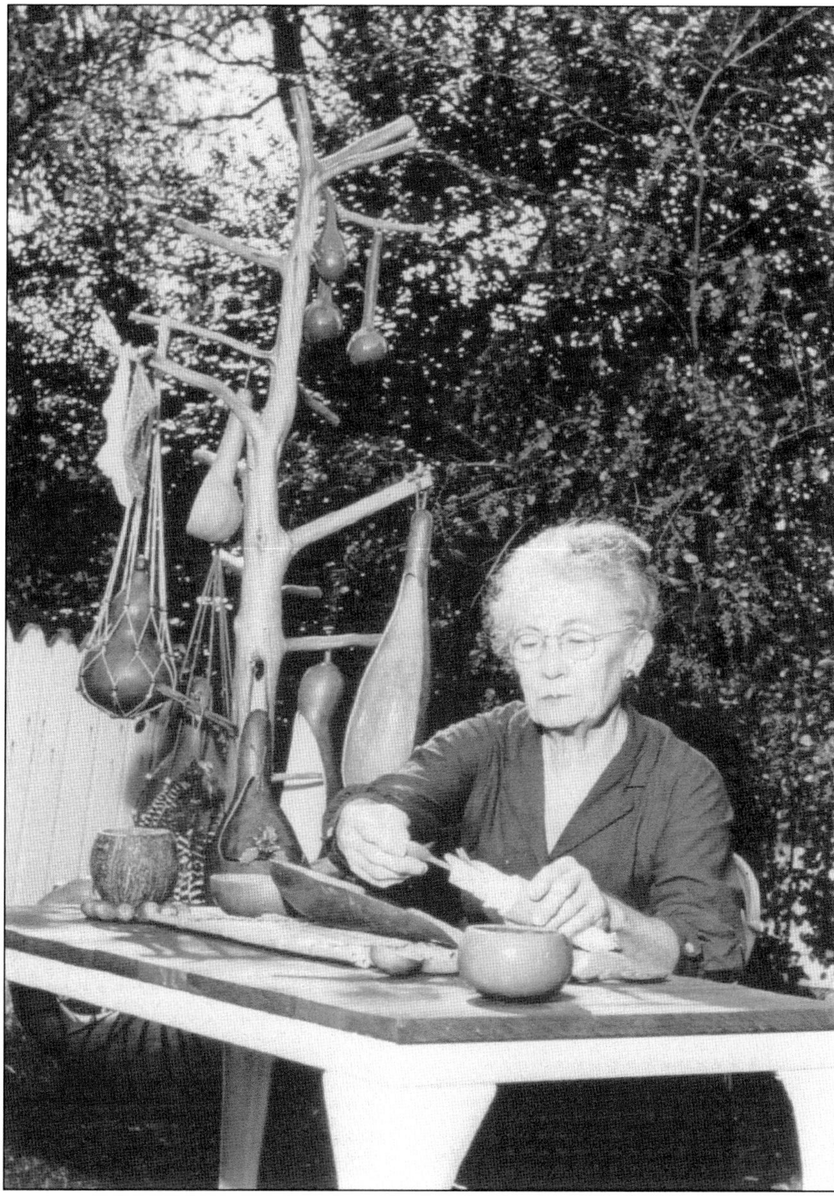

Lyda Smith White was born in 1895 in the territory now called Oklahoma. White received a degree in home economics at the College of Industrial Arts in Denton, now called Texas Woman's University. During the Depression, she used her degree to work in a program for the WPA called Housekeeping Aids, which provided women help if they fell ill or just had a baby. Another interest of Lyda's was the gourds she collected and cured that had various functions based on the uses of the frontier. (Courtesy Joyce Gibson Roach.)

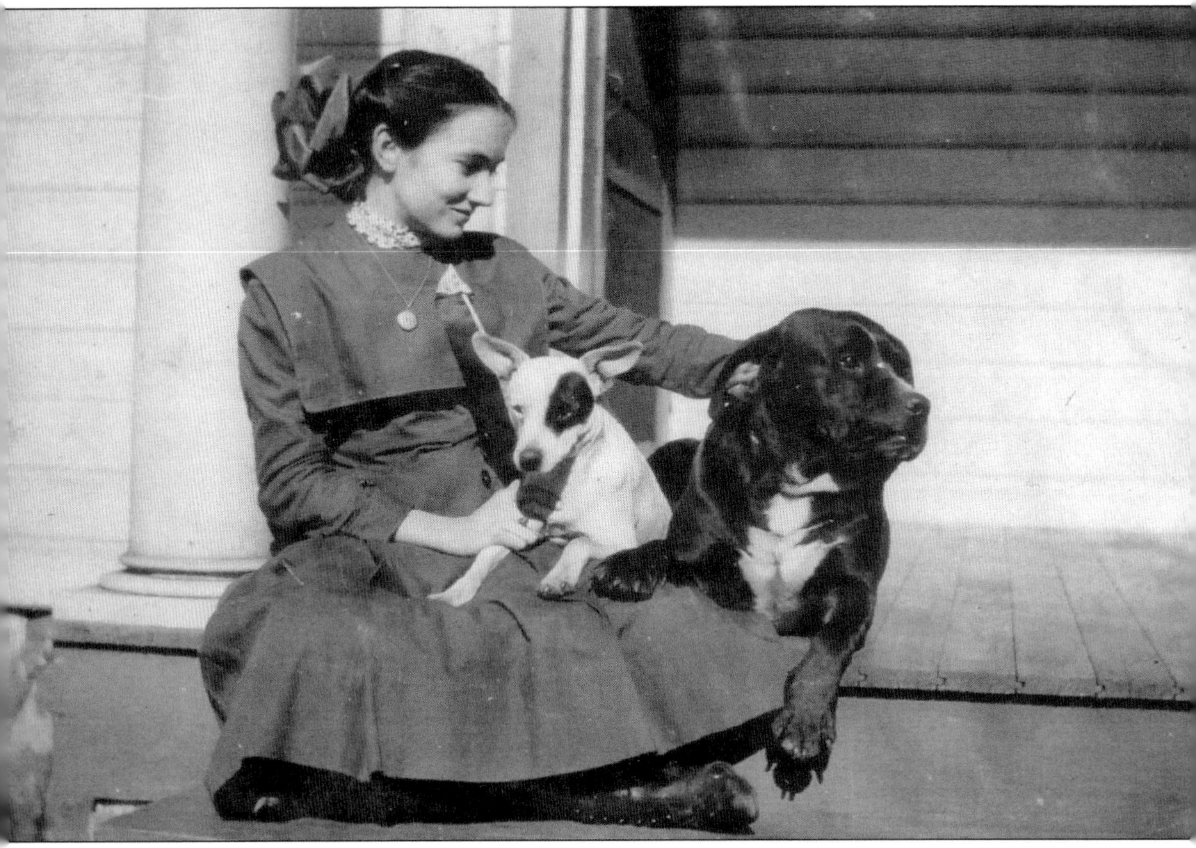

Pictured here is Lyda as a young girl with her dogs. (Courtesy Joyce Gibson Roach.)

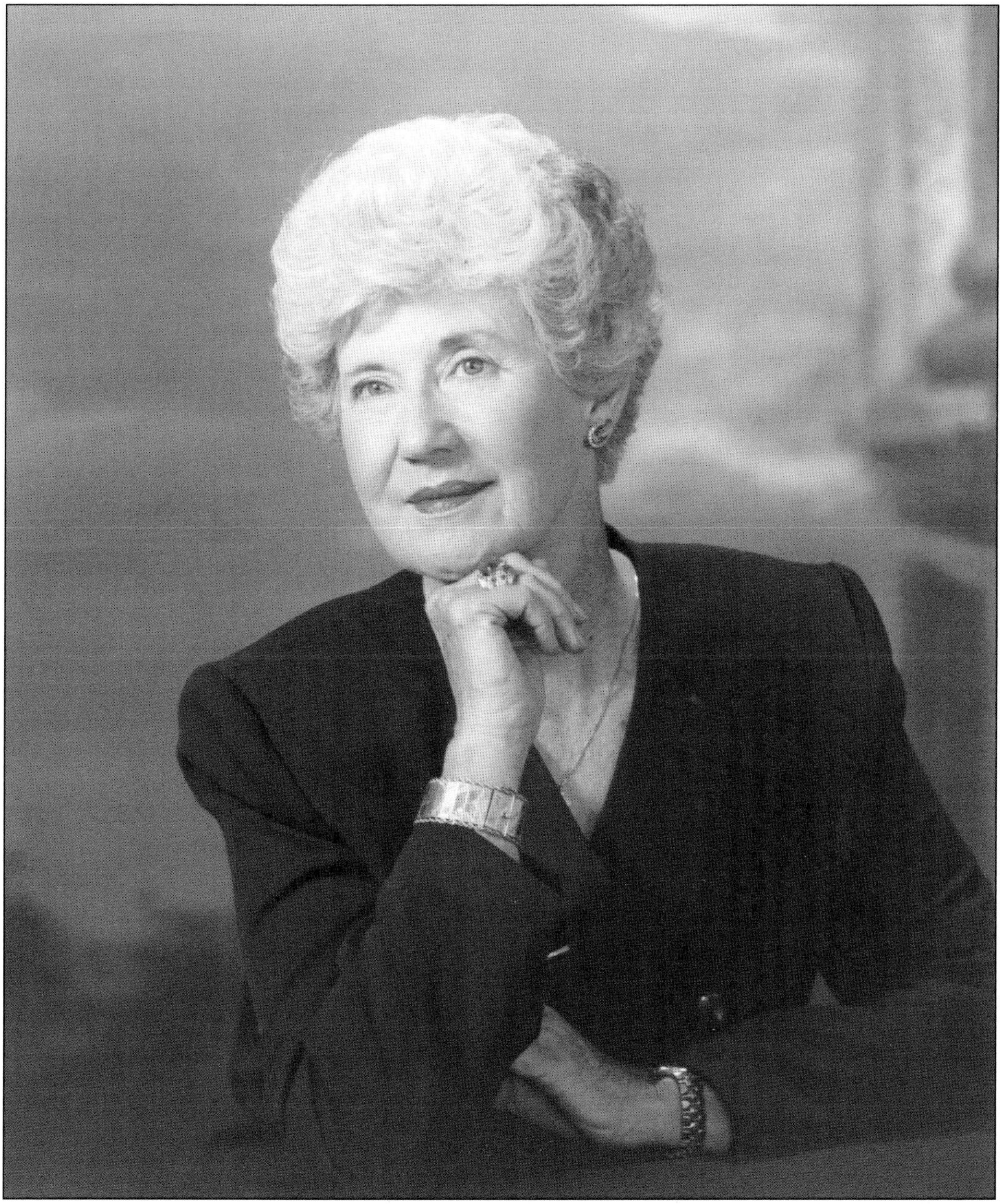

Joyce Ann Roach (nee Gibson) was born December 18, 1935, in Cleburne, Texas, to David Henry and Ann Hartman Gibson. She grew up in Jacksboro, Texas, graduating from Jacksboro High School in 1954. She holds B.F.A. and M.A. degrees in English from Texas Christian University and did post-graduate work in English at the University of North Texas. She taught from 1958 to 1962 in the Fort Worth Independent School District, in Keller High School from 1976 to 1985 (English and history), and as an adjunct English professor at Texas Christian University, specializing in Western novels and literature of the Southwest, and she taught composition, survey courses in both English and American literature, and folklore classes. A proud resident of Keller, Roach's book *Wild Rose: A Folk History of a Cross Timbers Settlement, Keller, Texas* explores in-depth the family history and stories of the early settlers in Keller.

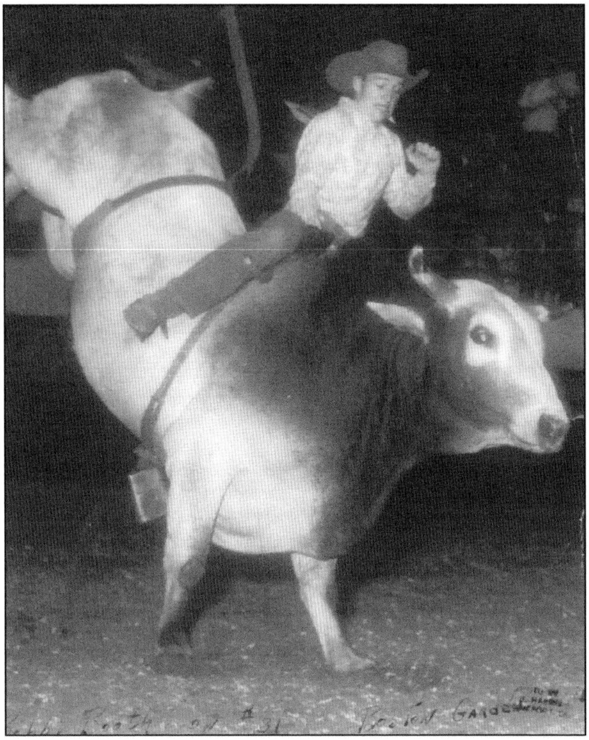

Many Keller residents became local legends, such as Bobby Booth, seen here riding his bull at Madison Square Garden. Booth was inducted into the Cowboy Hall of Fame in 2000. (Courtesy Bobby Booth.)

Here is another shot of Bobby Booth in action. (Courtesy Bobby Booth.)

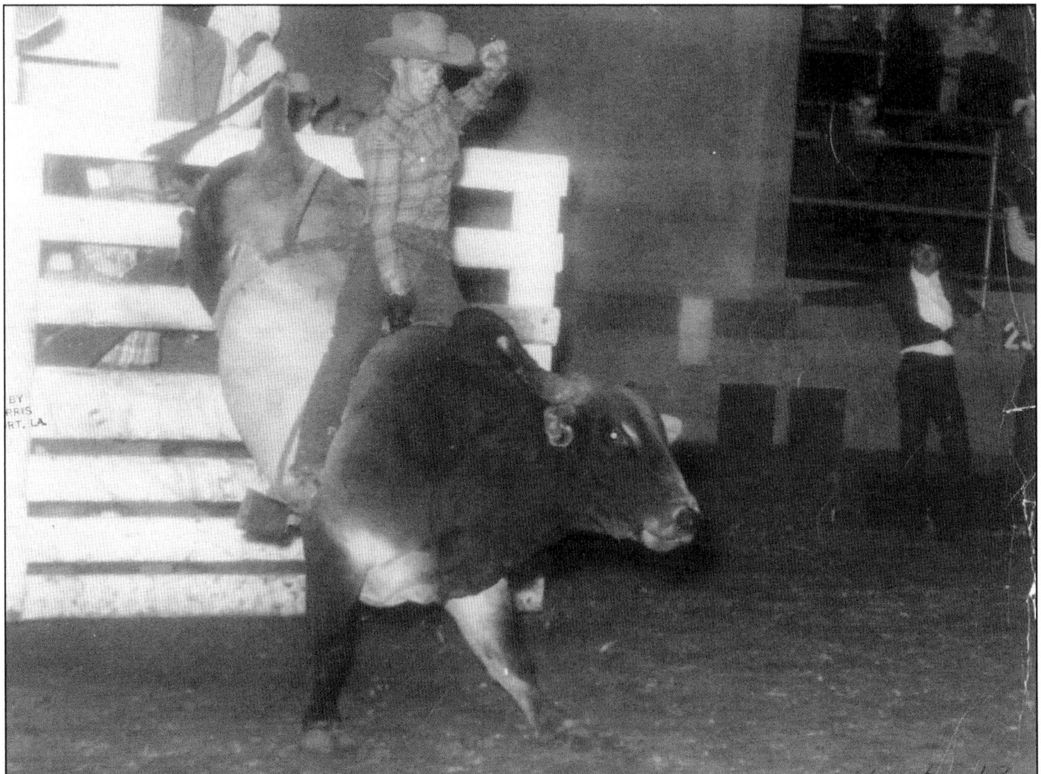

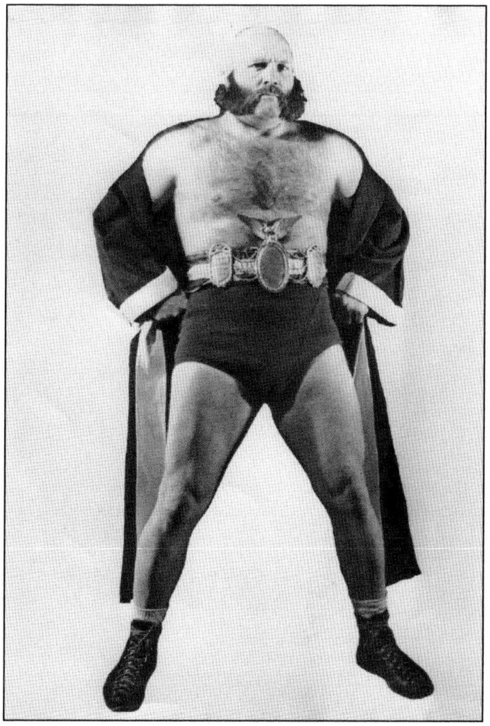

Jack Jacobs traveled all over the world wrestling. His wrestling name was Jack O'Brien, and his nickname was the "Mayor of Keller." He wrestled for over 30 years and moved to Keller in 1948 with his wife and three sons, Bobby, Donnie, and Jack. Many Keller residents remember gathering in front of a TV, whoever had one on the block, and watching the Mayor of Keller wrestle live from the North Side Coliseum in Fort Worth. Jack Jacobs passed away in 1978 at the age of 78.

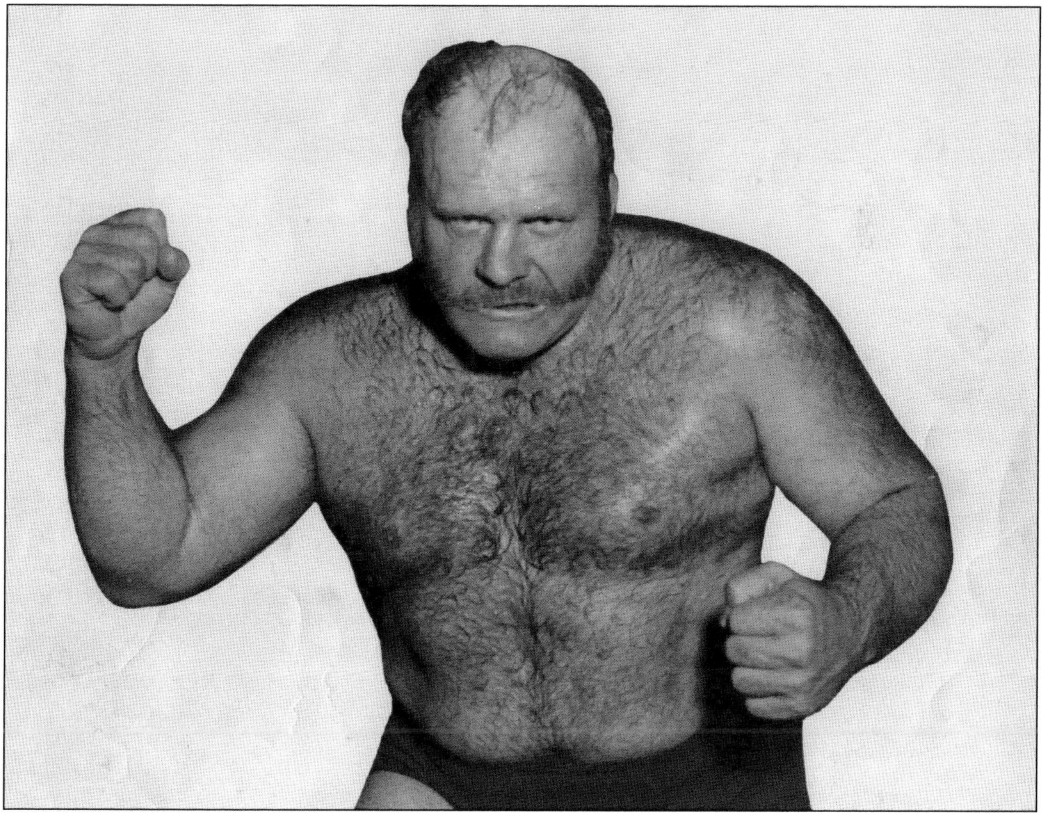

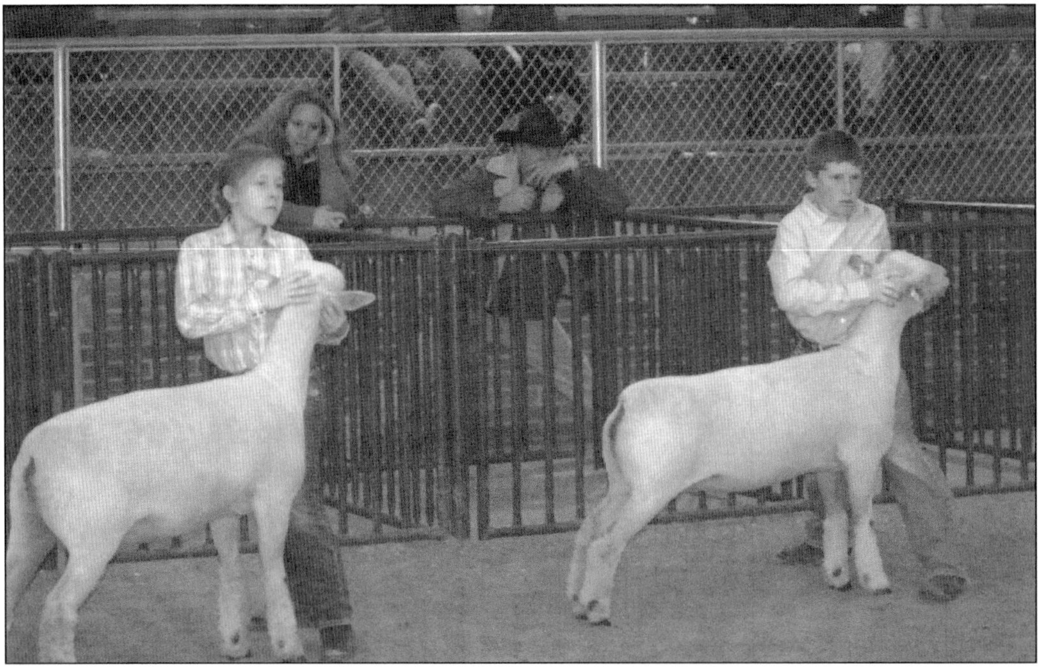

Tarrant County 4-H of Keller continues to grow and while carrying on the many traditions from the 1960s. Pictured here are Kathyrn (left) and Colter Stephens. (Courtesy Tarrant County 4-H.)

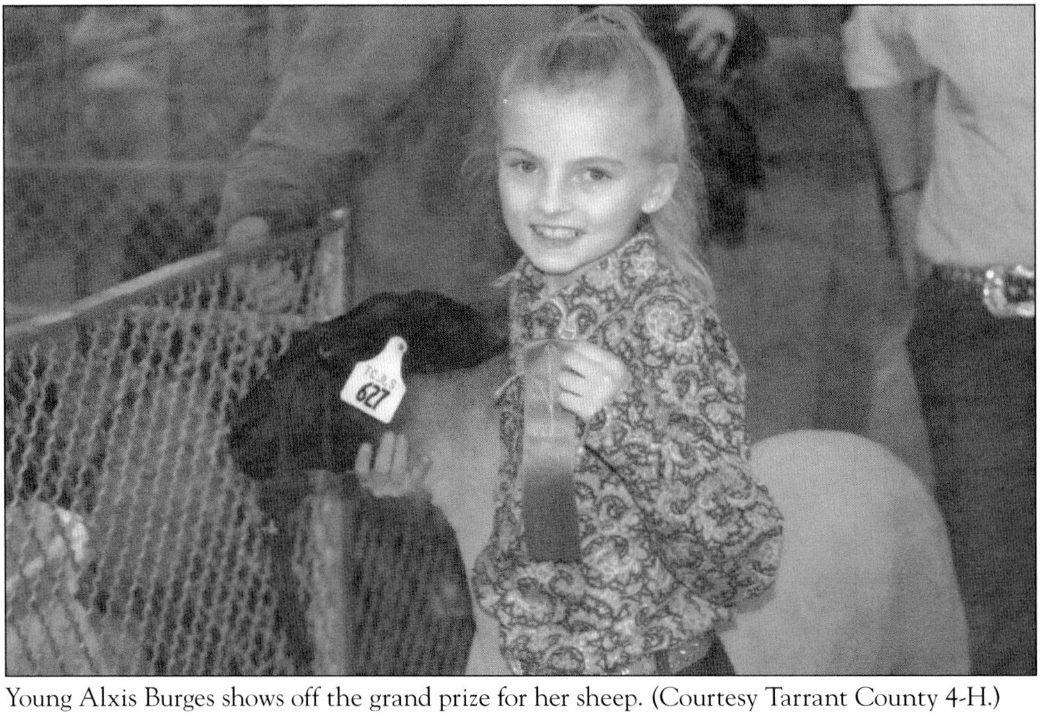

Young Alxis Burges shows off the grand prize for her sheep. (Courtesy Tarrant County 4-H.)

This is Ashton Bradberry and her prize-winning hog. (Courtesy Tarrant County 4-H.)

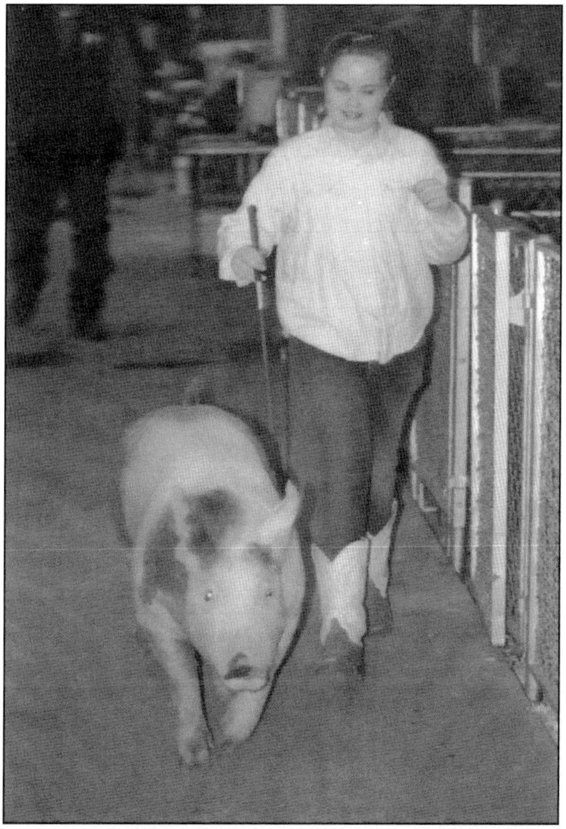

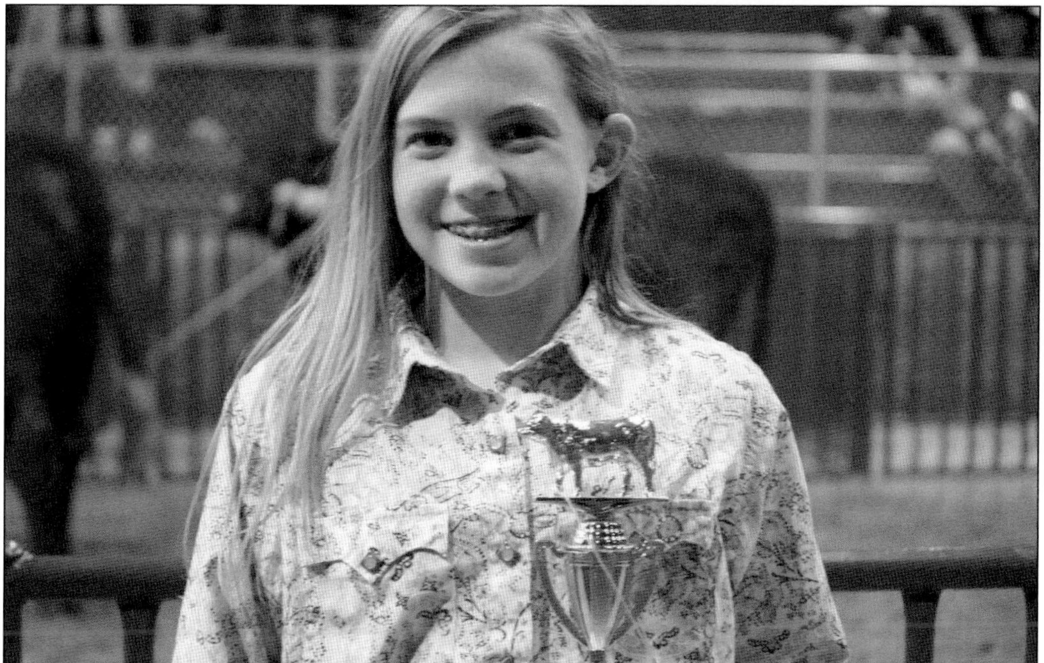

Hollyann Roach and her steer trophy are pictured here. (Courtesy Tarrant County 4-H.)

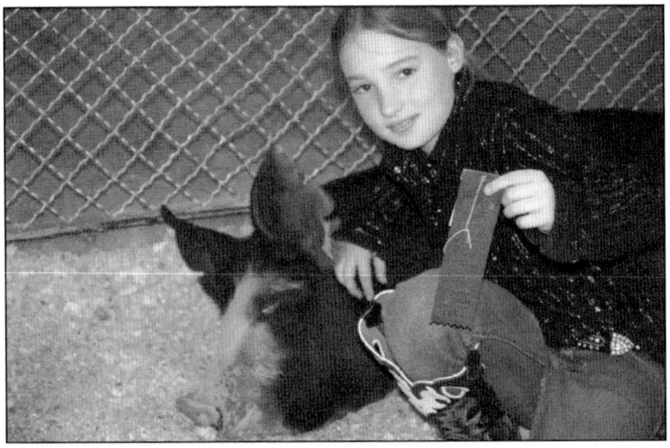

Cheyenne Bradberry poses with her winning pig. (Courtesy Tarrant County 4-H.)

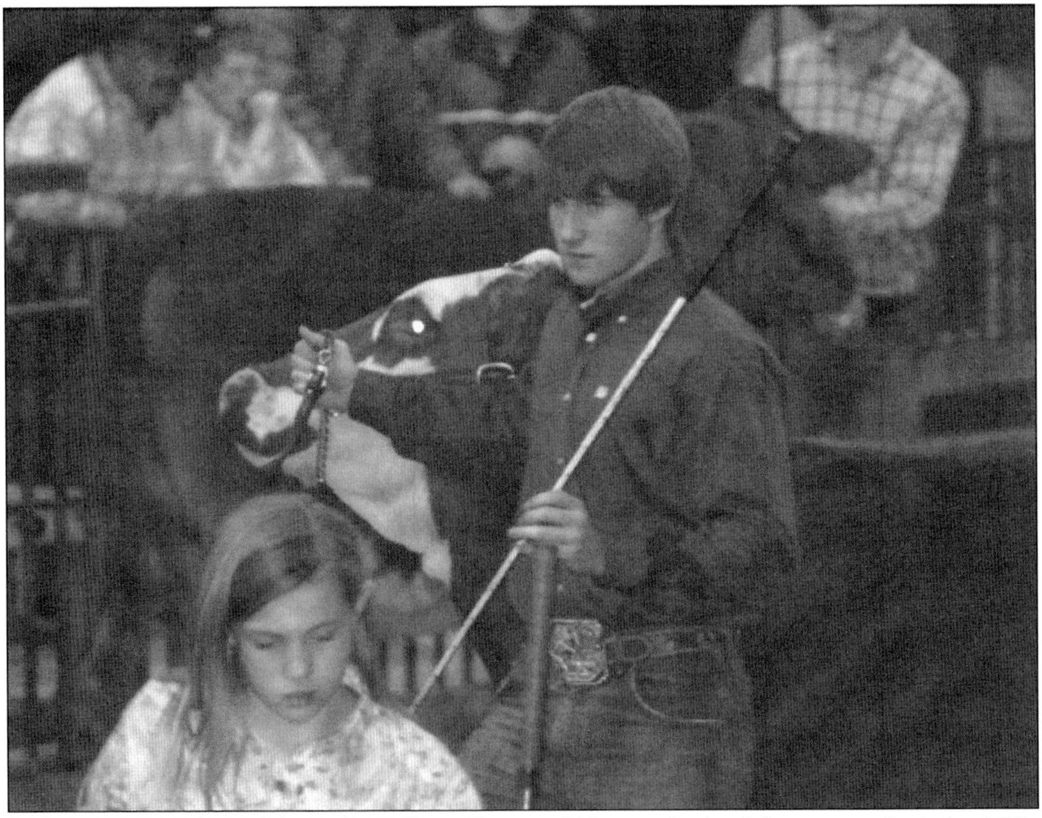

Trey Roach, president of the Keller 4-H, is 16 years old here as he leads his steer to be judged. His sister Hollyann is in the foreground. (Courtesy Tarrant County 4-H.)

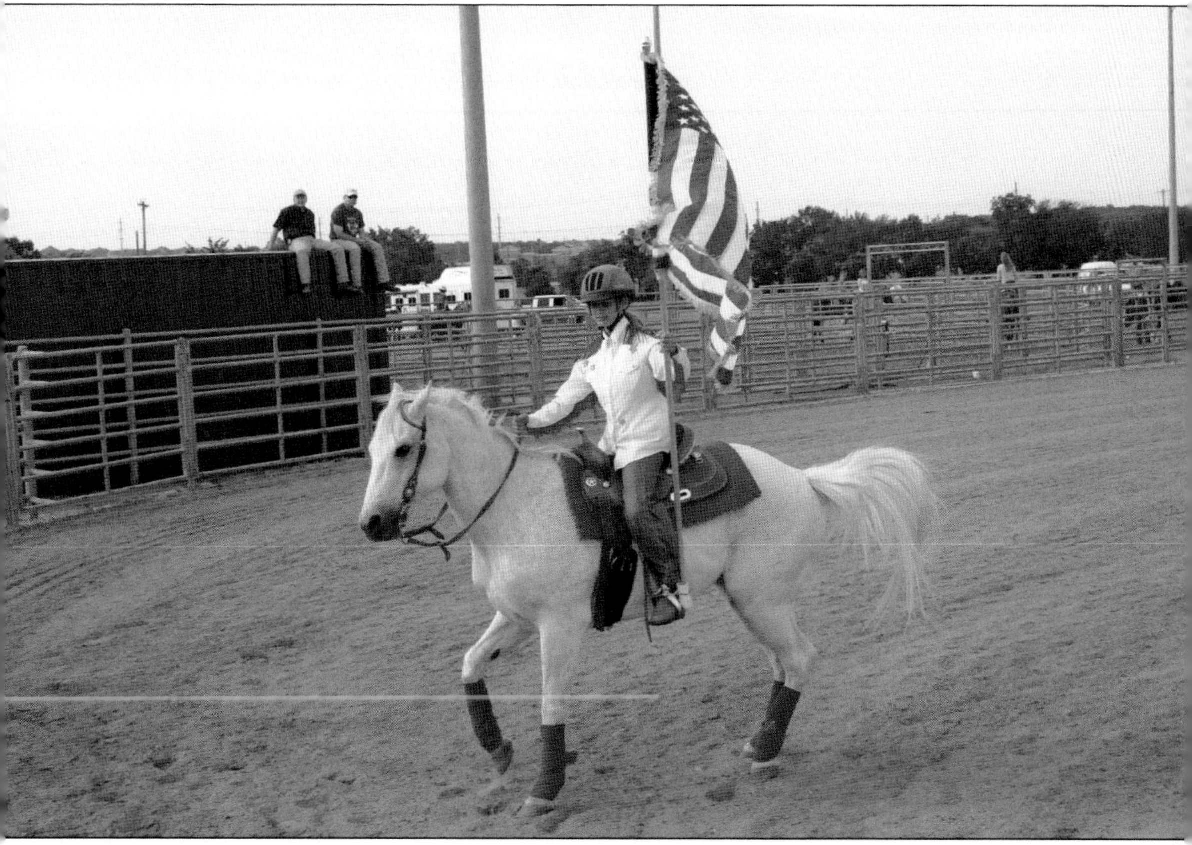

A member of the Keller Saddle Club performs at the Keller Arena. Alyssa Stephenson is carrying the flag at Keller Playday, a yearly equestrian event. The Keller Saddle Club was established in March 2008 as a nonprofit equestrian organization that promotes horsemanship, sportsmanship, and citizenship. Riders of all skill levels and ages are welcome to ride for fun or competition. (Courtesy Keller Saddle Club.)

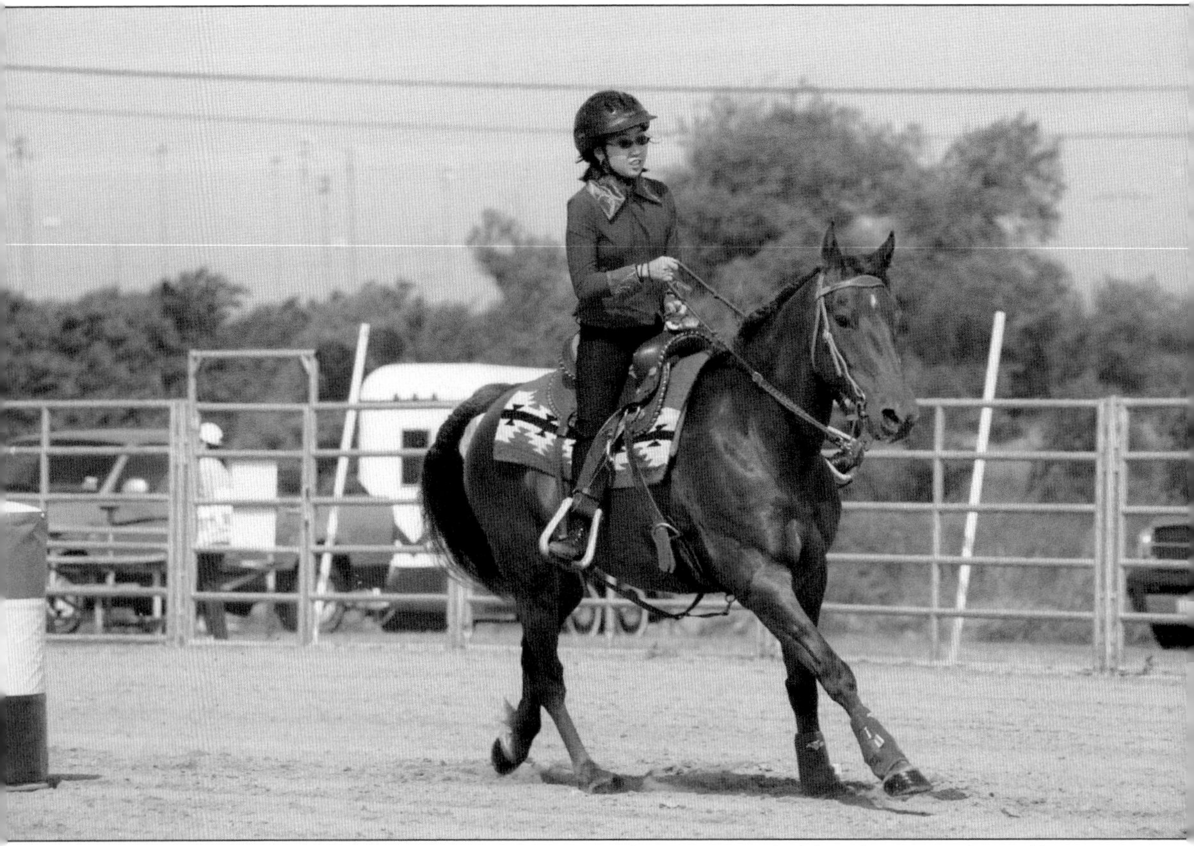

Katy Dare runs her horse, Willow, at Keller Playday, an event held each year at the Keller Arena. (Courtesy Keller Saddle Club.)

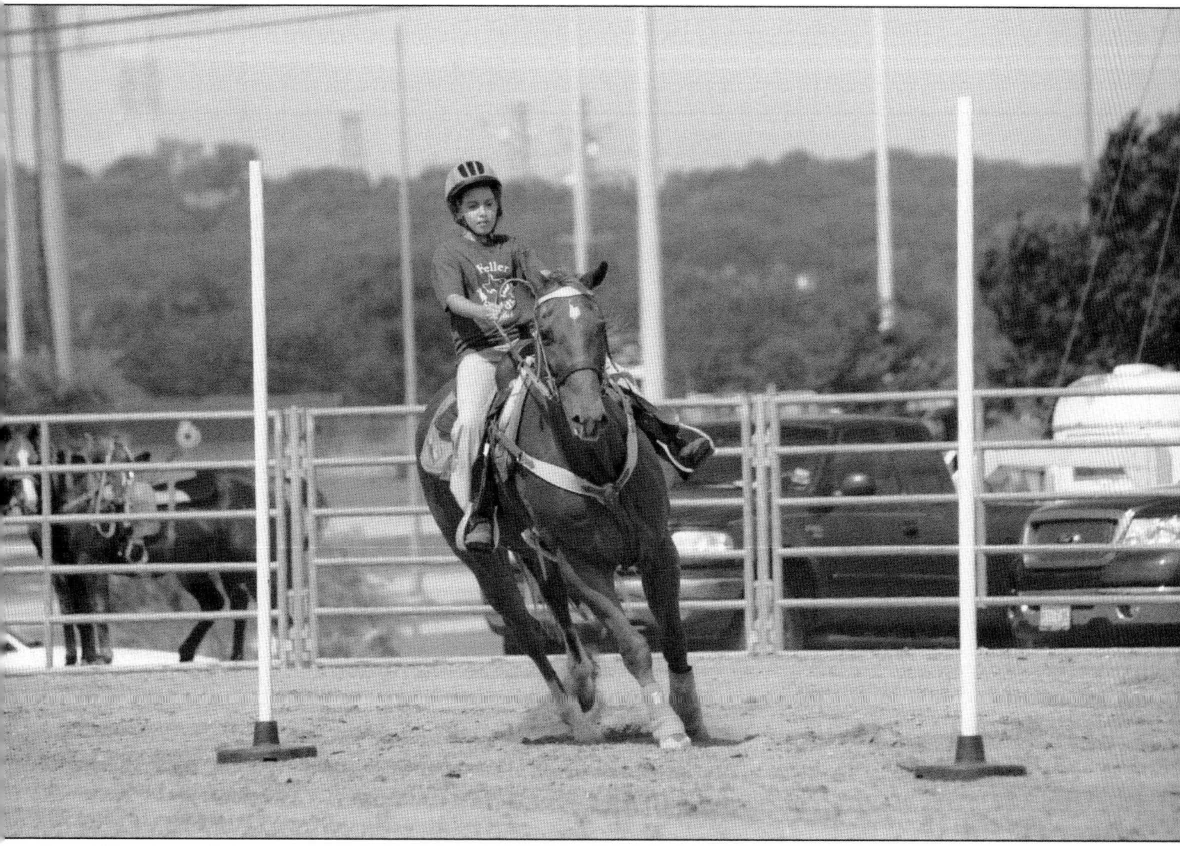

Barrel racer Sydney Metzinger is on her horse, Call 911, while showing her skills at the Keller Arena. (Courtesy Donna McWilliam.)

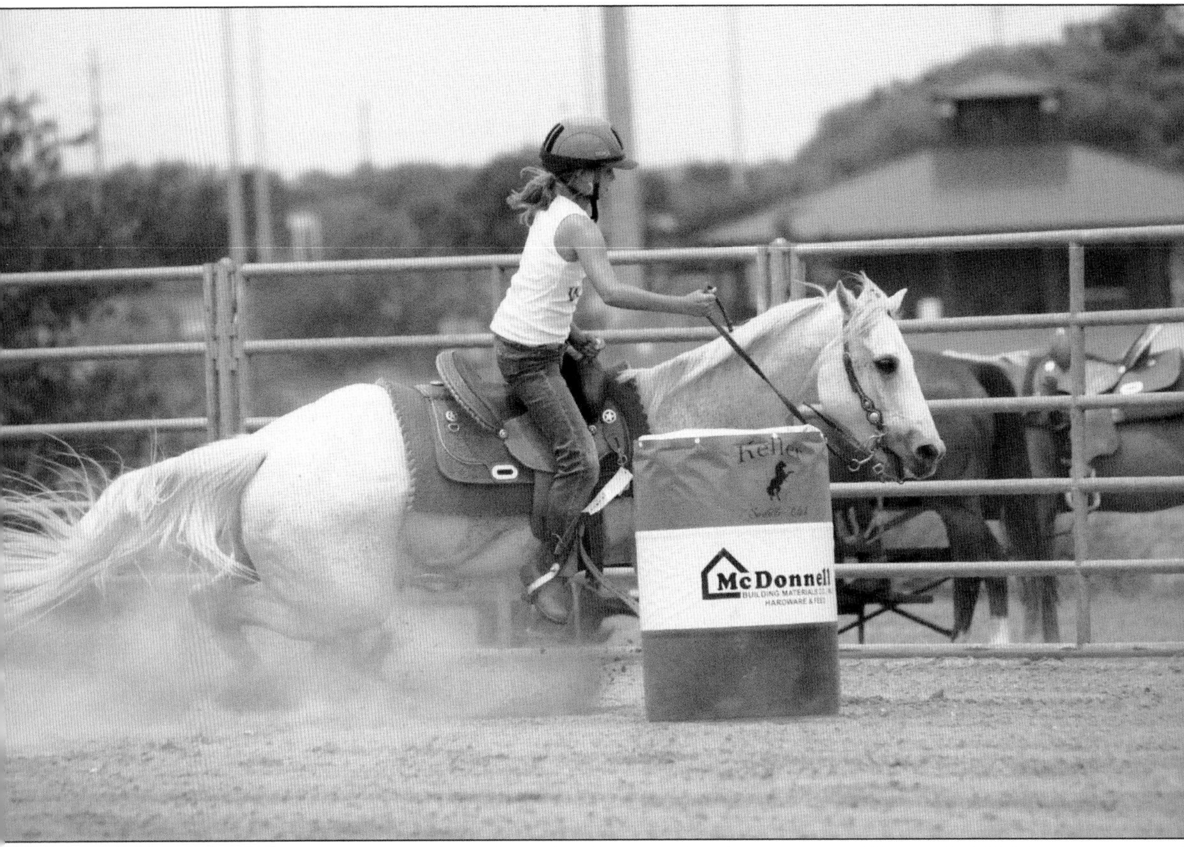

Alyssa Stephenson is running barrels on her horse, Skunk. (Courtesy Donna McWilliam.)

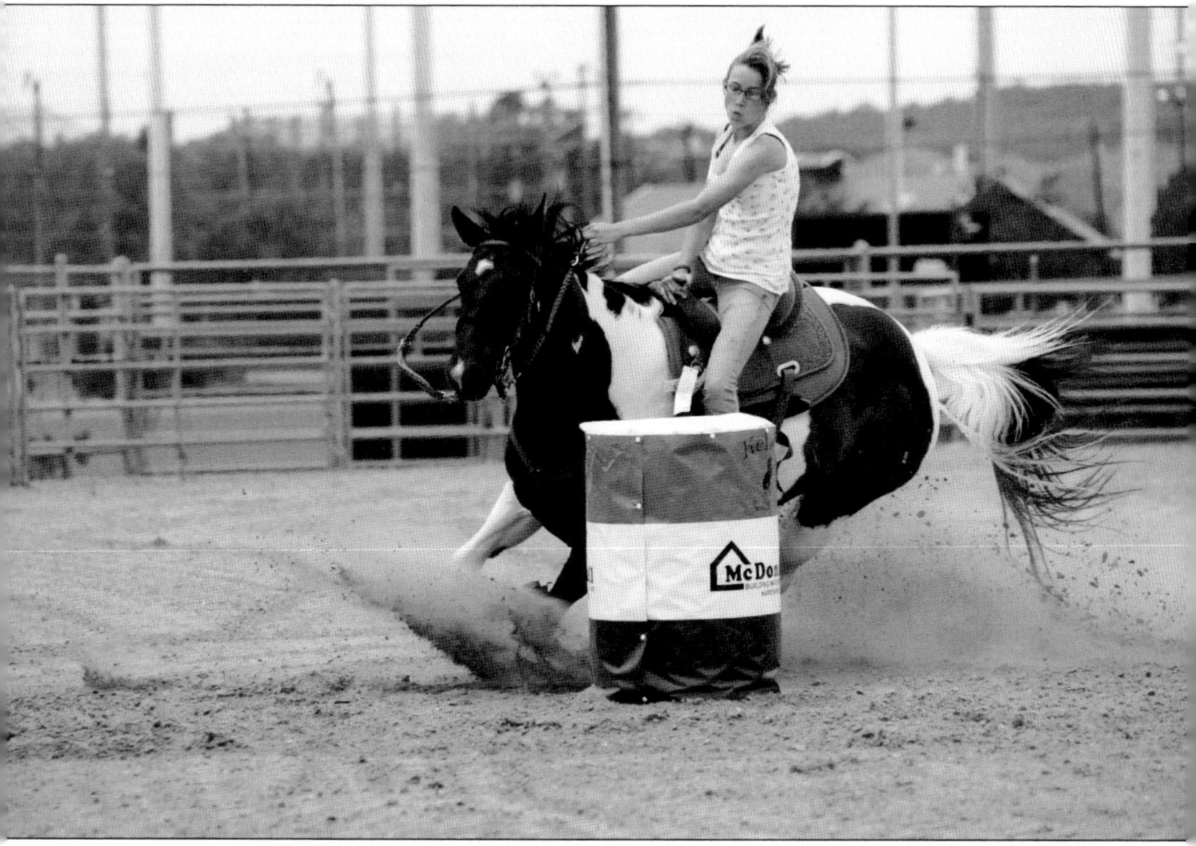

Courtney Foust competes in the barrel-racing event. (Courtesy Donna McWilliam.)

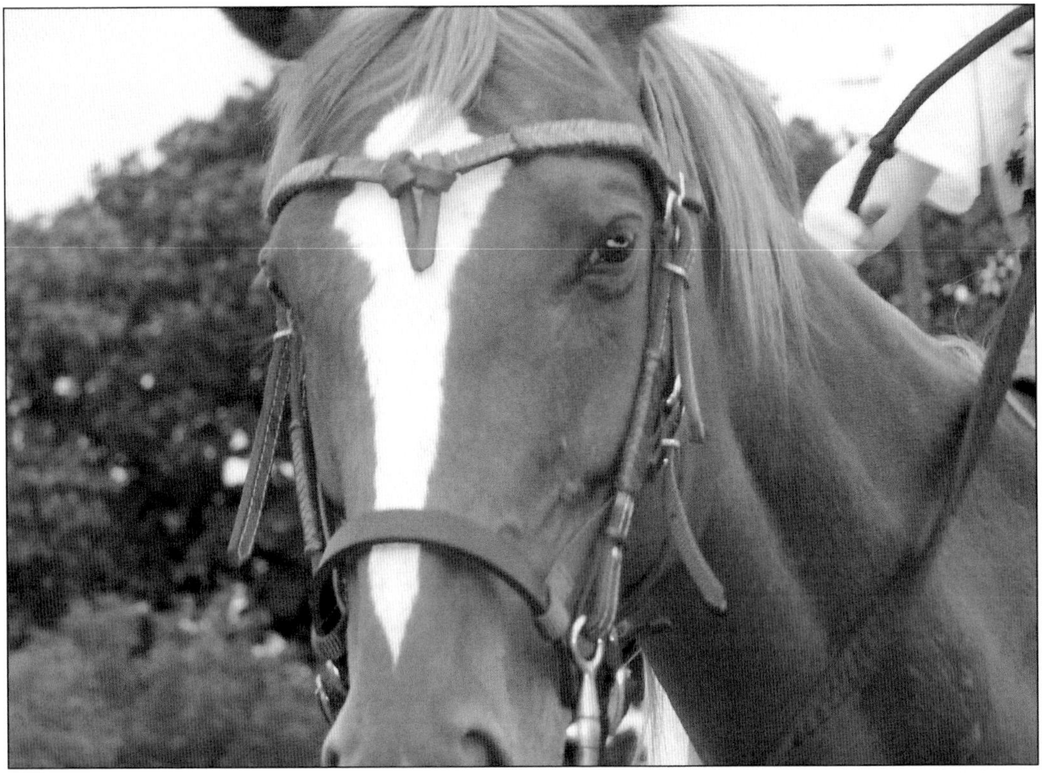

A Keller Saddle Club horse is relaxing before the horse show. (Courtesy Keller Saddle Club.)

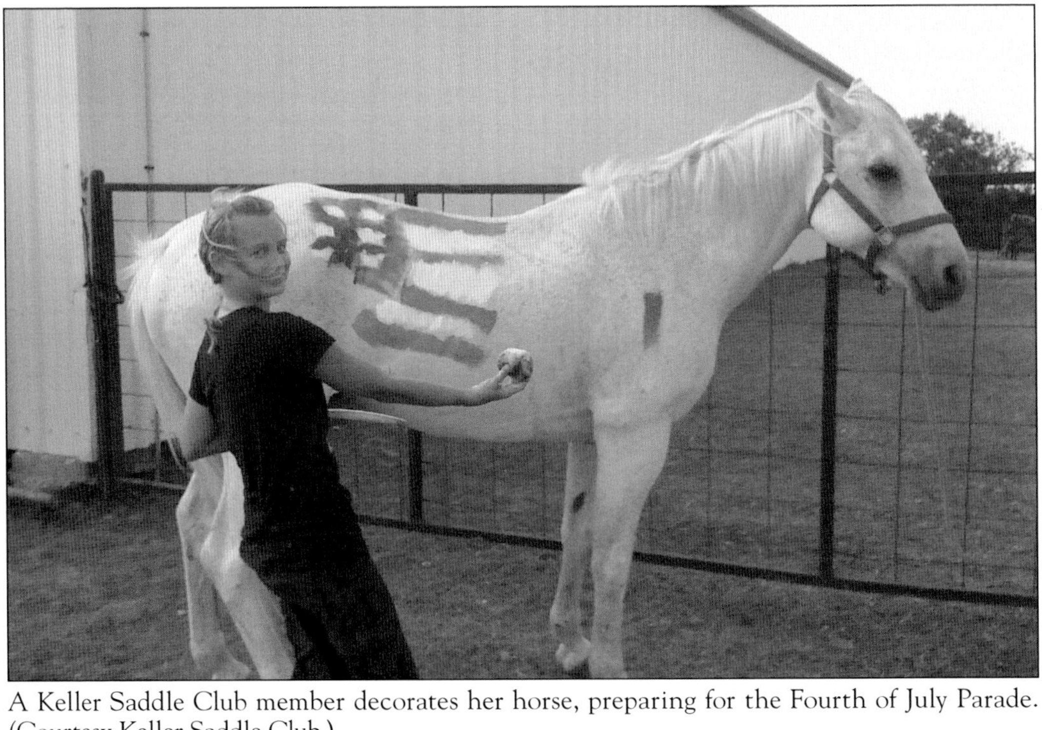

A Keller Saddle Club member decorates her horse, preparing for the Fourth of July Parade. (Courtesy Keller Saddle Club.)

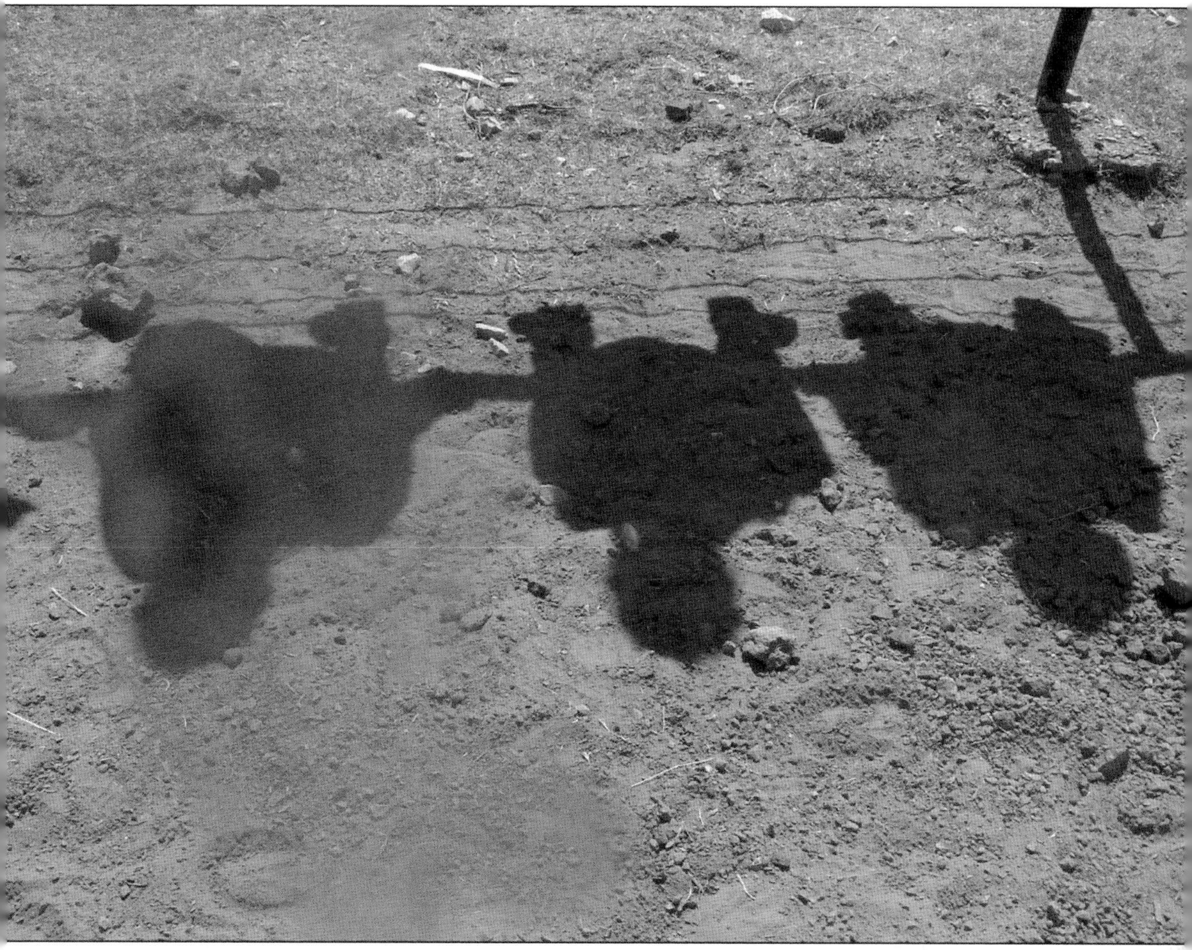

Kids are enjoying the events at the Keller Arena while casting a shadow sitting on the fence. (Courtesy Keller Saddle Club.)

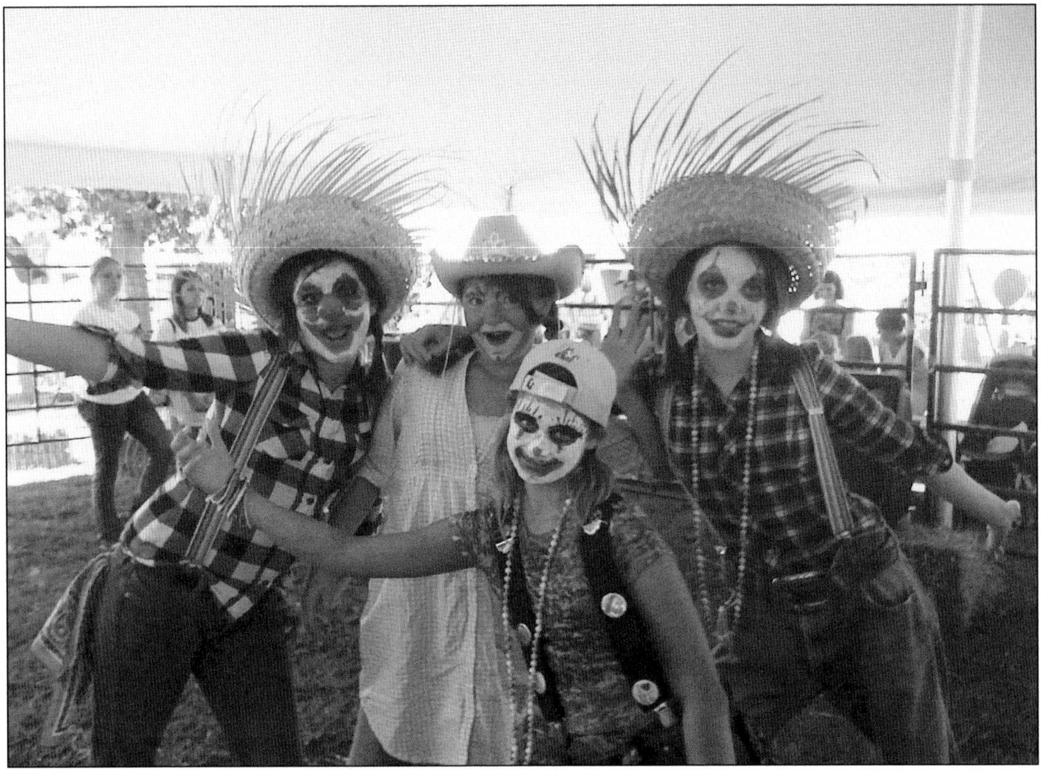

Keller Saddle Clubs kids are being clowns for the Wild West Fest in Keller. From left to right are Alyssa Stephenson, Liz Phelan, Kelsy Thomason, and Meredith Thomason. (Courtesy Keller Saddle Club.)

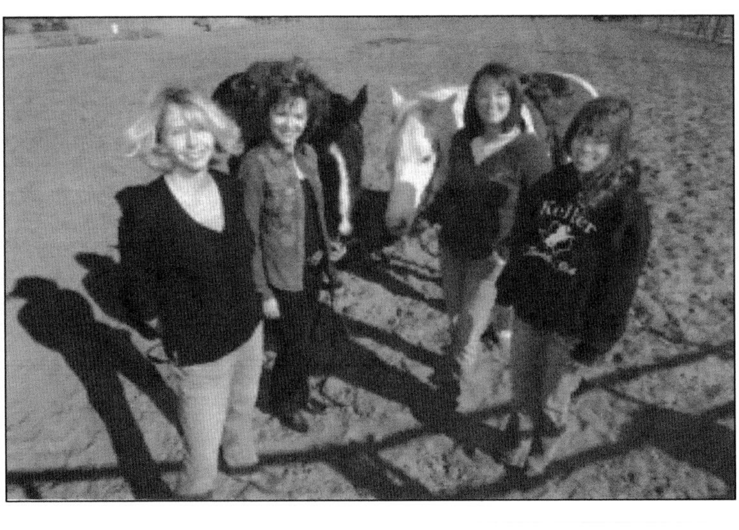

Founders of Keller Saddle Club include, from left to right, Ginny Worthingten, Nancy Del Mar, Sherri Eubanks, and Karen Suesens. (Courtesy Keller Saddle Club.)

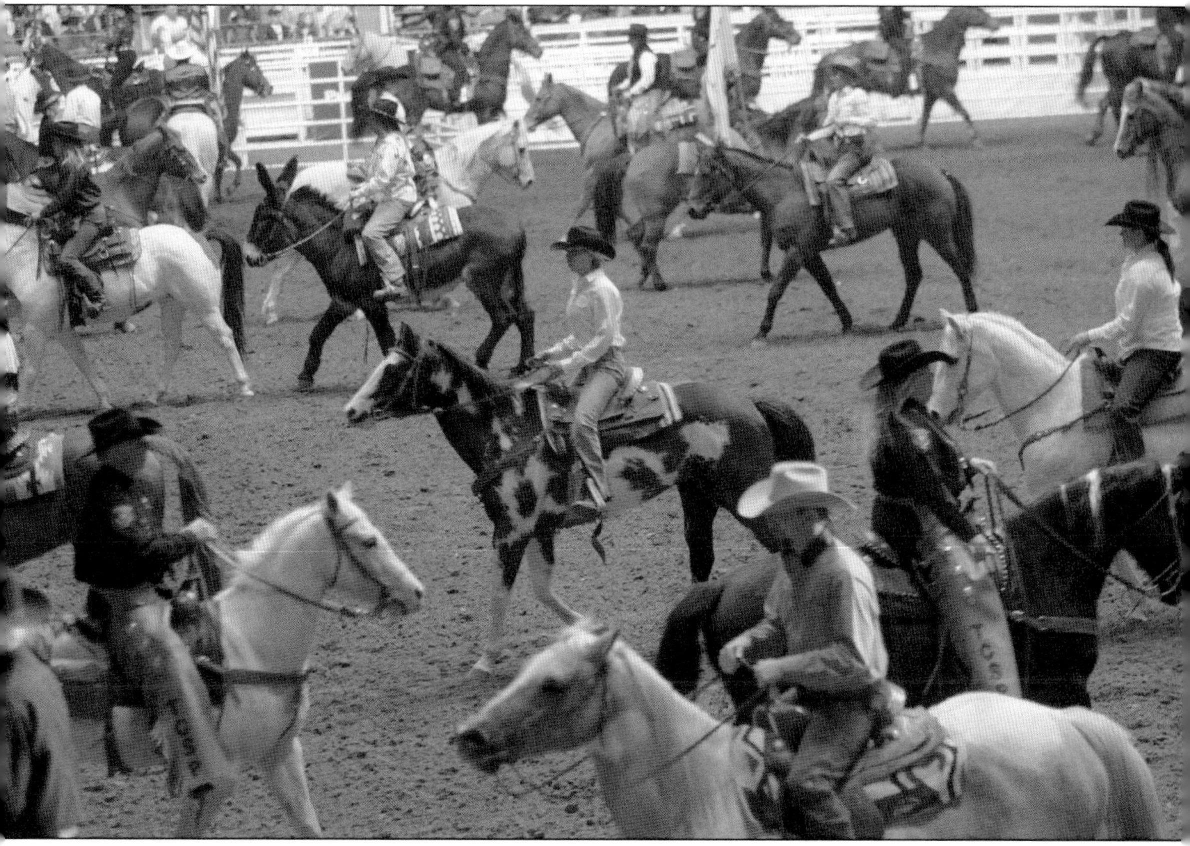

Keller Saddle Club members are at the Grand Entry Fort Worth Stockshow Rodeo. (Courtesy Keller Saddle Club.)

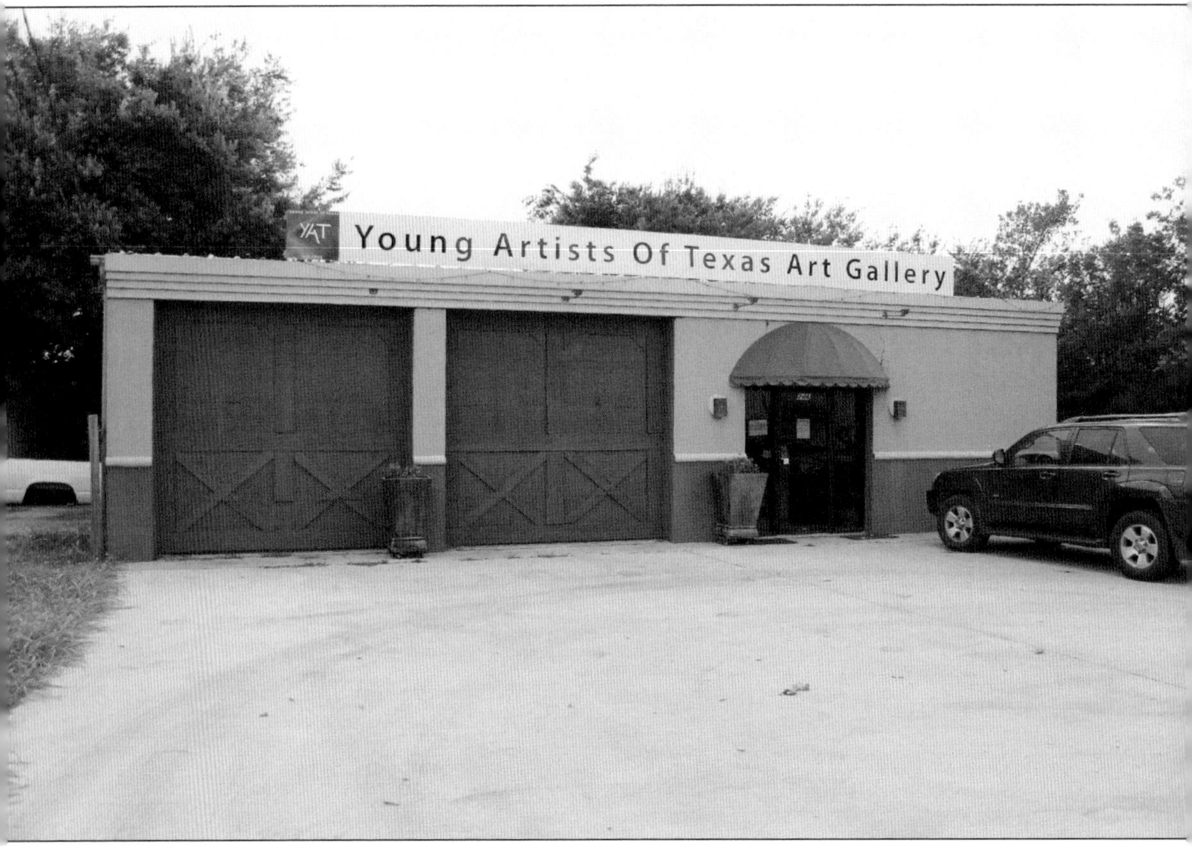

The Young Artists of Texas (YAT) Gallery, located at 246 Main Street in Keller, was established in 2005 with its opening in 2006. YAT is a nonprofit organization whose mission is to educate and promote young Texas artists by providing college scholarships to high school seniors planning to major in art. (Courtesy Jenny Tilbury.)

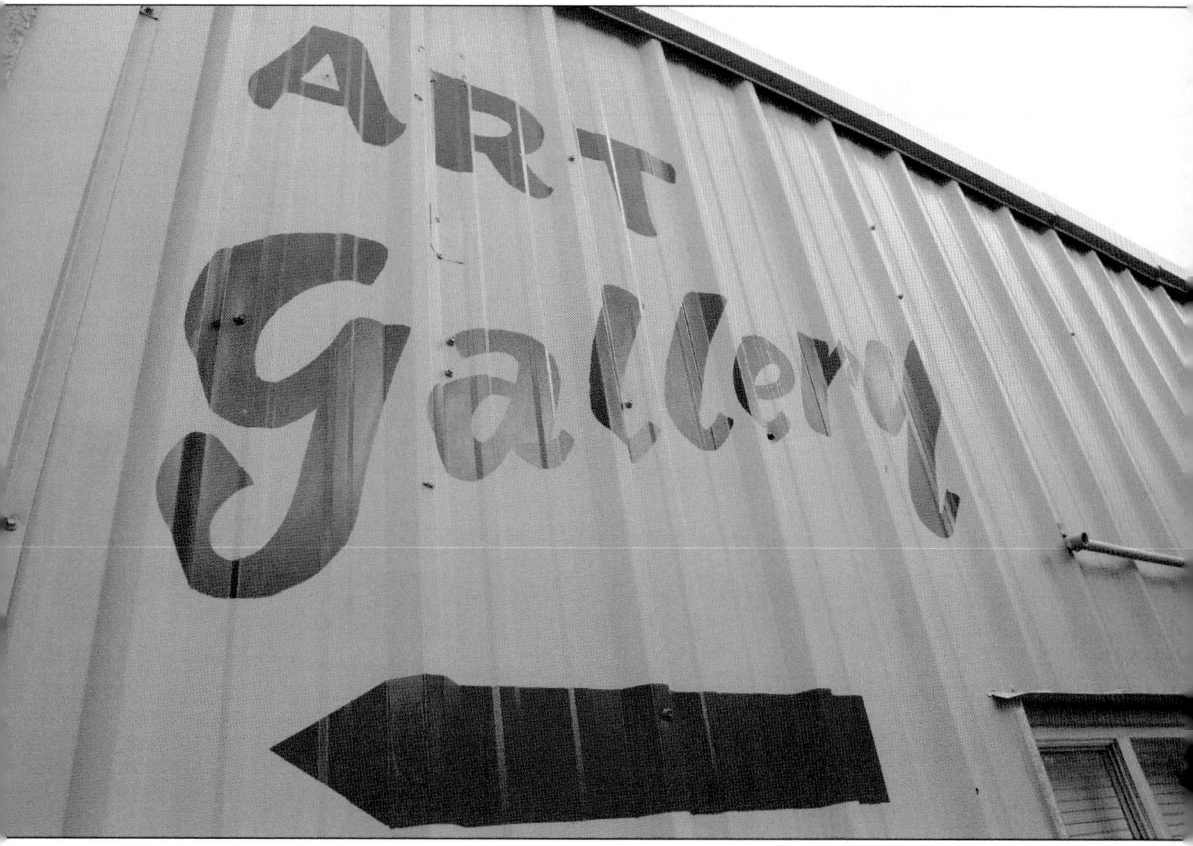

A sign outside the gallery directs viewers to the latest showcase. (Courtesy Jenny Tilbury.)

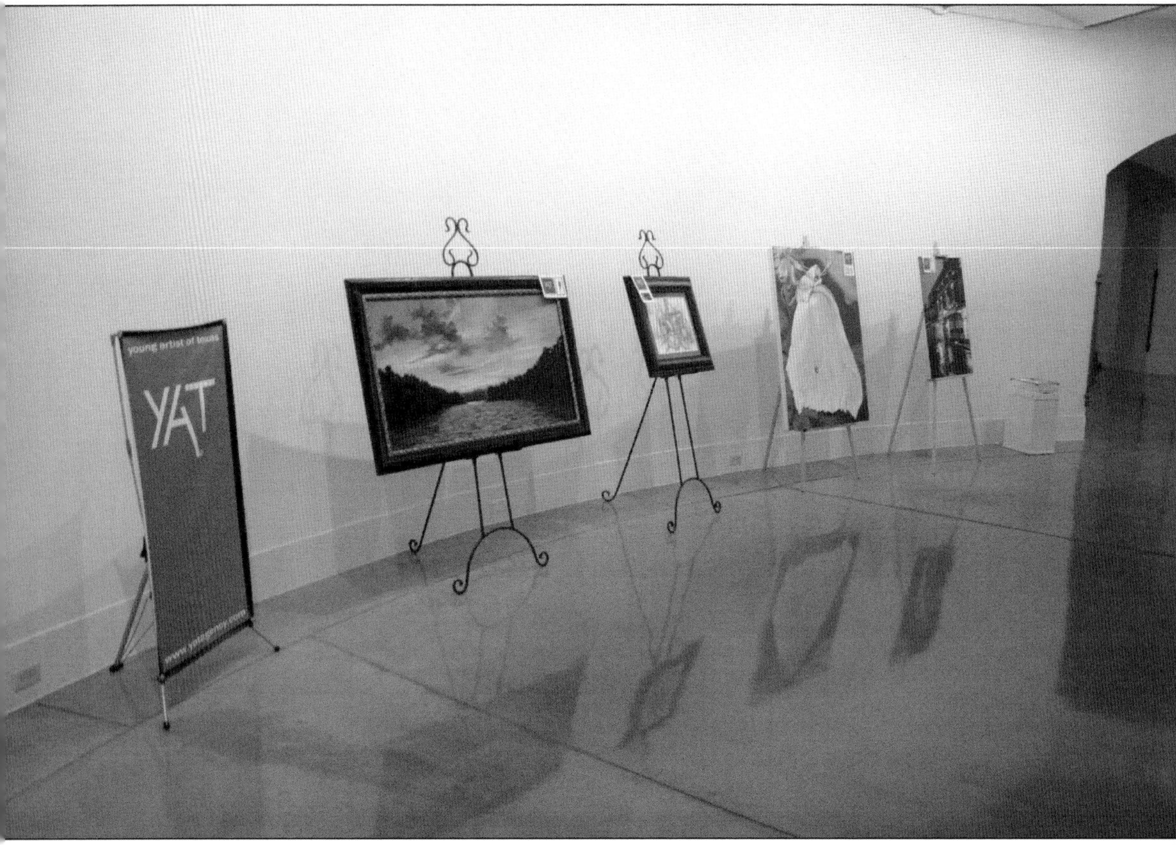

YAT Gallery provides artists with the opportunity to participate in 12 off-site shows annually. (Courtesy Jenny Tilbury.)

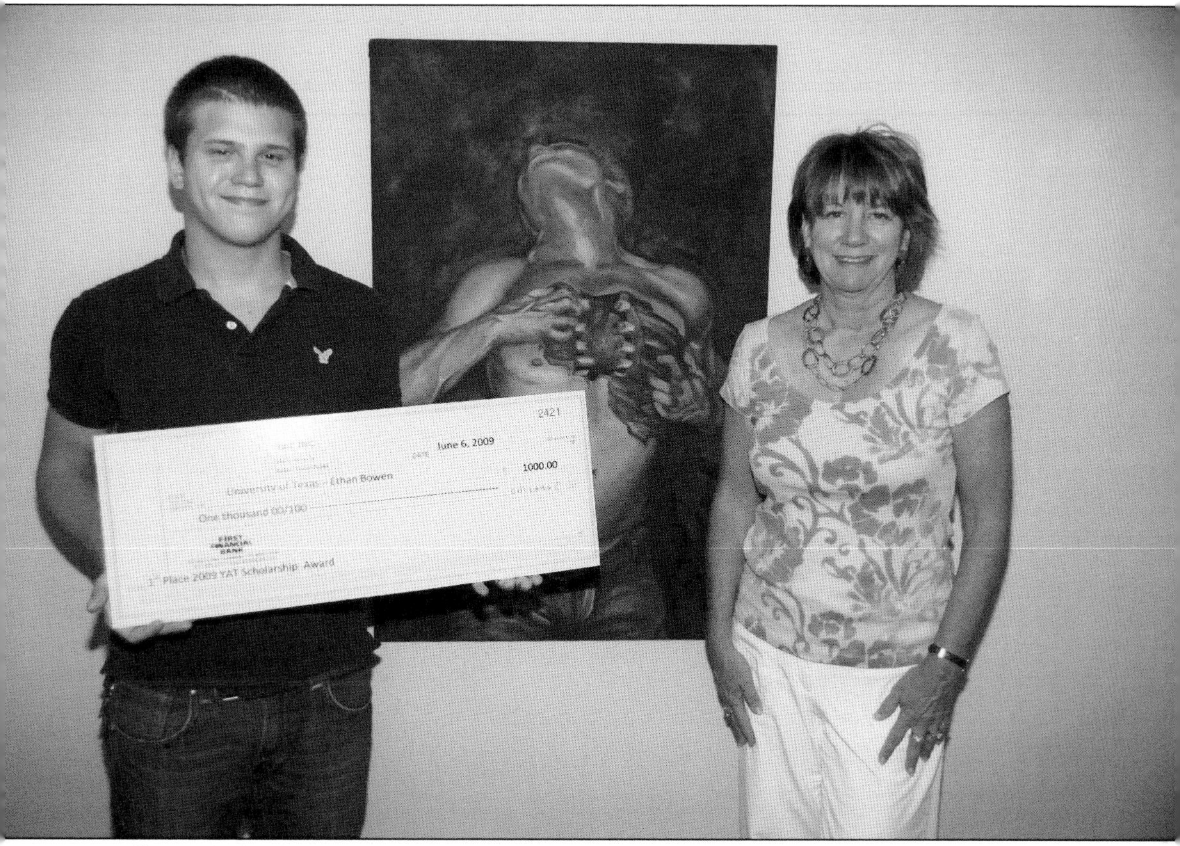

YAT Gallery scholarship winner Ethan Bowen is pictured with YAT Gallery founder Jenny Tilbury. (Courtesy Jenny Tilbury.)

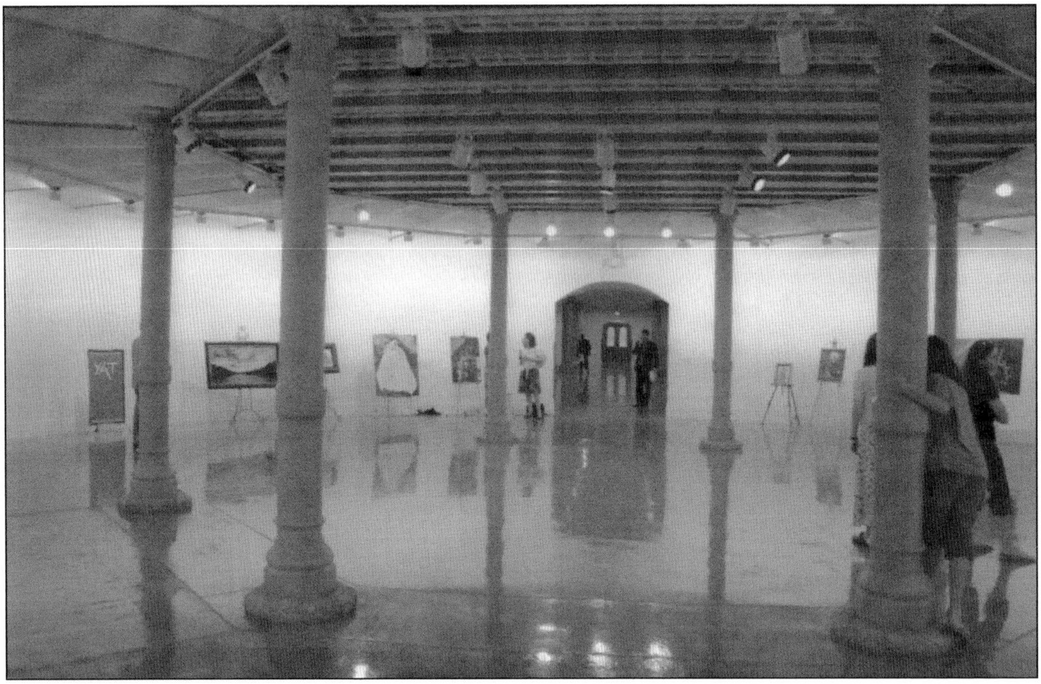

A YAT Gallery show displays art at the Texas state capitol building in Austin, Texas. (Courtesy Jenny Tilbury.)

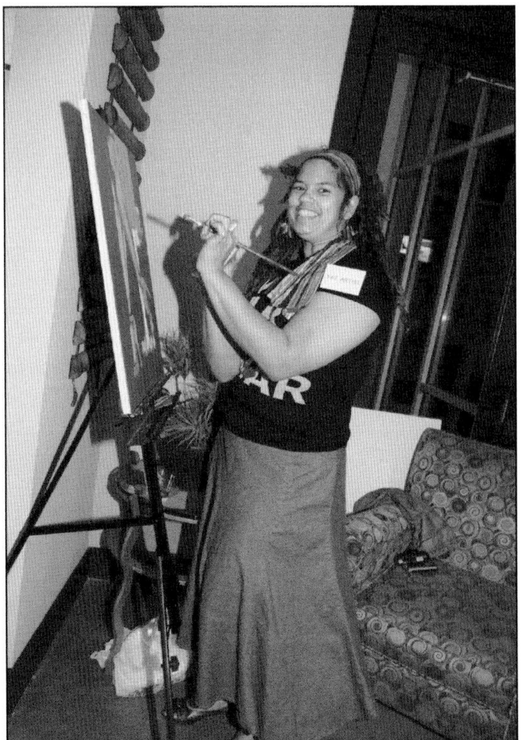

Artist Ricki Johnson is painting at the 2008 YAT Gallery Gala. (Courtesy Jenny Tilbury.)

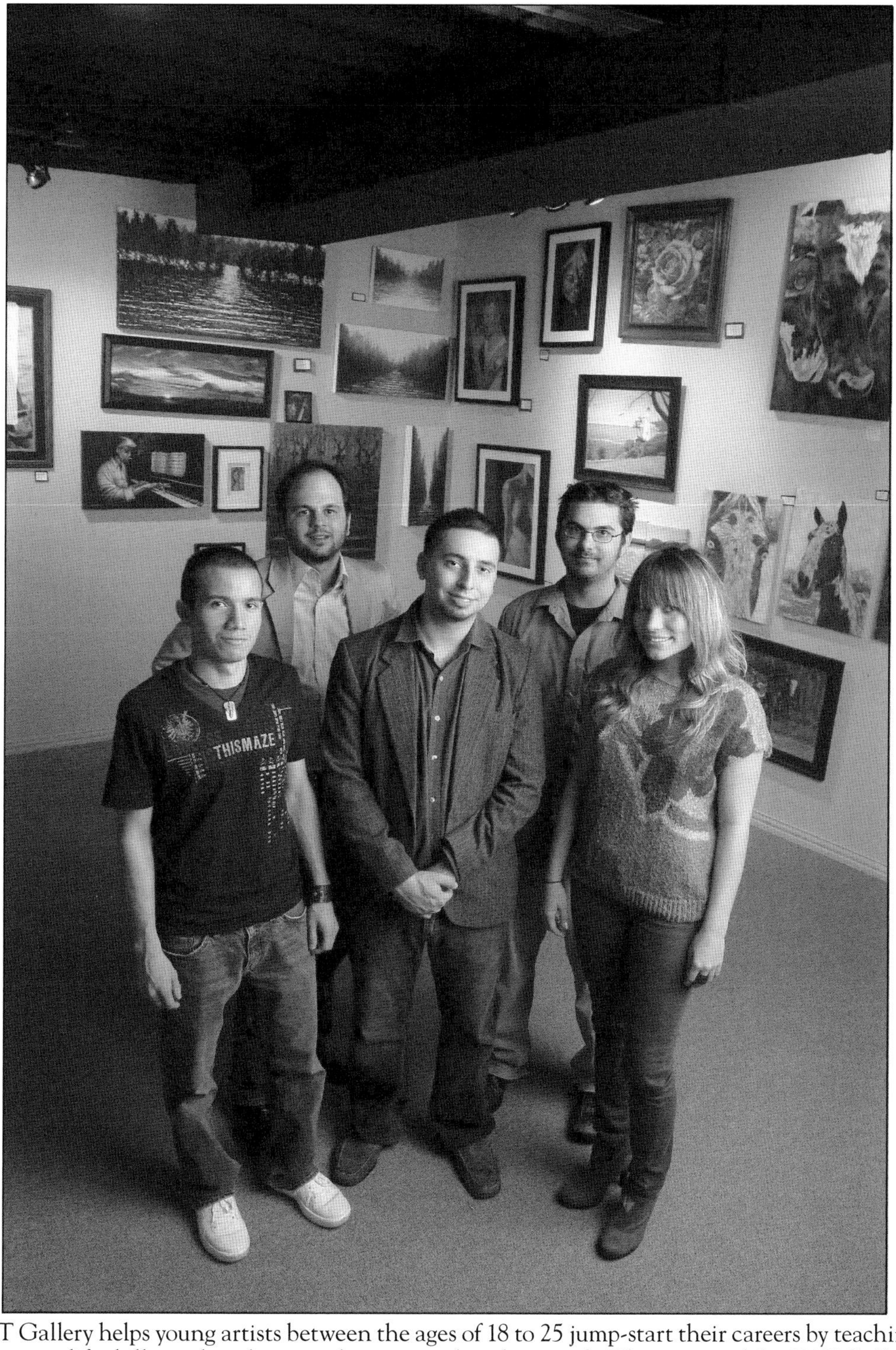

YAT Gallery helps young artists between the ages of 18 to 25 jump-start their careers by teaching necessary life skills, such as learning how to market their work. The artists of the YAT Gallery are, from left to right, Matthew Tilbury, Pedro Salano, Eric Soto, Albert Bourland, and Leslie Marshall. (Courtesy Jenny Tilbury.)

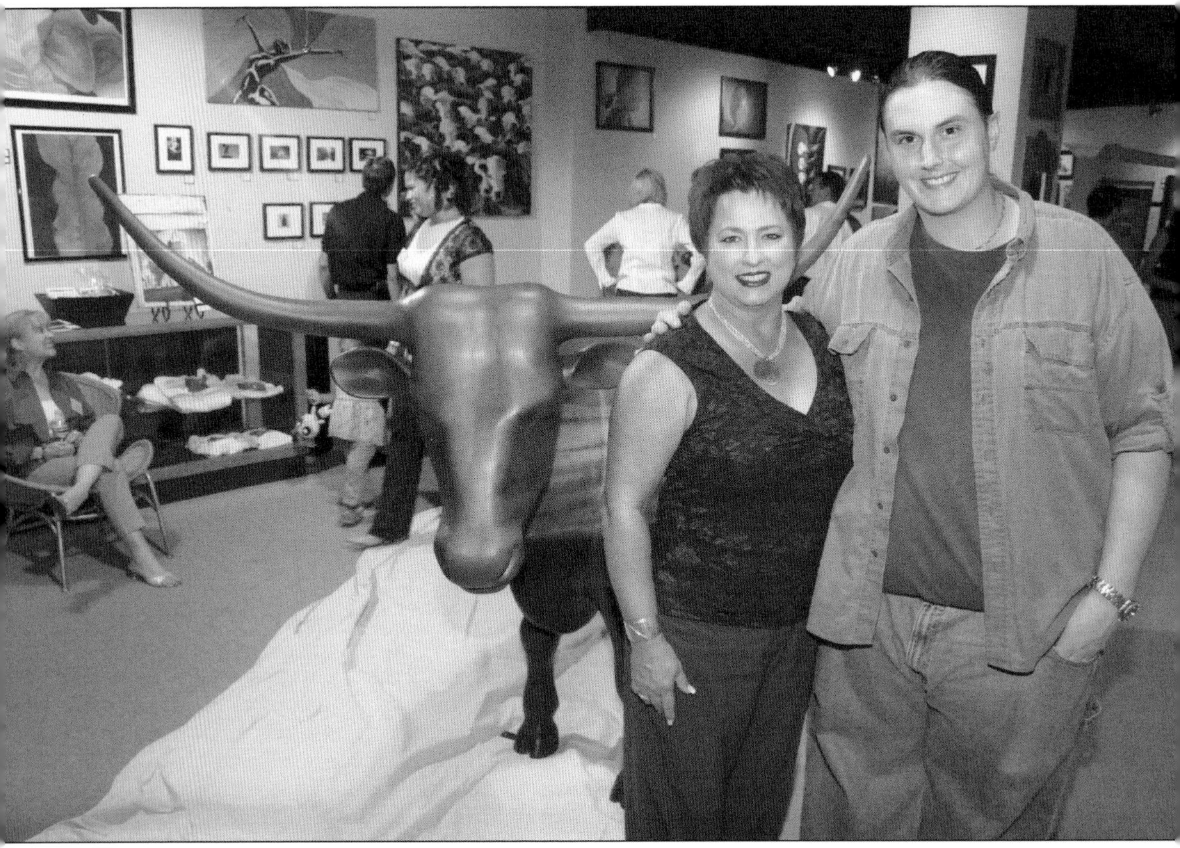

YAT artist Ben Purvis is pictured with state representative Viki Truitt. (Courtesy Jenny Tilbury.)

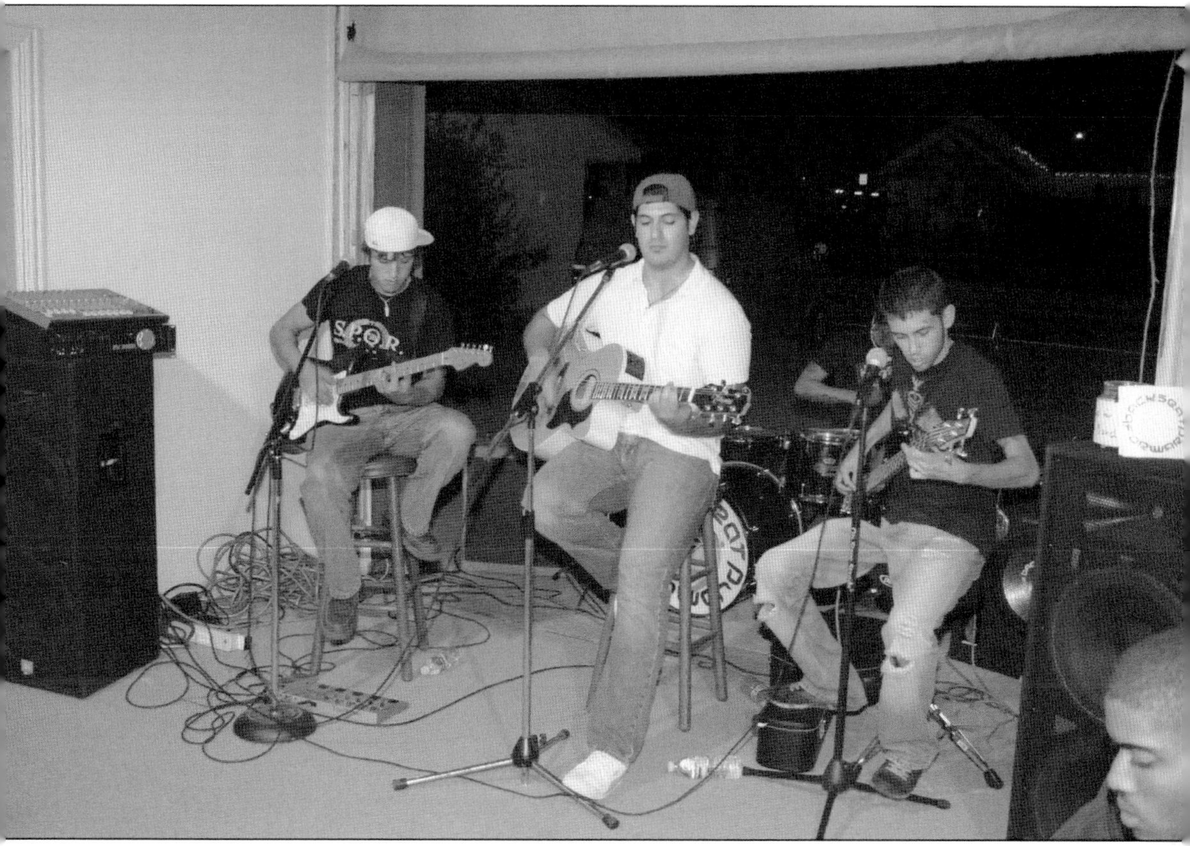

The band Backseat Forward plays at the YAT Gallery grand opening in 2006. (Courtesy Jenny Tilbury.)

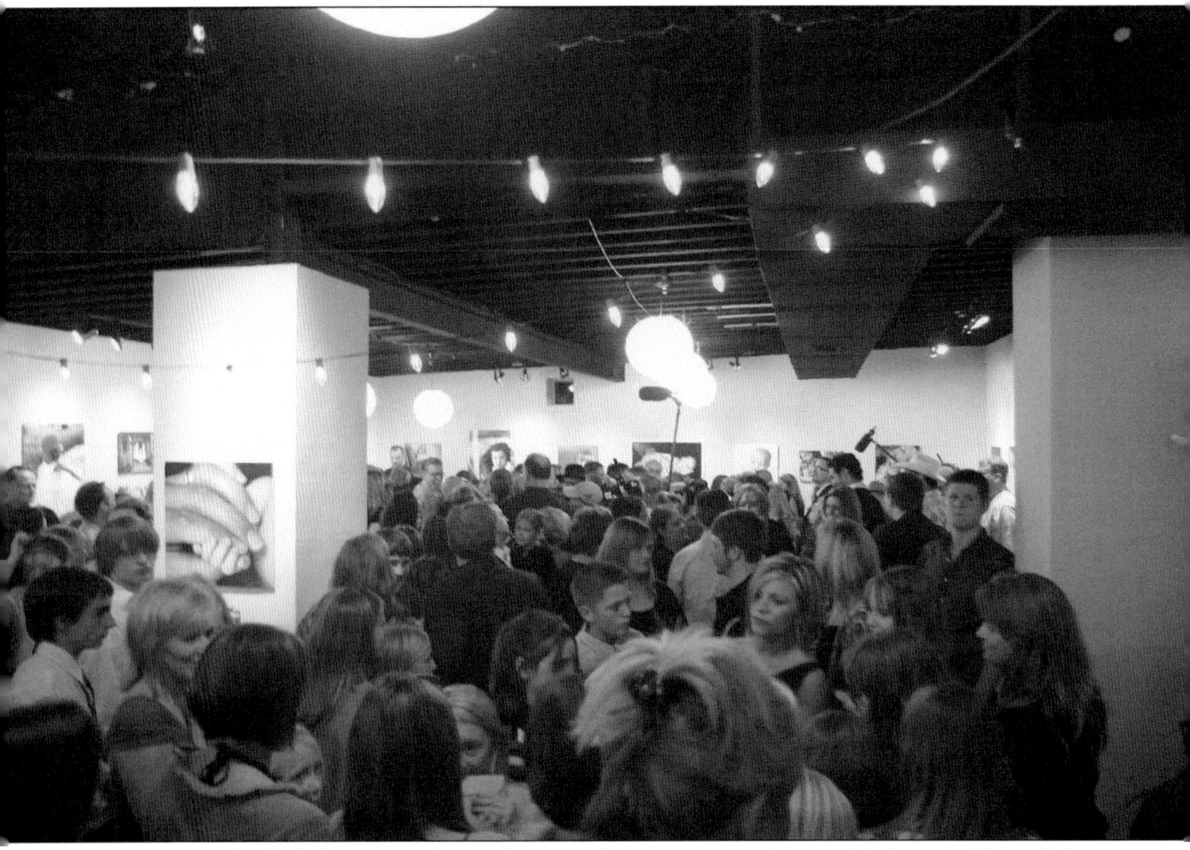

The 2009 YAT Gallery was chosen by the television show *Extreme Makeover: Home Edition* to feature a local photographer, Amber Augustin, who takes pictures of premature babies in the neonatal care unit for family keepsakes.

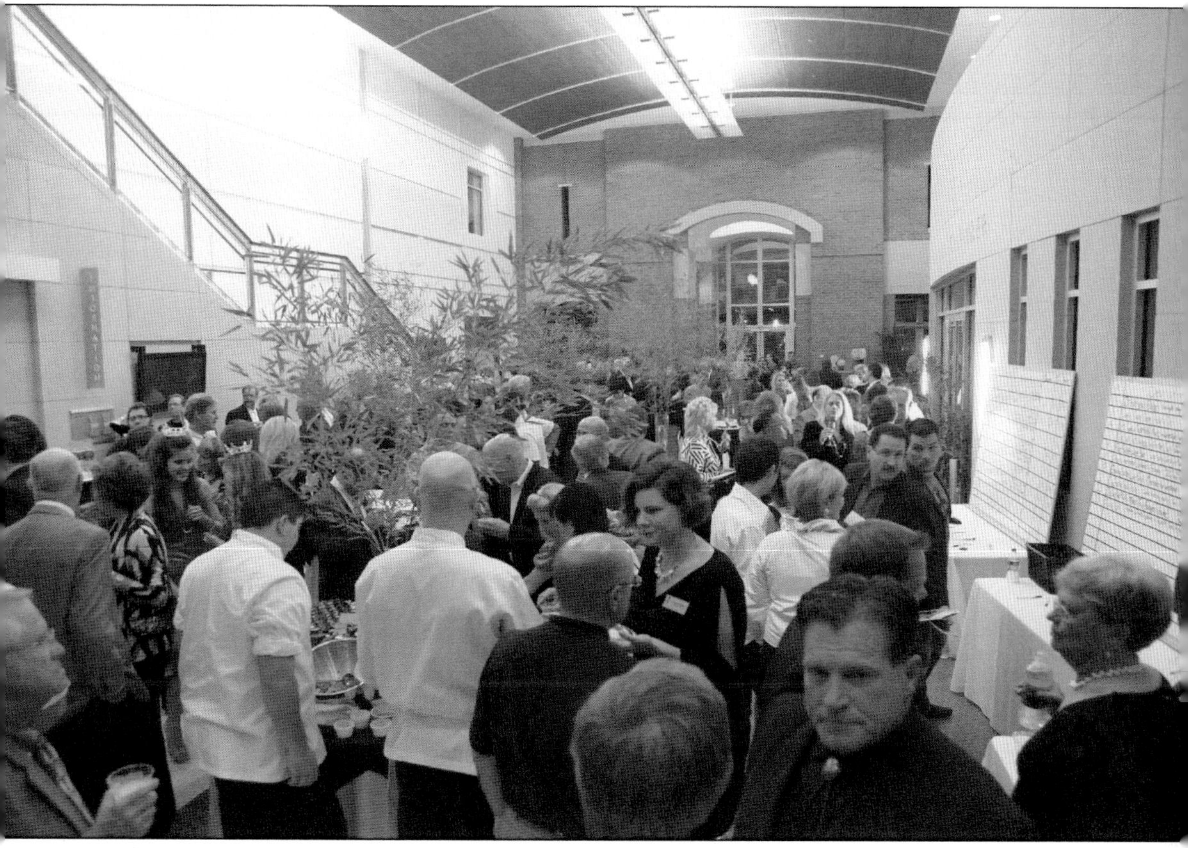

YAT Gala is a celebration each year to help earn scholarship money for the many young artists in Keller and other surrounding areas. This photograph is of the 2009 gala.

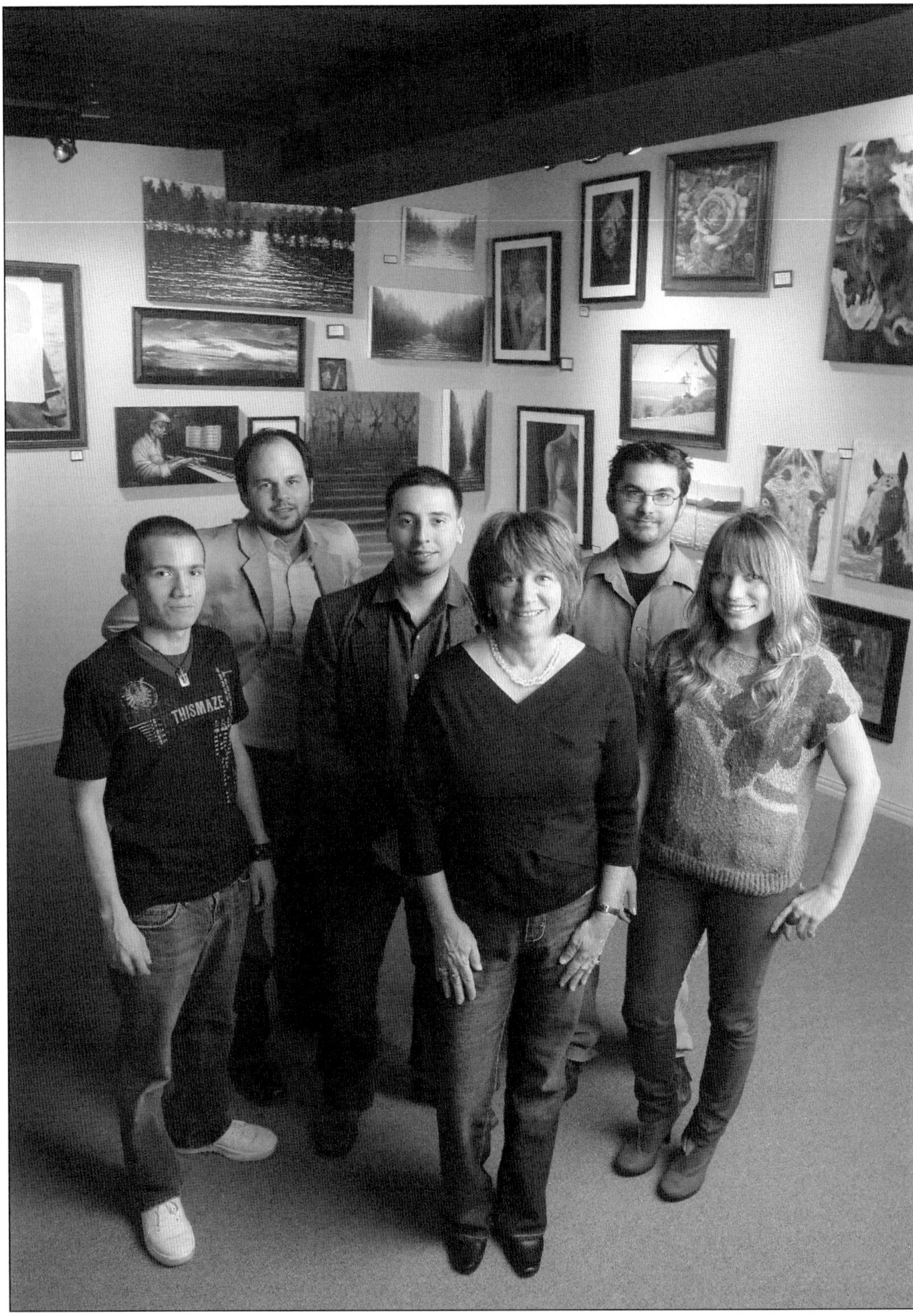

Jenny Tilbury, founder of YAT Gallery, poses with YAT artists. From left to right are Matthew Tilbury, Pedro Salano, Erick Soto, Jenny Tilbury, Albert Bourland, and Leslie Marshall.

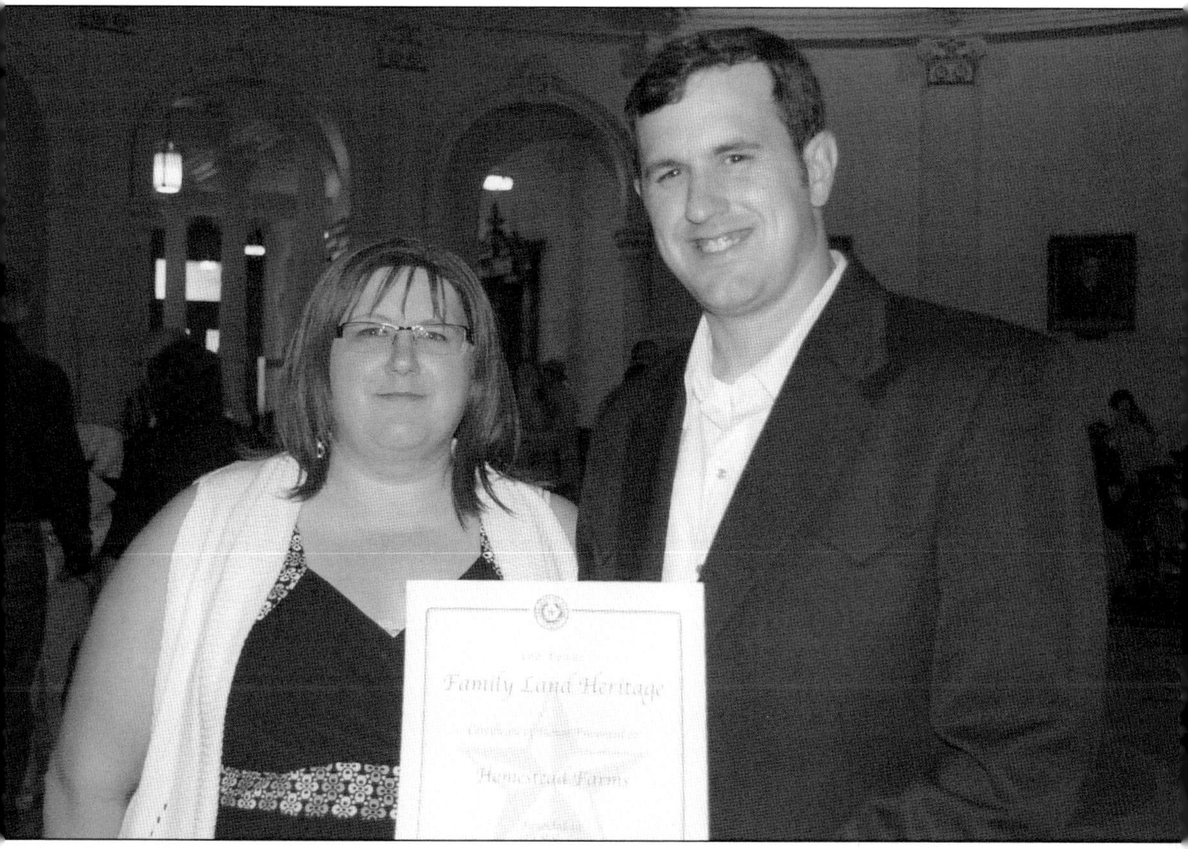

Brother and sister Michael Farris and Mindalyn Looper, grandchildren of the Browning family, receive the Century Farm Award from the Texas Department of Agriculture for their hard work and dedication in keeping Homestead Farms alive and well for 100 years. (Courtesy Homestead Farms.)

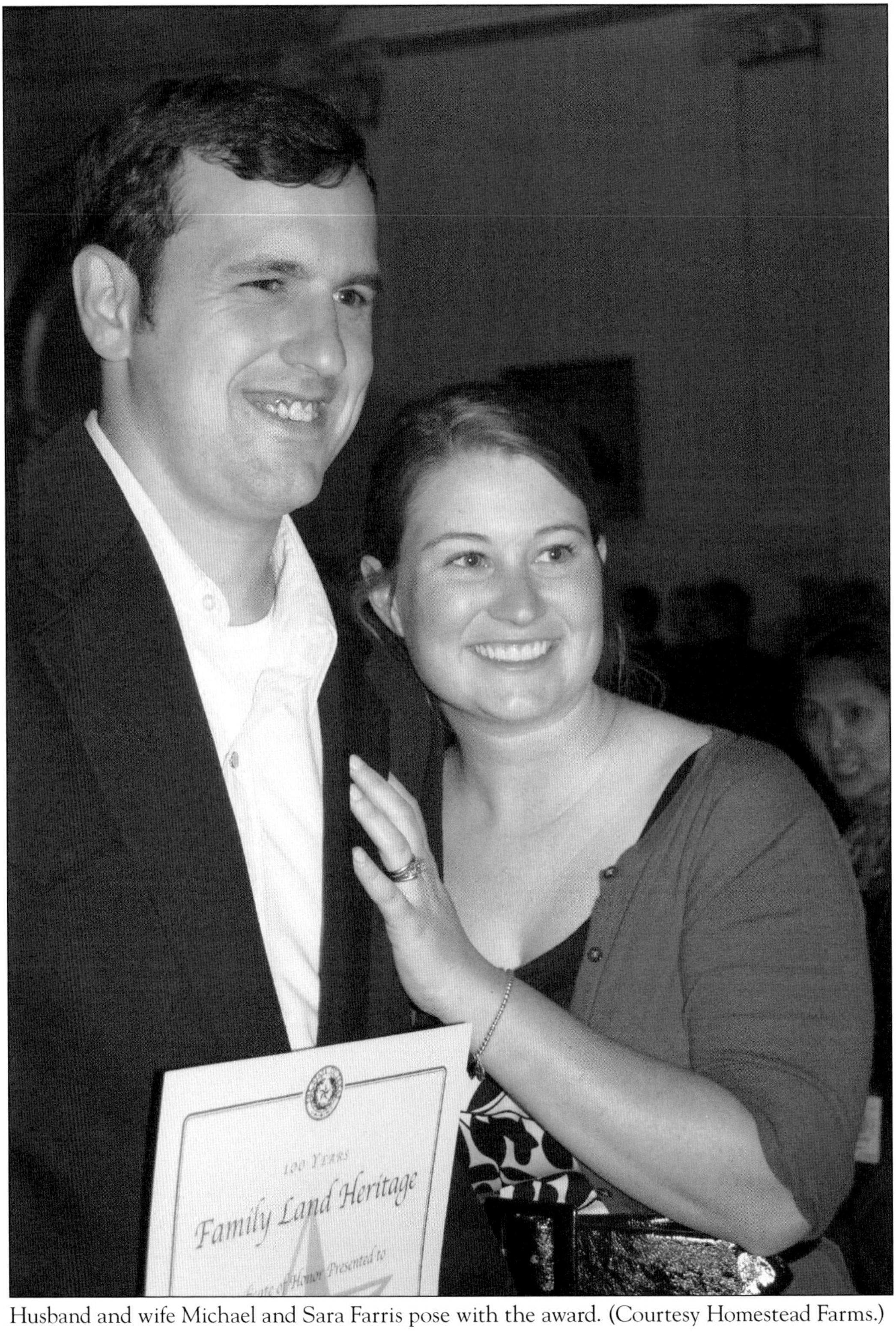

Husband and wife Michael and Sara Farris pose with the award. (Courtesy Homestead Farms.)

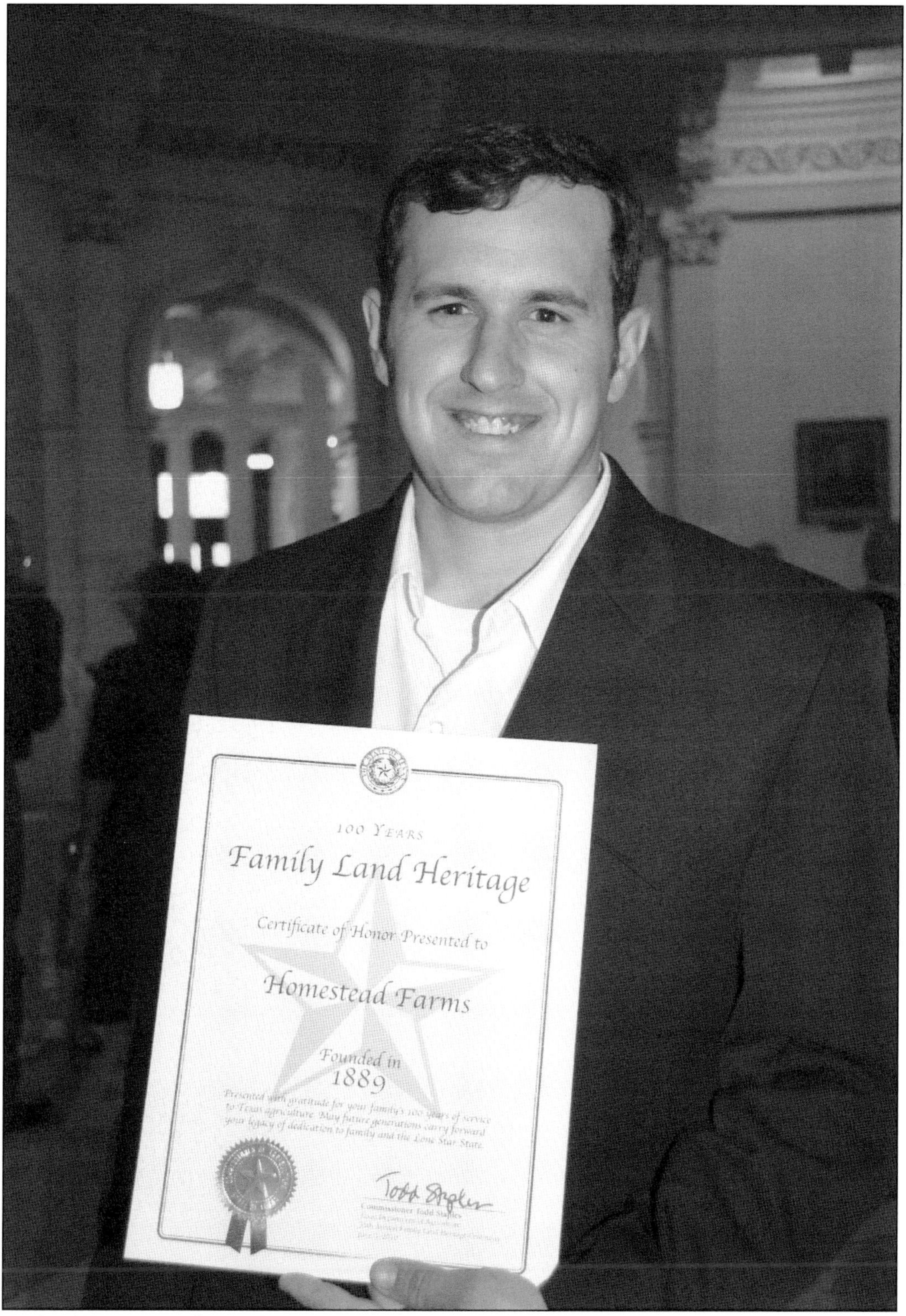

Michael Farris proudly displays the award. (Courtesy Homestead Farms.)

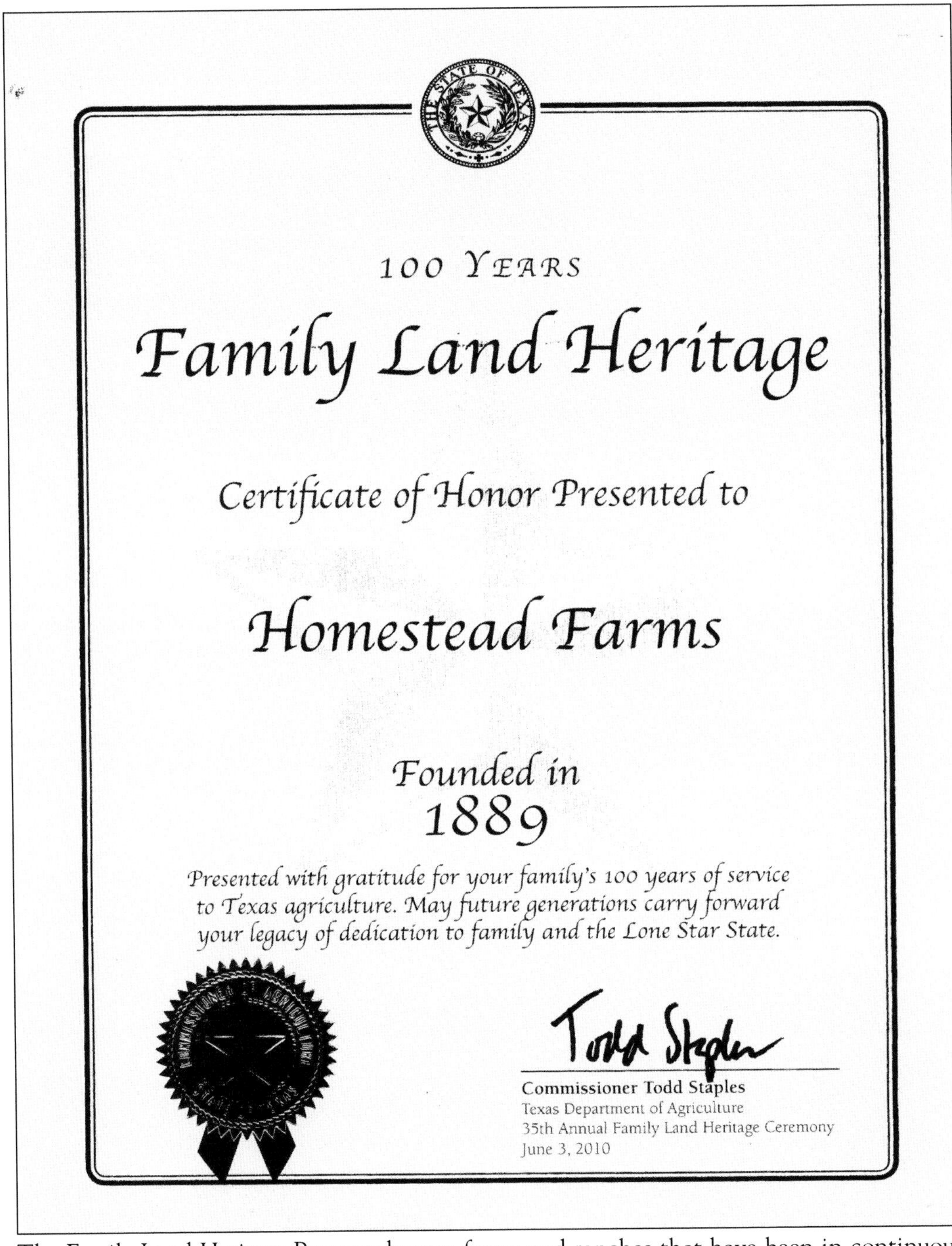

THE STATE OF TEXAS

100 YEARS

Family Land Heritage

Certificate of Honor Presented to

Homestead Farms

Founded in
1889

Presented with gratitude for your family's 100 years of service to Texas agriculture. May future generations carry forward your legacy of dedication to family and the Lone Star State.

Todd Staples

Commissioner Todd Staples
Texas Department of Agriculture
35th Annual Family Land Heritage Ceremony
June 3, 2010

The Family Land Heritage Program honors farms and ranches that have been in continuous agricultural operation by the same family for 100 years or more. The program is designed to recognize and chronicle the unique history of Texas agriculture and the men and women who settled this great state and continue the tradition today. Each year a ceremony is held to recognize the farms and ranches accepted into the Family Land Heritage Program. Participants whose farm or ranch qualifies receive a certificate of honor in the name of the farm or ranch. (Courtesy Homestead Farms.)

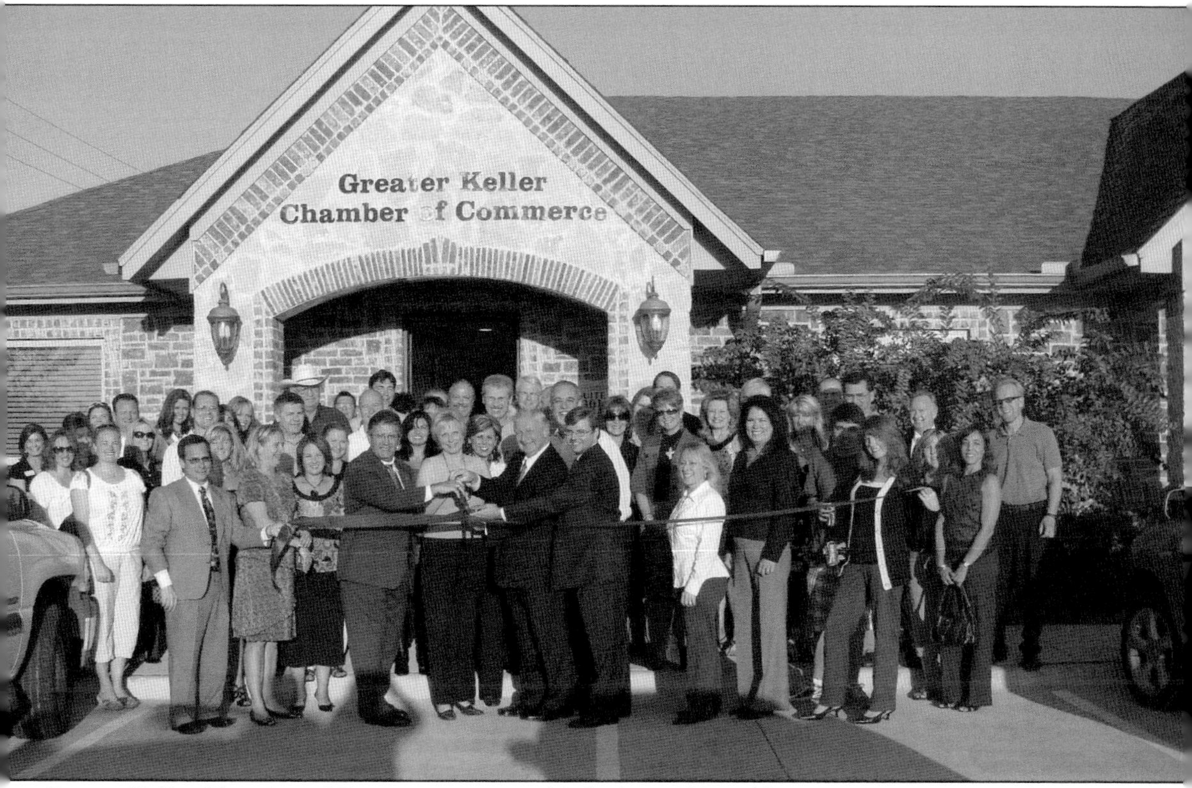

Greater Keller Chamber of Commerce was established in 1979 and has over 600 active members. The chamber is a nonprofit organization and relies solely on its events to fund the organization; without the support of the community and the many active businesses, the highly visible events would not be possible. The chamber office moved locations in 2009, from Main Street to 420 Johnson Road, Suite 301, adjacent to the Keller Library and Senior Center. Susanne Johnson has been the president of the Keller Chamber since 2005 and continues to grow the chamber each year in membership. Rhonda Seyfried is the events and programs manager and has been with the chamber since 2008. Her many programs include Leadership Keller and the Ambassador Program, which networks businesses with community members. Holding the ribbon in the front row are, from left to right, Rhonda Seyfried, Cara Gray, Steve Taylor, Susanne Johnson, Charla Kitch, Mayor Pat McGrail, Greg Kocian, Tiffanie VanAusdoll, Alison Benton, and Kathy Young. (Courtesy Greater Keller Chamber of Commerce.)

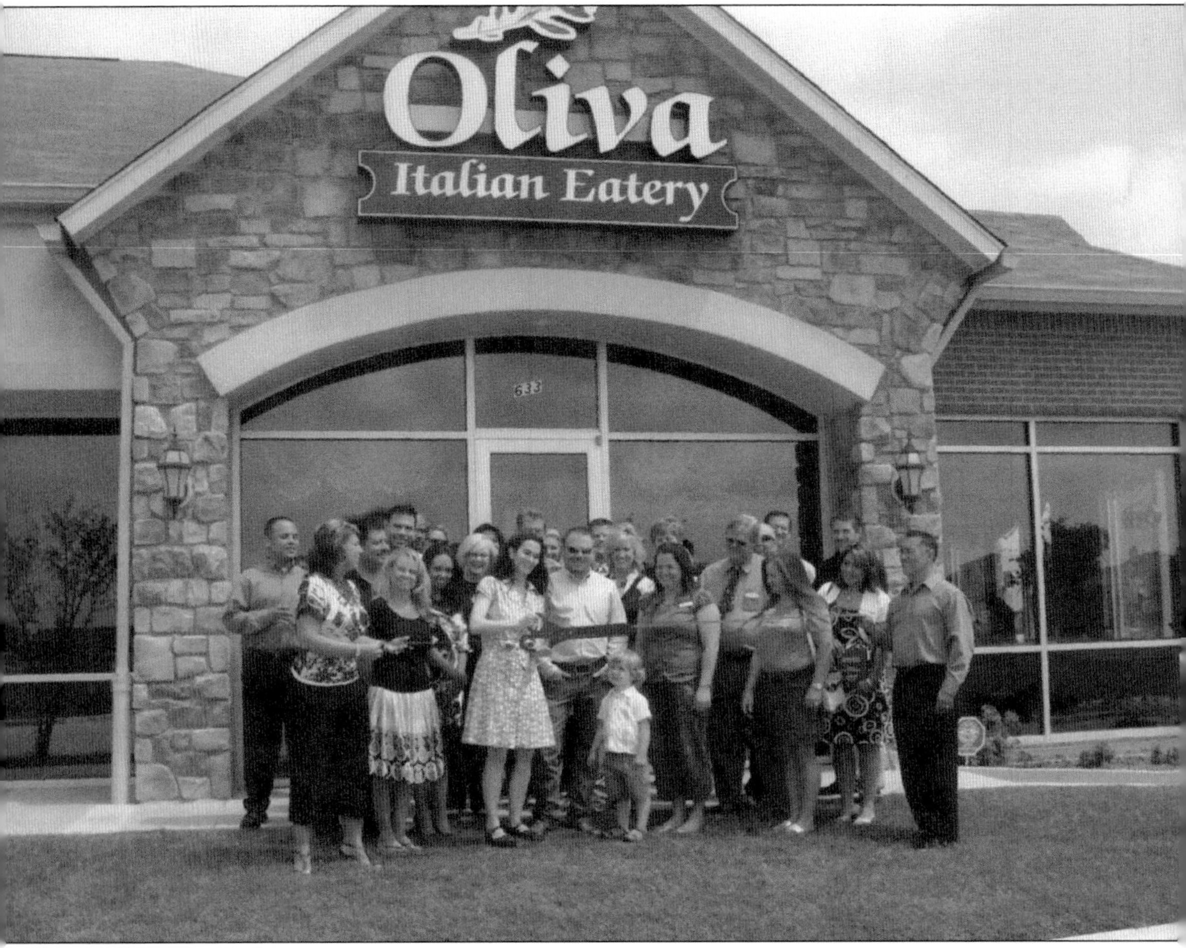

Ribbon-cutting ceremonies are the responsibility of the Greater Keller Chamber of Commerce and provide new businesses an opportunity to be welcomed into the community. Oliva Italian Eatery is a new restaurant located on Alta Vista Road and Timberland Boulevard. Holding the ribbon in the first row are, from left to right, Charla Kitch, Terri Schrobilgen, Rev. Kathryn Cox, owner Cynthia Loeb, Stacy Rountree, Donna Kirkwood, and Jaime Blanco. (Courtesy Greater Keller Chamber of Commerce.)

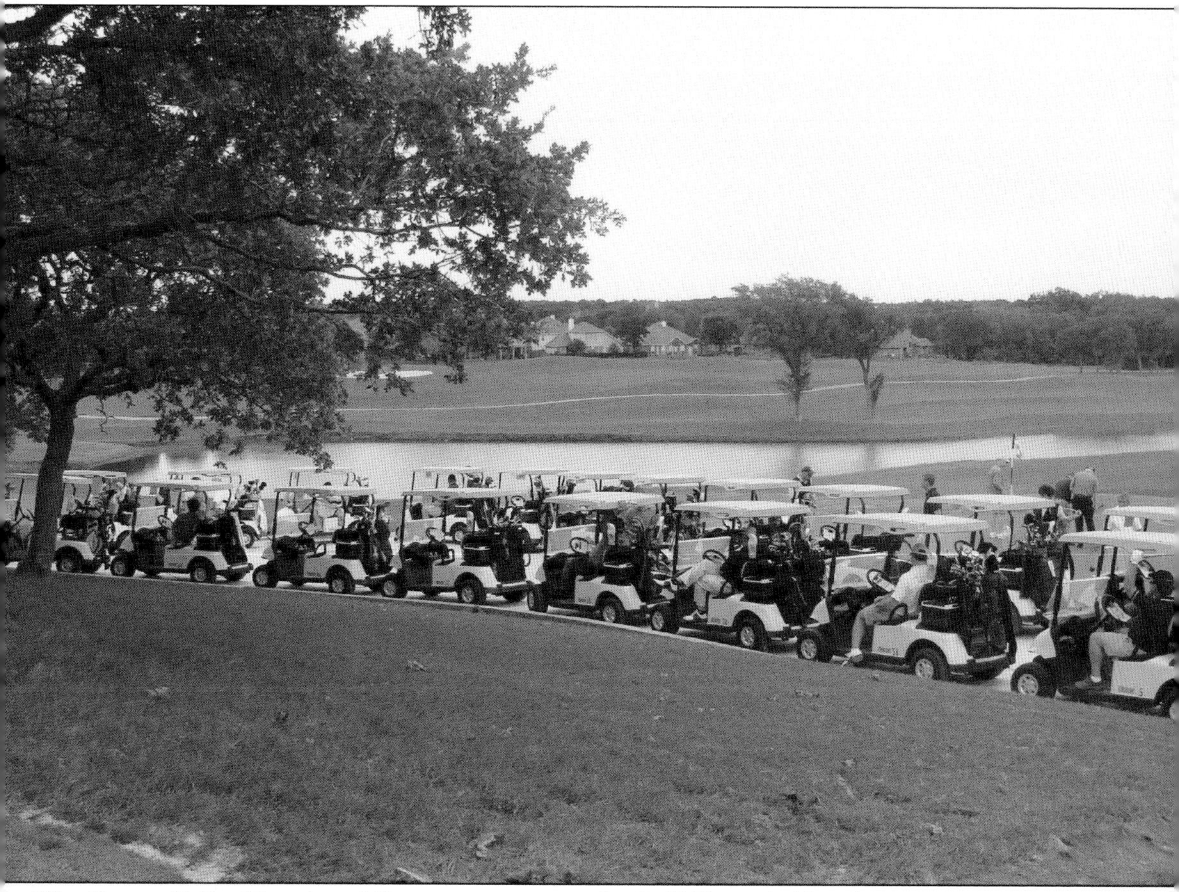

The Greater Keller Chamber of Commerce sponsors the Golf Classic held each year in September, which offers an opportunity to strengthen customer relations and network with community leaders and friends to promote a business product or service. The classic is played on the beautiful course of Sky Creek Ranch Golf Club in Keller. (Courtesy Greater Keller Chamber of Commerce.)

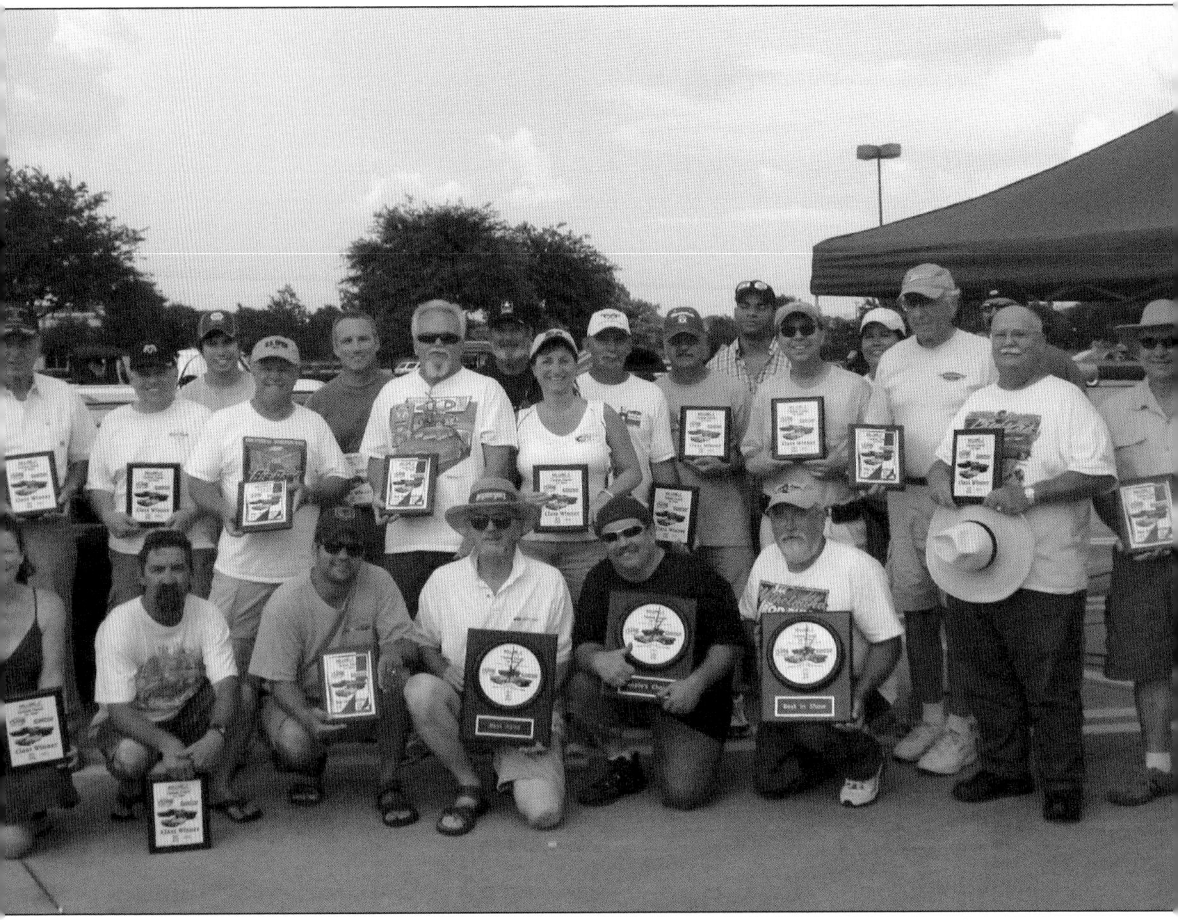

The Custom Classic Car Show is put on by the Keller Chamber of Commerce and features custom and classic cars from all eras. This car show is held in conjunction with KellerFest and features about 100 exhibitors. (Courtesy Greater Keller Chamber of Commerce.)

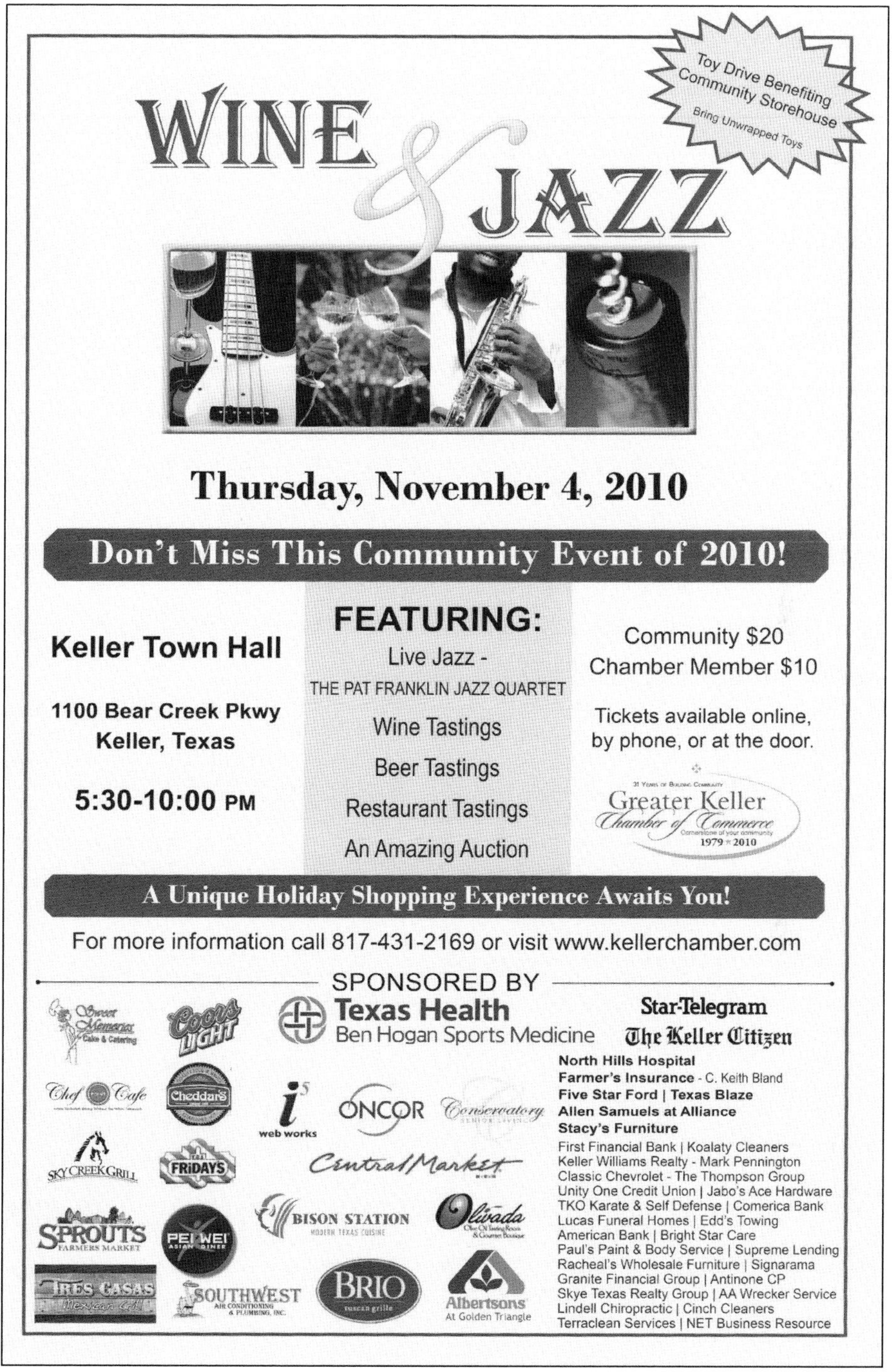

The Wine and Jazz Festival is held each year in November and features an evening of great jazz, food tasting from local restaurants, and a live auction. Proceeds benefit the Greater Keller Chamber of Commerce to fund its exciting community events. This Wine and Jazz poster announces the many activities of the program sponsored by the chamber. (Courtesy Greater Keller Chamber of Commerce.)

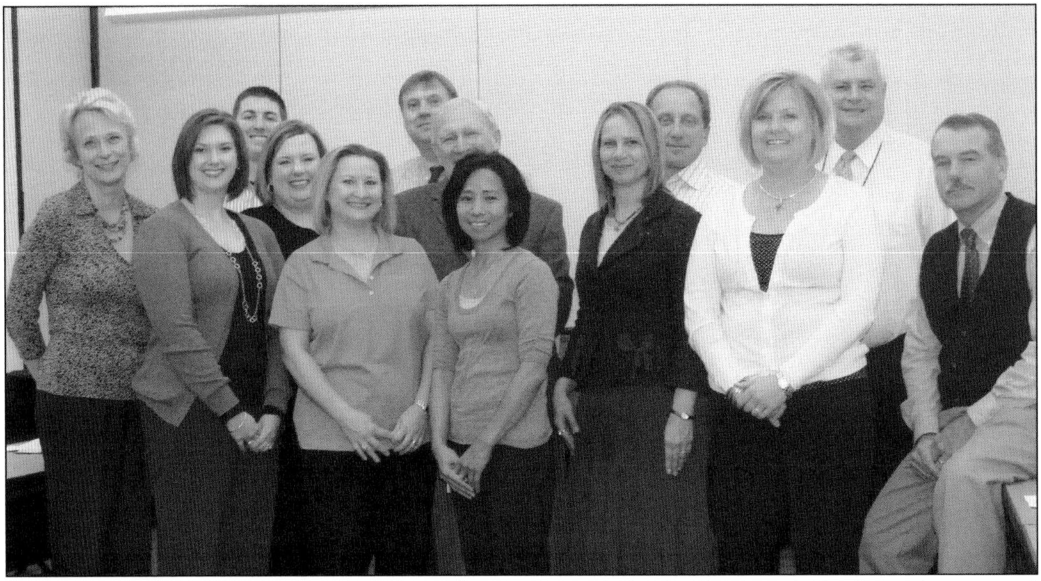

Leadership Keller is a dynamic program that enhances the leadership skills through personal and professional development and promotes understanding of many sectors such as business, government, health care, arts, human services, and education. Leadership Keller brings together a small group of area professionals for an intensive eight-month study to gain insight into the different sectors as well as provide information about local resources. Pictured from left to right are (first row) chamber president Susanne Johnson, Rachel Nobles, Diane Hildreth, Daisy Harsa, Rhonda Seyfried, Cindy Willis, and Greg Dickens; (second row) Amanda Bigbee, Mayor Pat McGrail, Brad Ender, and Dan O'Leary; (third row) Kevin Auten and Steve Polasek. (Courtesy Greater Keller Chamber of Commerce.)

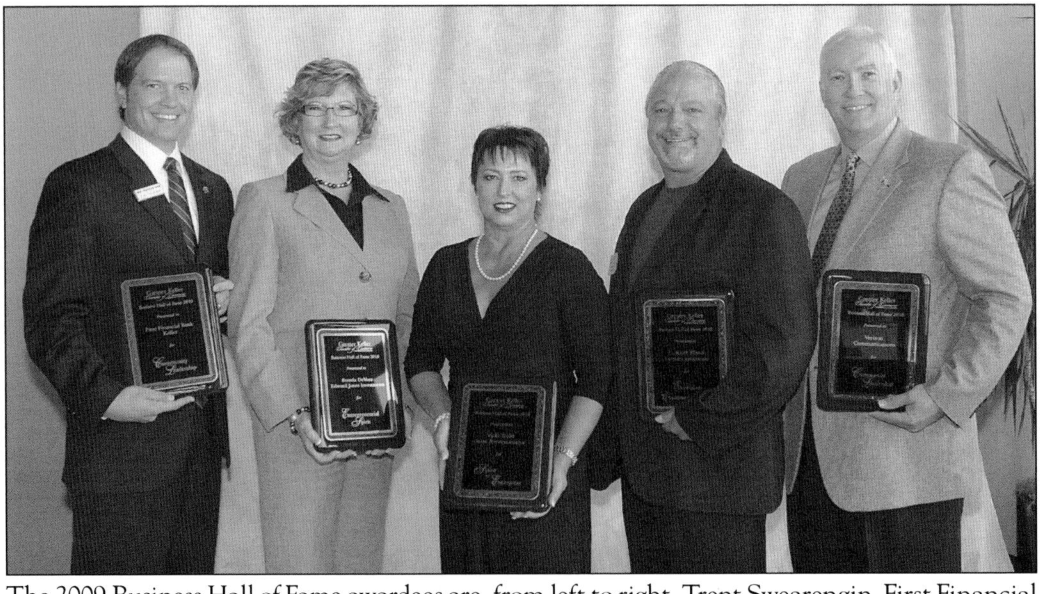

The 2009 Business Hall of Fame awardees are, from left to right, Trent Swearengin, First Financial Bank; Breda DeVore, Edward Jones Investments; state representative Vicki Truitt, District 98; C. Keith Bland, Farmers Insurance; and David Russell, Verizon Communications. (Courtesy Greater Keller Chamber of Commerce.)

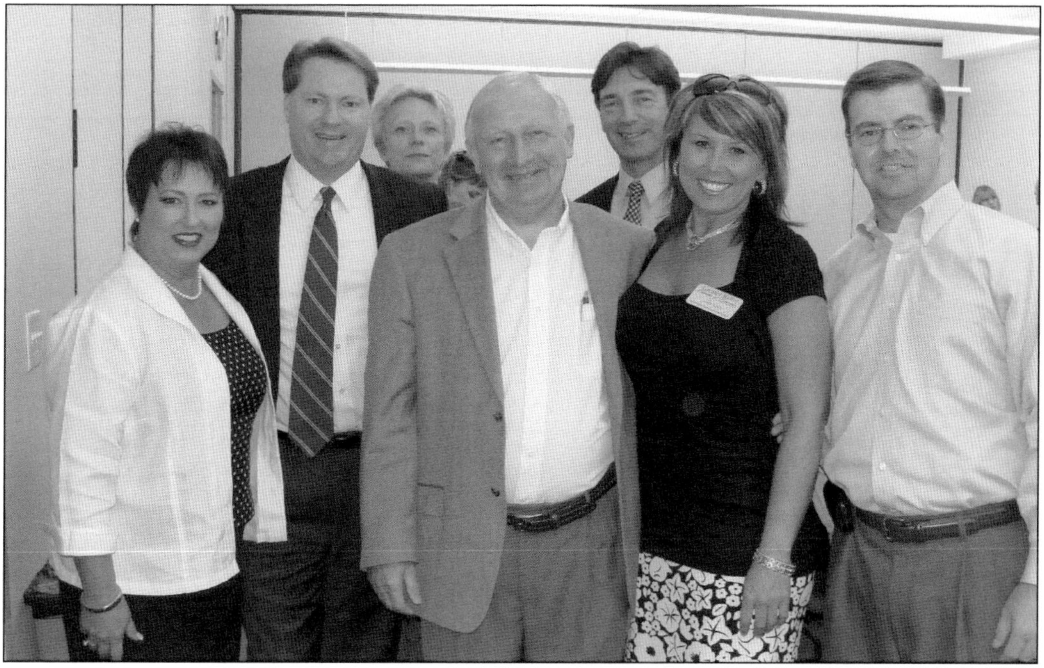

The Elected Official Roundtable offers Keller chamber members the ability to meet in a small group with elected officials to discuss topics of interest that impact the community. Elected officials include, from left to right, (first row) state representative Vicki Truitt, David Lehde, Mayor Pat McGrail, Charla Kitch and Greg Kocian; (second row) chamber president Susanne Johnson and Erik Wulfers. (Courtesy Greater Keller Chamber of Commerce.)

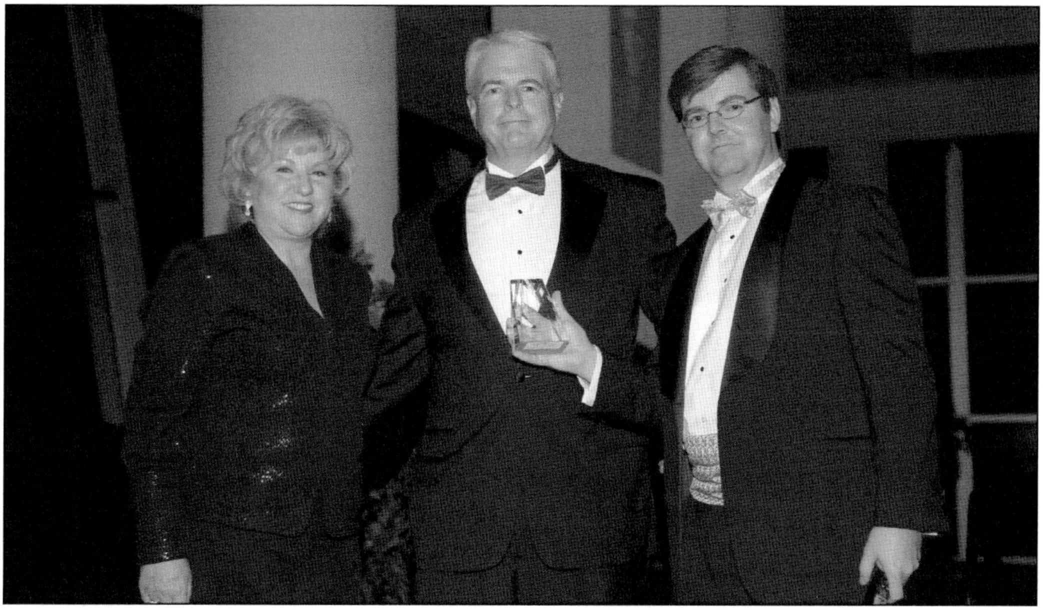

The Greater Keller Chamber of Commerce Awards Gala is a black-tie event held in January at the famous Texas Motor Speedway. It acknowledges the businesses and community members of the year. From left to right are state senator Jane Nelson, Bill Dodge, and Greg Kocian. (Courtesy Greater Keller Chamber of Commerce.)

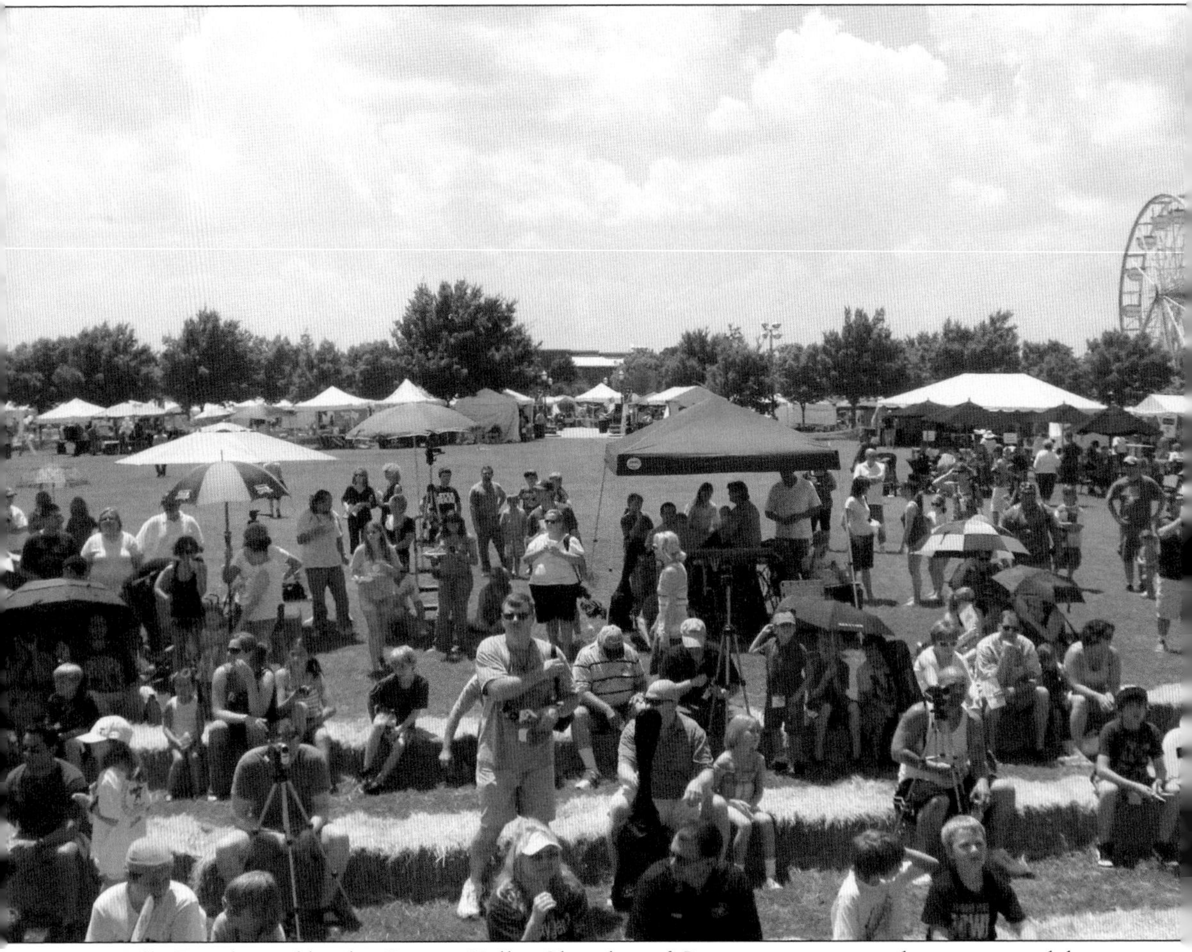

KellerFest, hosted by the Greater Keller Chamber of Commerce, is a true hometown celebration with activities for all ages held each year in May on the grounds of Keller Town Hall Plaza. Activities include concerts from local bands, a fireworks show, arts and crafts, business booths, carnival rides, petting zoo, bounce houses, food, and much more. (Courtesy Greater Keller Chamber of Commerce.)

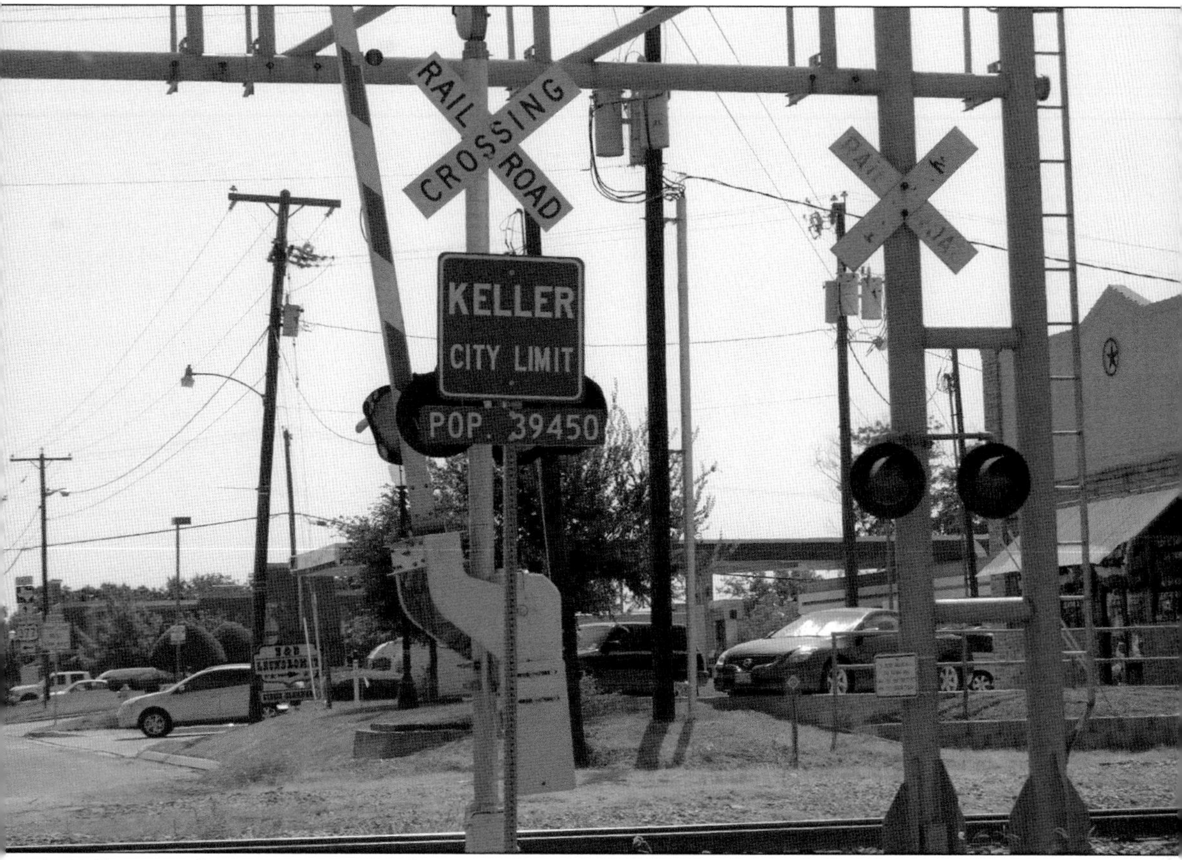

A Keller population sign sits at the railroad tracks on Golden Triangle Boulevard and U.S. Highway 377 (Main Street). The town continues to prosper with 39,450 residents, a number that will surely grow. New housing developments have made it an affordable city for residents. Old Town Keller is currently going through revitalization, and the Old Town Keller Association has been working for the past 11 years to make sure that merchants in this area maintain their historic roots. (Courtesy Jennifer Featherston.)

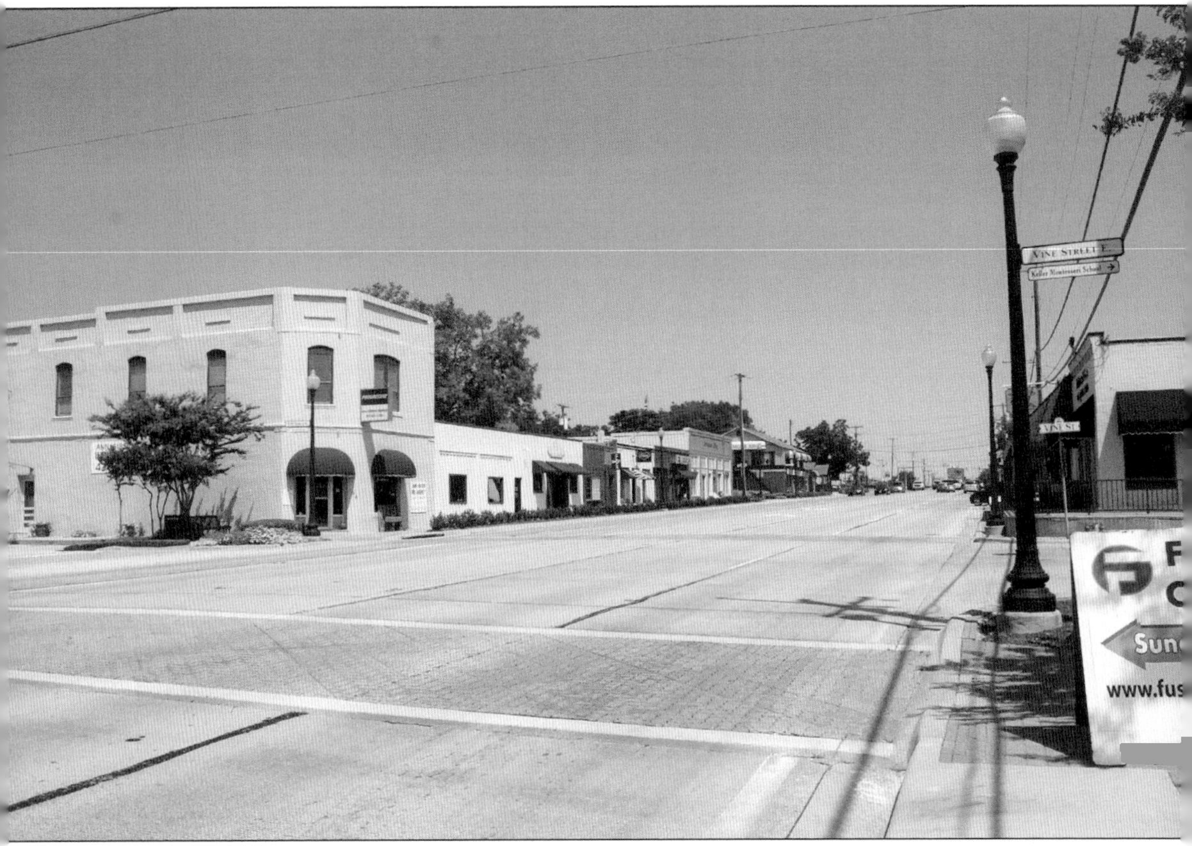

This is the view looking north from Main and Vine Streets. A lot has changed since the original picture was taken in the early 1900s. In 2009, CNN's *Money Magazine* ranked Keller seventh in its article, "Top 100 Best Places to Live." True American grit has always run through Keller and continues today with its vast array of local retail shops and restaurants. Keller has been and continues to be a great place to live. (Courtesy Jennifer Featherston.)

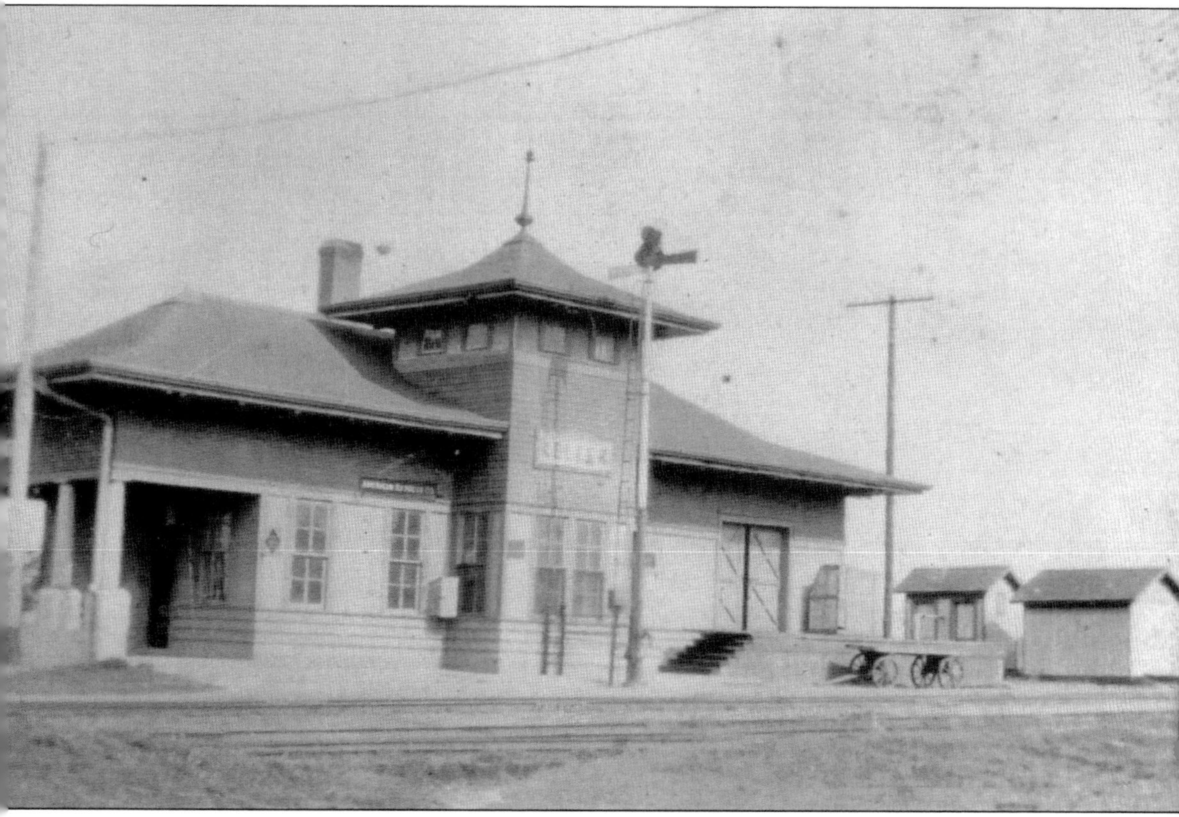

It all started because a train came to town and made Keller a home. From the pioneers to its current residents, Keller continues to prosper. (Courtesy Joyce Gibson.)

Bibliography

Dale, Edward Everett. *Cross Timbers: Memories of a North Texas Boyhood*. Austin, TX: University of Texas Press, 1967.
"History of the Town of Keller, Tarrant County, Texas." Unpublished paper, 1959.
Maps. General Land Office: Austin, Texas.
Martin, Jay Cy. *Chisholm Trail, Déjà Vu*. Self-published, 1992.
Roach, Joyce Gibson. *Wild Rose: A Folk History of a Cross Timbers Settlement Keller, Texas*. Virginia Beach: the Donning Company Publishers, 1996.
University of Texas at Arlington Library Special Collections, Lyda Smith White Collection.

About the Organization

The Keller Lions Club has served the Keller community for the last 62 years and has helped make Keller what it is today. The Keller Lions Club was formed in 1948 and provides many Keller Independent School District (KISD) students with scholarships as well as eye exams and eyeglasses each year at no cost to the students. The club is able to underwrite this and many other programs by holding the annual Keller Fair. The club also supports Casey's Kids, which help needy KISD students purchase school clothing, as well as Rocky Top Therapeutic Riding Center, which utilizes horses in their treatment for special-needs children. The Lions Club facilities host many Keller events throughout the year, which aid in raising funds for the many great deeds done by the club.